RETREAT

RETREAT

DUNKIRK AND THE EVACUATION OF WESTERN EUROPE

Henry Buckton

AMBERLEY

First published 2017

Amberley Publishing
The Hill, Stroud
Gloucestershire, GL5 4EP

www.amberley-books.com

Copyright © Henry Buckton, 2017

The right of Henry Buckton to be identified as
the Author of this work has been asserted in
accordance with the Copyrights, Designs and
Patents Act 1988.

ISBN 978 1 4456 6482 8 (paperback)
ISBN 978 1 4456 6483 5 (ebook)

British Library Cataloguing in Publication Data.
A catalogue record for this book is available
from the British Library.

Typesetting and Origination by Amberley
Publishing.
Printed in the UK.

MIX
Paper from
responsible sources
FSC® C013056

CONTENTS

INTRODUCTION

The word Dunkirk is undoubtedly part of Britain's identity. It not only refers to an event in history but is used to describe perceived traits of the British character, such as defiance, bravery, stoicism, all pulling together to overcome adversity: the so-called Dunkirk spirit.

In historical terms the Battle of Dunkirk is spoken about in the same exalted company as Agincourt, Waterloo and the Normandy Landings. However, unlike these other great occasions, it was in fact a defeat, which for some reason is talked about as though it was a victory.

Dunkirk is of course just one small chapter in a much larger story, that of the Battle of France of 1940, which itself was part of the Second World War. In this book I will try and explain its place in that story.

In basic terms the story of Dunkirk refers to the evacuation of British and other Allied troops from Western Europe in May and June 1940. I begin by describing the political situation in Germany that led to the deployment of the British Expeditionary Force (BEF) to France in 1939. We then examine how the troops were deployed, taken under the command of the French and totally mismanaged.

The Germans launched a new type of warfare: fast-paced and direct, it took the Allies by complete surprise. They were digging in expecting a long drawn-out campaign similar to the trenches of the First World War, but the Nazis had other ideas.

One by one countries and armies fell before the German onslaught and the BEF was evacuated to fight another day, first from Dunkirk in Operation Dynamo and then from other French ports in operations Cycle and Aerial.

The story of the Battle of France is full of intrigue and surprises. Many of the famous characters associated with the Second World War on both the political and military fronts had important parts to play in it, and when it was over the civilised world hung on a knife's edge. The British armed forces, having retreated back to the safety of their home islands had learnt important lessons both on the ground and in the air. However, they had survived and would now face an even bigger challenge: the defence of their homeland in the subsequent Battle of Britain.

I

REVOLUTION, REPARATIONS AND REVENGE

To understand exactly where the evacuation of Dunkirk sits in history and why British troops were deployed on the European mainland in May 1940, we need to go right back to the final days of the First World War, which ended for Great Britain with the general armistice in November 1918 and the signing of the Treaty of Versailles on 28 June 1919.

Shortly before the end of hostilities there had been a revolt in Germany, inspired by the Communist revolution in Russia, which had resulted in the replacement of Germany's imperial government with a republic.

By the summer of 1918 it was clear to most people in Germany that the war was reaching its climax and that negotiations would have to take place with their enemies, sooner rather than later, to decide upon a post-war settlement, even though the country's politicians and military leaders largely remained stubborn to such a prospect. Perhaps they feared the worst – that Germany would ultimately be held responsible for the carnage and destruction of the last four years.

Germany was a very different place in 1918 than it was in 1914 when it went to war overflowing with arrogance and confidence. Then, it was one of the richest countries in the world, both an industrial and economic powerhouse. Four years later it was on the verge of total ruin and starvation, with its infrastructure in tatters. The people of the nation began to despise their leaders for the predicament in which they found themselves: Germany was ripe for a revolution.

The situation came to a head on 3 November 1918, when sailors in a naval base at Kiel, on Germany's Baltic shore, refused to embark on what they saw as a suicide mission to attack the British fleet just in order to uphold the martial honour of their senior commanders.

Rumours about the mutiny quickly spread to other naval bases and port facilities, where their comrades began to take similar actions. This unplanned uprising was soon affecting the other military services and even factory workers engaged in wartime manufacturing, so much so that the government found itself losing control of the situation. Local groups established Soviet-inspired councils in order to organise their activities; the word 'soviet' is derived from a Russian word quite literally meaning 'council'.

Bavaria, although once an independent kingdom, had been part of the German empire, or Reich, since its formation in 1871, although it continued to have its own monarchy, the House of Wittelsbach. This arrangement had proved controversial from the onset as the state was mainly Catholic, so its population resented being dictated to by their Protestant neighbours in Prussia. So it certainly did not take much effort to establish revolutionary groups here that would quickly seize control in the area, and who proceeded to expel their monarch, King Ludwig III, who signed a document relinquishing his government's authority in favour of a socialist administration led by Kurt Eisner, a German-Jewish journalist who had coordinated the revolt in the region. Eisner interpreted the document to be an abdication by King Ludwig, although it did not actually state this; interestingly, no member of the House of Wittelsbach has ever formally declared its renunciation of the throne.

Soon what had occurred in Bavaria would be mirrored in the rest of Germany, where increasingly the populace called for the abdication of the kaiser, Wilhelm II, who had been King of Prussia and Emperor of the German Reich since 1888. In 1918 the chancellor of Germany, the equivalent of the prime minister in the British government, was Prince Maximilian Alexander Friedrich Wilhelm Margrave of Baden, better known to history as Max von Baden. He was appointed chancellor by the kaiser on

3 October 1918 to head a new coalition government represented by the majority parties of the Reichstag National Assembly; the Reichstag was the name of the building in Berlin built to house the imperial 'diet', or parliament. He was soon given the task, contrary to his own personal views, to approach the Allies and sue for peace, as by then most of those in authority had come to appreciate that this might be inevitable. The message asking for an armistice was sent to the Allies on 4 October.

However the ongoing unrest put Baden in a difficult position. He had been appointed by the kaiser and certainly did not wish to remove him from office, but the revolution left him with little alternative, and on 9 November 1918 the imperial government was replaced by a provisional one led by Friedrich Ebert and formed from the Social Democratic Party of Germany (SPD) and the Independent Social Democratic Party of Germany (USPD). The following day the armed forces agreed to work with the stand-in establishment in their task of running the nation until elections could be held. The kaiser, who had previously left the country and escaped to Belgium, finally accepted that his throne and empire were gone. He effectively exiled himself to Holland, from where he officially abdicated on 28 November.

So Germany now found itself with a left-wing provisional government led by Ebert. By far the largest part of the new authority was drawn from Ebert's own party, the SPD, who called for a democratically elected socialist republic; the USPD were a splinter group of the SPD who sought more radical reforms.

Then there was the even more extreme Spartacus League, another splinter from the SPD led by Rosa Luxemburg and Karl Liebknecht. Luxemburg is described as a Marxist philosopher and revolutionary. She was of Polish-Jewish descent but had become a naturalised German citizen. Liebknecht was a German-born lawyer and socialist politician. Together they are credited with founding the German Communist Party.

Luxemburg and Liebknecht believed that Germany should follow the Russian example, by first taking control in a communist revolution and thereafter creating a state run through regional soviets. Luxemburg herself was certainly uneasy about the violence caused by the Russian model and hoped that in Germany a similar state could be achieved without the horrors inflicted by Lenin's regime.

On 1 January 1919 the German Communist Party, known as the KPD, was created from the Spartacus League announcing that they would not support the forthcoming elections and instead would instigate an armed uprising in order to take charge by force.

The KPD began their campaign in the capital city, Berlin, where they seized key buildings and formed a revolutionary committee. For some reason they imagined that most working men would back them, thinking that the disgruntled populace would support their call to arms. However they had profoundly misjudged the situation, and after three days the army alongside units of ruthless paramilitary volunteers, known as Freikorps, had crushed Germany's communist revolution once and for all. Both Luxemburg and Liebknecht were arrested, tortured and shot.

Towards the end of January, the promised elections finally took place, with an astounding 83 per cent of the population casting their votes. Three quarters of the votes went to democratic parties, who formed the Weimar Coalition, with several parties working together to carry on sorting out the country's issues. Ebert's SPD had the biggest share so he continued to head the new administration as Germany's first president.

Ultimately however, the internal politics of Germany, those which had successfully transformed the country from an autocracy to a republic with very little bloodshed, were secondary to what was taking place elsewhere in Europe, as the country's wider future was being decided upon by representatives of other nations through the dictates of the Treaty of Versailles.

The First World War had been hugely destructive to both the landscape of north-west Europe and its populations, particularly its manhood. Vast areas of France and Belgium had changed beyond recognition, with verdant fields and woodlands left as what can best be described as cratered lunar landscapes. Entire towns and villages were wiped from the face of the earth, their histories and cultures consigned to dust. It is believed that the French alone suffered over 1,000,000 military deaths and the loss of 300,000 civilians. As well as the dead, another 4,000,000 had been wounded, many left incapacitated. Irrespective of what was occurring politically within Germany itself, those most affected by the war demanded revenge.

The Treaty of Versailles was signed by representatives of the major Allied powers that had brought Germany to its knees, although of course never actually defeated it militarily. The signing took place at the Palace of Versailles, near Paris, although most of the lengthy negotiations had actually taken place in the city itself, on the Quai d'Orsay at the Ministry of Foreign Affairs. The Allies were represented by what were termed 'The Big Three' of Great Britain, France and the United States of America, in the persons of the British prime minister David Lloyd George, French prime minister Georges Clemenceau and the US president Thomas Woodrow Wilson.

Interestingly, the three powers that would decide the post-war fate of Germany all had slightly different views on how to go about it. The French were determined that Germany should accept full responsibility for the war and devastation of their country. Their voice, of which Clemenceau's was amongst the most vehement, demanded that Germany be both militarily and economically crushed, so that in the future it would be unable to cause any further aggression on the Continent. They thought the best way to achieve this was to force severe reparations on their old enemy and to make them pay huge sums of money: in this way the other governments concerned would be able to keep Germany under tight control.

The British were also in favour of reparations but Lloyd George himself advocated a slightly more lenient approach. Whilst he wanted to quench the national thirst for revenge and make sure the post-war German state was in no position to cause further military action, at the same time he had the foresight to understand that if Germany were left destitute, it could easily become a breeding ground for extreme left-wing politics. His biggest fear was a further communist uprising, and in order to guard against this he believed that Germany should pay realistic reparations and not be destroyed by them.

Similar to Lloyd George, President Woodrow Wilson was slightly more sympathetic to Germany's plight as well as being conscious of public opinion in America, where the population increasingly supported isolationism, in other words keeping out of European affairs altogether. He staunchly believed that the best way to keep the peace in Europe was reconciliation between countries rather than simple revenge. He therefore submitted what were known as the 'Fourteen Points', which were in effect his own blueprint for the post-war world. Among its main ambitions, it called for the self-determination of all European powers and the creation of an international peacekeeping organisation.

By the end of June 1919, Germany was presented with the final treaty setting out her fate, which had been painstakingly agreed by the three powers. She would lose 13 per cent of her territory, most notably the area of Alsace-Lorraine, which was returned to France. This territory had been ceded by France to Germany in 1871 after the Franco-German War and historically had been inhabited by German-speaking citizens since the time of the Holy Roman Empire.

There were also territorial losses to Poland, while large numbers of Sudeten Germans – ethnic Germans who had traditionally lived in lands ruled over by the Bohemian crown – were absorbed by the newly formed Republic of Czechoslovakia; the part of Czechoslovakia in which they now found themselves residing was known as the Sudetenland. Collectively these areas stripped Germany of a massive 10 per cent of her population. On an industrial level, it removed 75 per cent of her iron ore capacity and 26 per cent of her coal and potash. She also lost all of her overseas colonies, most notably in East Africa, South West Africa, and West Africa, with other territories in what we now call Oceania affected.

Other restrictions were placed on the size of the army and navy Germany could maintain, and these further could only be used for internal security purposes. Particularly relevant to the events that lay ahead was the fact that she was forbidden to have an air force, submarine force, or to design and build armoured vehicles.

The Germans also had to officially accept war guilt and pay reparations to the tune of £6,000,000,000, although the sums actually paid in the coming years remain a matter of debate.

In order to maintain the peace and ensure the future of world security, the League of Nations was established on 10 January 1920. It was essentially the first international organisation whose principal mission was to maintain world peace. Its primary goals, as stated in its covenant, included preventing wars through collective security and disarmament and settling international disputes through negotiation and arbitration. At its height between September 1934 and February 1935, it had fifty-eight member states. However, it did not have its own military arm and depended on the great powers to enforce its resolutions. This would ultimately prove to be its biggest drawback.

A part of Germany known as the Rhineland would also be policed by a joint occupation force from Great Britain, the United States, Belgium and France for stipulated periods. The Rhineland encompasses a loosely defined area in the west of the country which straddles the River Rhine. The main objective of the occupation force was to control all the bridgeheads across the river. The entire area became a demilitarised zone, and it was forbidden for the Germans to have any troops to the left of the Rhine or within thirty miles of its right bank.

The British contingent entered the Rhineland on 3 December 1918 from which the British Army of the Rhine (BAOR) was established, in March 1919, under the command of Lieutenant General Sir William Robertson. This new force was initially made up of five corps, each consisting of two divisions of infantry soldiers; there was also one separate cavalry division. They were deployed to the area for five years.

In August 1920 Winston Churchill, then Secretary of State for War and Air, told the British parliament that the BAOR consisted of approximately 13,360 troops, made up of staff, cavalry, Royal Artillery, Royal Engineers, infantry, Machine Gun Corps, tanks, and the usual ancillary services. He stated that these units were located principally in the vicinity of Cologne at an approximate cost of £300,000 per month.

Over the coming years, the BAOR seems to have been a political football that few people at high level were really interested in, and its makeup was constantly changing – usually in a downward spiral of numbers. The final vestige of this occupation army would leave the area in 1929 and was thereafter disbanded. Although it left under a much reduced strength, it had in actual fact stayed for double the period originally intended.

The United States initially provided around 240,000 men in eight divisions, which was nearly a third of the total occupying force. General John Joseph Pershing, who had commanded American forces in Europe during the war, established the US 3rd Army for the purpose, under the command of Major General Joseph Dickman, which became known as American Forces in Germany (AFG), headquartered at the commanding Ehrenbreitstein Fortress near the city of Koblenz, which itself sat at the confluence of the rivers Rhine and Moselle. They had been given a ten year mission.

Pershing later added two further divisions to secure the line of communication that would run through Luxembourg from France to Germany. In total they covered a 2,500-square-mile section of the Rhineland inhabited by slightly less than 1,000,000 people. He also sent another 50,000 troops to Luxembourg. However, similar to Britain's, the force constantly shifted and dwindled. By January 1923 they were down to a 1,000 men, and by February of that same year all US soldiers had gone, to be replaced by the French. In contrast to the British, the US forces left six years ahead of schedule.

The original Belgian contingent consisted of five divisions, with their headquarters at Aachen. But understandably, it was the French who took the occupation most seriously: in the long term, especially after the withdrawal of US troops, they would provide 75 per cent of the entire force. Their task was to overseer the area for fifteen years, which would mean deploying troops in the Rhineland until 1934.

At first the French sent the 8th and 10th Armies, which on 21 October 1919 combined to form the French Army of the Rhine, based in the south of the occupation zone around Mainz.

France would also station around 40,000 French colonial soldiers in the Rhineland, mainly Senegalese troops, a situation that would cause consternation in the months ahead, as this was seen as a kind of ultimate humiliation, to have black soldiers guarding white civilians. The press called this 'colonialism in reverse', and for a country whose imperial ambitions had largely been achieved in Africa, this was a bitter pill for the Germans to swallow.

In January 1919, following the events of the earlier revolution, the new democratic government was formally established. It was known as the Weimar Republic. However from the outset the people of Germany were profoundly unhappy with the post-war situation in their country. Territorial losses to Poland, the demilitarisation of the Rhineland and the incorporation of large numbers of Sudeten Germans within the state of Czechoslovakia provoked feelings of bitter resentment.

Perhaps the greatest anger, however, was caused by the war guilt clause, which forced Germany to accept full responsibility for causing the conflict. In a nation that had lost something like 2,000,000 men and considered that it had not been militarily defeated but betrayed by its politicians, this was hard to bear.

Due to the war guilt clause, the occupying forces reputedly treated the German populace with complete contempt. Alleged assaults by black soldiers in the French occupation army on local women led to fearmongering and accusations of systemic rape and other such atrocities targeted against the German civilian population, attributed mainly to the French-Senegalese.

These events resulted in a widespread campaign by the German right-wing press, which labeled these soldiers 'The Black Shame' and depicted them as a form of humiliation deliberately inflicted on the German nation by the French. There was also the scandal of German women having children by African soldiers out of wedlock. The newspapers dubbed these infants 'Rhineland Bastards' and considered them to represent the ultimate public disgrace.

General Henry Tureman Allen, the US commissioner in the Rhineland, reported to the US secretary of state that from the start of the occupation until June 1920 there were sixty-six cases of formal accusations against black colonial troops, out of which there were twenty-eight convictions. He did however also admit that there were probably many more unreported cases, where women felt ashamed to come forward.

However, although there were certainly some genuine cases of abuse towards German women, the widespread atrocities reported in the newspapers committed by French colonial troops, such as alleged abductions, followed by rape, mutilation, murder and concealment of the bodies, were largely fabricated by the right-wing press as political propaganda.

Although the idea of an international peacekeeping agency had been strongly endorsed by President Woodrow Wilson, ironically the US Senate retrospectively rejected the Versailles settlement and vetoed US membership of the League of Nations. This was a crippling blow to the other Allied nations and contributed to the League's failure as a force for good during the increasingly unstable and dangerous years leading up to the Second World War.

By 1923, Germany was beginning to default on the terms of the Treaty of Versailles, and on several occasions it failed to pay the required reparations, either in money or in goods such as coal or timber. After negotiations and against the desire of Great Britain, both France and Belgium reacted by occupying the industrial region of the Ruhr in Germany in order to force the Weimar Republic to pay what it owed. Most of the Ruhr was across the river on the right bank of the Rhine. The German public was outraged by this – a controversy that would benefit an emerging political party, the National Socialist German Workers' Party.

2

THE ROAD TO WAR

During the negotiations that led to the Treaty of Versailles, the British prime minister David Lloyd George had grave concerns about inflicting unrealistic reparations on Germany, as he was fearful that its economic suffocation could lead to a further rise in extreme left-wing politics, namely in the form of communism. Ironically, however, the state in which the country now found itself would actually be a breeding ground for extreme right-wing politics, in the shape of fascism.

Although it was not in Germany but in Italy that the first fascist movements began to emerge towards the end of the First World War. During the war years they had seen how the major countries had obliterated the distinction between military and civilian life in a total war that mobilised entire societies towards victory. As well as the military ranks, most other people were also involved in some capacity, perhaps making things for the war effort or growing food to sustain the troops and nation. Great advances in science and technology were also achieved through this system which might otherwise never have been financed.

Fascists believed that war was an end-in-itself, intrinsically good, and examined the probability that if countries in peacetime could be ruled under warlike conditions by a totalitarian one-party state, it would make them stronger. It would also give the state boundless authority to intervene in the lives of its citizens. They totally disregarded other political ideologies such as democracy, socialism and communism, and wherever they began to appear they had similarities, although they were not identical. Their common doctrines included their veneration of the State, devotion to a strong dictatorial leader and an emphasis on ultra-nationalism and militarism. Fascism viewed political violence, war and imperialism as a means to achieve national rejuvenation, and most alarmingly they promoted the idea that it was the right of stronger nations to expand their own territory by displacing those that were weaker than themselves.

In 1922 Benito Mussolini became prime minister of Italy, elevating his National Fascist Party to office. Until 1925 he ruled the country constitutionally but then established a legal dictatorship and began to pursue an aggressive foreign policy aimed at making Italy a world power. He envisaged a new Roman Empire with himself as its emperor, with the title Il Duce, 'the leader'.

Meanwhile in Germany the interwar period was not proving easy for the new Weimar Republic and its legitimacy would soon be challenged by right-wing elements including the fascist National Socialist German Workers' Party, commonly referred to in English as the Nazi Party, headed by Adolf Hitler.

The Nazi Party can be traced back to the final days of the First World War when a league called the Free Workers' Committee for a Good Peace was created in Bremen. Fiercely nationalist, a branch of this league was subsequently started in Munich in March 1918 by a local locksmith called Anton Drexler. It was bitterly opposed to both the Armistice and, later, the Treaty of Versailles. It was anti-Semitic, anti-monarchist and anti-Marxist. It promoted the idea of the superiority of Germans, whom they claimed to be part of an Aryan master race. Drexler also accused the nation's capitalists, whom he claimed were Jewish-dominated, of war profiteering while the nation had suffered.

Later in 1918, Drexler also formed the Political Workers' Circle with journalist Karl Harrer and several others. This was largely a discussion group with the main topics being nationalism and racism directed against the Jews. Then, in January 1919, Drexler combined the local branch of the Free Workers' Committee for a Good Peace with the Political Workers' Circle to create a new political party, which he proposed to call the German Socialist Workers' Party, but it was eventually amended to the German Workers' Party (DAP) as Harrer objected to the inclusion of the word 'socialist'.

What made this group different from other organisations identifying as socialist, and who mainly represented the interests of the working class, was that it also aimed itself at the country's middle class. Drexler made it clear that the party's socialist platform was meant to give social welfare to any German citizens deemed part of the Aryan race.

At its onset the DAP was a relatively insignificant group but because of its known subversive tendencies, it soon began to attract the attention of the German authorities. The army's education and propaganda department decided to investigate and sent one of their intelligence agents to infiltrate the organisation. The agent in question was an army *gefreiter* called Adolf Hitler (the rank of *gefreiter* was roughly equivalent to that of a lance corporal in the British army). Little did his superior Captain Karl Mayr suspect, that as well as infiltrating the group, he would be seduced by its ideology.

In September 1919, Hitler was involved in a heated argument at a DAP meeting and impressed party members with his oratorical skills so much that Drexler invited him to become a member. Hitler accepted and was given the membership number 555; apparently the party began counting membership at 500 to make it appear bigger than it actually was.

Hitler proved to be a talented orator and attracted large crowds to hear him speak. Soon he had become chief of propaganda and helped to give the party a more public profile. On 24 February 1920 he organised their biggest gathering to date, when 2,000 people heard him enumerate the twenty-five points of the party's manifesto in Munich. If anyone from a neighbouring democracy had heard this speech it would have sent a shiver down their spine.

Hitler set out a clear foreign policy that included ignoring the Treaty of Versailles, taking back the land Germany had lost at the end of the war, and expanding its own borders to the east by occupying other countries in order to colonise them with German settlers, while at the same time displacing the people who already lived there. This policy was known as *Lebensraum*, which literally meant 'living space', and it would see a new German Reich devour states like Poland and

Czechoslovakia, eventually as well as large swathes of Soviet Russia. Another disturbing point in the party manifesto was the exclusion of Jews from citizenship and the confiscation of what they deemed their war profits.

On the same day that Hitler made this speech, in an attempt to appeal to a wider audience the DAP finally changed its name to the National Socialist German Workers' Party (NSDAP or 'Nazi' Party).

Before long Hitler had become the face of the party and people would flock to hear his speeches. Despite this, he was not without his enemies: some members found him too overbearing, and while he was away on a fundraising trip to Berlin, in June 1921, the executive committee went behind his back and attempted a merger with the DSP. On his return Hitler angrily tendered his resignation. However, the party faithful knew that Hitler was their greatest asset and that without him they would return to being a fringe minority. So after deliberation they asked him to reconsider. He accepted on the condition that he was appointed party chairman in place of Drexler.

Hitler was formally elected party chairman at the end of July 1921, with only one opposing vote. The committee was dissolved and he was granted almost absolute power, taking the title of Führer, which translates as 'leader'. He would hold this position for the rest of his life.

He immediately instated a regime notorious for its violent reprisals against anyone who opposed him, even founding his own party militia called the *Sturmabteilung* (SA), better known as the 'Brownshirts'. He would thereafter use violence as a legitimate tool of fascist rule. After his appointment the Nazi Party grew rapidly. This was partly due to Hitler's charisma but also partly because many young men wanted to join the ranks of the SA.

The rise of the Nazi Party might well have floundered had it not been for the fact that Germany by now was in severe economic meltdown due to the reparations it had to pay to the Allies. Because of its failure to pay these reparations, in January 1923 forces from Belgium and France occupied the industrial Ruhr area. This led to an upsurge of nationalist sentiment and Nazi Party membership shot up to around 20,000.

In November 1923 Hitler decided that the time was right for an attempt to seize power in Munich and bring down the Weimar authority, in what became known as the Beer Hall Putsch. Around 2,000 men marched to the city centre and in the ensuing confrontation sixteen Nazis and four policemen were killed. Hitler was arrested and charged with treason. The failure of the putsch brought Hitler his first significant publicity, and after a trial lasting for twenty-four days he was sentenced to five years imprisonment. However, he was released having served only nine months of his sentence.

Although a failure the Beer Hall Putsch and Hitler's incarceration all helped the Nazi propaganda machine, so when Germany was affected by the Great Depression of 1929 and its economy collapsed, the people looked towards the Nazis and their nationalistic agenda as the answer to their problems.

In 1933 an election was held in Germany after which Hitler was appointed chancellor. Fortuitously for him an event then occurred that allowed him to constitute his totalitarian single-party state, ruled over by the Nazis. The event in question was a fire at the Reichstag government building.

The Nazis accused the communists of starting the blaze, who were their principal political opponents. As chancellor, Hitler urged the Weimar president Paul von Hindenburg to pass an emergency decree to suspend civil liberties in order to counter the communist threat. Mass arrests of known communists followed, including all parliamentary delegates. So, with their bitterest rivals eliminated, the National Socialist German Workers' Party suddenly found itself in a majority.

A year later another thing happened that indirectly aided the Nazi cause: Paul von Hindenburg died. Hitler declared that the office of president was vacant and would not be filled, effectively making him in his capacity as chancellor the head of state.

Hitler was now able to implement his radical and racially motivated vision of the world order. Openly ignoring the restraints of the Treaty of Versailles, he began a massive rearmament campaign and introduced conscription. He also set in motion his plan to take back German territories from those who had benefitted from them after the settlements of the First World War. In early 1935 the first of these was the Saar Basin; it was at this time that multiple political analysts began to predict that an upset to the geopolitical world order, and perhaps even a Second World War, was now almost inevitable.

The Saar Basin, or Saarland as it is more commonly known, is a highly industrialised area in the south-west of Germany rich with coal deposits. Under the Treaty of Versailles it was occupied and governed jointly by Great Britain and France under a League of Nations mandate, although in reality the area was administered by France alone. After fifteen years the people of the area were promised a plebiscite, a type of referendum, that would decide whether they returned to German control or remained under French authority.

During the 1930s the Saarland was the only part of Germany that remained under foreign administration. Because of this a large number of political opponents of the Nazis, including communists, had moved there. As the date of the plebiscite drew near these anti-Nazi groups began to campaign for the area to remain under French administration, while Hitler instigated a propaganda war to allure voters to the extreme right. As most of the region's native population was German and exhibited strong nationalistic sentiments, the anti-Nazi voice fell on deaf ears; when the plebiscite occurred, on 13 January 1935, over 90 per cent voted in favour of reunification with the fatherland.

Although the Saarland had been legally reunited with Germany the situation began to ring alarm bells among some western politicians, who were by now well aware of Hitler's rhetoric. They were fearful that this would be just the start of his plans for expansion and worried that his next goal would be to bring Austria under German control.

On 14 April 1935, in an attempt to curtail the Nazis, Great Britain, France and Italy formed an alliance. This became known as 'The Stresa Front', which took its name from the Italian town on the banks of Lake Maggiore in which the agreement was formally sealed between Pierre Laval, the prime minister of France, Ramsay MacDonald, the prime minister of Great Britain, and Benito Mussolini, the self-styled prime minister of Italy. The aim of this agreement was to reassert the treaties of Versailles and Locarno and make sure that Germany could not make amendments to them. They also agreed to support the independence of Austria. The Pact of Locarno, which had been agreed at Locarno in Switzerland and signed in London in December 1925, was a series of agreements whereby Germany, France, Belgium, Great Britain and Italy had mutually agreed to guarantee peace in Western Europe.

In reality, though, many of the doctrines behind the Stresa agreement were rendered unworkable in June 1935 when the United Kingdom made an independent naval agreement with Germany that eased some of the prior restrictions placed on it. At the same time France signed a treaty of mutual assistance with the Soviet Union, which was concerned by Hitler's threats that he would acquire vast areas of Eastern Europe and repopulate these with German nationals. This flurry of alliances also prompted the United States of America to reaffirm its own position over Europe, and in August 1935, in an attempt to stay clear of any potential involvement, they passed the Neutrality Act.

However, it was not only Germany that was beginning to cause problems on the world stage, as Italy was commencing its own campaign of empire building. Italy at that point was still regarded as a friendly power, posing even greater difficulties for France and Great Britain in their position as her allies. In Africa, Italy already held territory in Somaliland and now wished to include Ethiopia (also known as Abyssinia) in its empire. Italy invaded Ethiopia in October 1935 and, keen to keep Mussolini as an ally, Great Britain and France did little in response. Germany on the other hand openly supported the move, which resulted in Italy dropping its own objections to Hitler's goal of annexing Austria. The Stresa Front was already falling apart before the ink had even dried.

Italy's justification for the attack was an incident that had occurred in December 1934 between Italian-Somali and Ethiopian troops at the Walwal Oasis, on the border between the territories of the two nations, where 107 Ethiopians and fifty Italian and Somali soldiers had died. The Ethiopians had claimed that an Italian fort was situated on their side of the border. Although both parties were exonerated, Mussolini felt that Ethiopia should have been held accountable, which provided him with an excuse to invade the country; he also saw it as an opportunity to provide land for Italian settlers and acquire rich mineral resources to help fight off the effects of the Great Depression.

The war lasted until May 1936 with Ethiopia becoming part of the colony of Italian East Africa as a result. Politically, it is best remembered for exposing the weakness of the League of Nations. Both countries were member states yet the League failed to control Italy or protect Ethiopia.

Hitler looked on, emboldened by events. Under the terms of Versailles, Germany was of course forbidden to field troops within the Rhineland. Hitler was well aware that any violation of this would be regarded as committing a hostile act and the Allies would be obliged to react. Yet, with the League's treatment of Italy surely in mind, on 7 March 1936, in direct contravention to the treaty, 32,000 German soldiers and armed policemen occupied the demilitarised zone. The Allies did nothing to prevent them.

Why Great Britain and France failed to react remains something of a mystery. In the case of the former, it is probable that the British government supported the view that the section of the Treaty of Versailles covering this incursion was unenforceable and agreed that in this instance Germany was behaving in an acceptable manner. Having also recently made a private agreement with the Germans, they perhaps naively hoped that this would now be the extent of their expansion. As for France, at that time they were themselves going through a period of internal political crisis so this sideshow was of little interest at home. It was a time when communists on the left and royalists and fascists on the right were openly advocating regime change in France. Hitler later commented that this had been one of the most nerve-wracking forty-eight hours of his life, but from this episode he had learned that as far as Britain was concerned there was certainly room for negotiation with regards to Versailles.

In July 1936 a civil war erupted in Spain, which would give both Italy and Germany the opportunity to pursue further military action. Despite the restrictions placed on it, by this time Germany had built up considerable military reserves. Most alarming was the capability of its air force, which under the terms of the Treaty of Versailles it was forbidden to have.

At the end of the First World War it is fair to say that military aviation did not actually cease in Germany, in spite of the Allied order to disband their flying corps and prohibit the construction of military aircraft in the country. The commander of the German army, Hans von Seeckt, laid the basis for both a strong provisional national army and navy called the Reichswehr, the security forces for the Weimar Republic. By disguising their true purpose he had laid the foundation of a highly skilled professional officer class, well versed in mechanised warfare, even before the Nazis came to power.

Aircraft were often constructed abroad or under the guise of being civilian or sports machines. Rigorous training was undertaken, which included the use of a secret air base at Lipetsk within the Soviet Union. The German government also provided subsidies during the 1920s for a successful civilian aircraft industry. Knowledge of air combat gained in the First World War was put to good use while developing new civil aircraft; the designers of these were under instruction to view them as potential military machines of the future.

When Hitler came to power, in 1934, Hermann Göring (Goering) was made Reich Minister for Aviation and the expansion of military aviation became a priority. By 1935, when the Luftwaffe was formally established, it already had over 1,800 aircraft and 20,000 personnel. By 1936 most of the aircraft that would participate in both the battles of France and Britain four years later were already in prototype form and undergoing testing.

In 1936 at the start of the Spanish Civil War both Hitler and Mussolini came out in support of the fascist, nationalist forces led by General Francisco Franco against the existing government, the Soviet-backed Spanish Republic. Italy and Germany would use the conflict to test new weapons and methods of warfare, and in October 1936 they formed the Rome-Berlin Axis.

On 26 April 1937 an event would occur that proved to be a foretaste of what lay ahead for London and other British cities during the Second World War. Franco invited his fascist allies to attack the small town of Guernica, the spiritual capital of the Basque people in the north of Spain. The Condor Legion of the combined German and Italian air forces carried out Operation *Rügen*, an aerial bombardment that caused widespread destruction and many civilian deaths. This attack is considered to be the first substantial raid in aviation history on a civilian target, although Madrid had been bombed several times previously to a lesser extent. It also demonstrated to the Allies the awesome weaponry and military power that had become available to Germany even under tight sanctions.

The nationalists would eventually win the civil war, in April 1939. But despite this Spain remained neutral during the Second World War, and even though Franco sent volunteers to fight on the Eastern Front under German command, he did not permit either side to use Spanish territory.

In March 1938, Germany finally annexed Austria, again provoking little response from other European powers. Earlier that year Austrian Nazis had conspired to seize the country by force and to unite their nation with Nazi Germany. Learning of the conspiracy, Austrian chancellor Kurt Schuschnigg met with Hitler in the hope of reasserting his country's independence, but instead named several top Austrian Nazis in his Cabinet as a result of political bullying. On 9 March Schuschnigg called a national vote to resolve the question of annexation, or *Anschluss*, once and for all. However, before the plebiscite could take place Schuschnigg gave in to pressure from Hitler and resigned, on 11 March. In his resignation address, under coercion from the Nazis, he pleaded with Austrian forces not to resist a German occupation of the country.

The following day, 12 March, Hitler, an Austrian himself by birth, accompanied German troops as they entered Austria, where enthusiastic crowds met them. Hitler appointed a new Nazi government, and on 13 March the *Anschluss* was proclaimed and the two nations were united to create one Greater Germany.

Encouraged by this, Hitler began pressing German claims on the Sudetenland, an area of Czechoslovakia predominantly populated by ethnic Germans. The British prime minister Neville Chamberlain and French prime minister Édouard Daladier went to Germany to meet both Hitler and Mussolini to try and resolve the situation diplomatically. A deal was finally agreed on 29 September 1938, and at about 1:30 a.m. on 30 September the four leaders signed what became known as the Munich Agreement. Against the wishes of the Czechoslovakian government, in this document Great Britain and France conceded the disputed territory to Germany in exchange for a promise of no further territorial demands. Following the summit, Chamberlain returned to Great Britain where he infamously declared that the Munich Agreement had secured 'peace for our time'.

Although Hitler's demands had been met by the Munich Agreement, in March 1939 his troops invaded the rest of Czechoslovakia, capturing it with little resistance and subsequently splitting it in two as the German protectorate of Bohemia and Moravia and a pro-German client state called the Slovak Republic.

In spite of this provocation, Great Britain and France still did relatively little to remonstrate; but then Hitler issued new demands on the free city of Danzig, a semi-autonomous state within Poland also mainly occupied by Germans. Alarmed at this, France and Britain gave their guarantee to support Poland if its territory was violated. Similarly, when Italy conquered Albania in April 1939, the same guarantee was extended to Romania and Greece.

Shortly after the Franco-British pledge to Poland had been made, Germany and Italy formalised their own alliance, known as the Pact of Steel. Hitler then renounced the Anglo-German naval agreement and the German-Polish non-aggression pact. He then presented Poland with new terms and agreed to recognise the country's borders if it granted Danzig to Germany. The Poles declined the offer as they felt the city was vital for their own security.

Knowing by now that any further escalation would lead to war between the Allies and Germany, Hitler edged his bets with the Soviet Union – he did not wish to fight on two fronts at the same time, even though his ultimate plan was still to expand his empire east into Russian territory. The Molotov–Ribbentrop Pact was a non-aggression treaty in which Germany and the Soviet Union agreed to each other's rights to spheres of influence. This basically meant that Germany could invade western Poland and Lithuania without Soviet interference as long as Germany had no objection to Russia's claims on eastern Poland, Finland, Estonia, Latvia and Bessarabia.

With a Russian agreement secured, Hitler ordered the attack on Poland to start on 26 August, but upon hearing that Great Britain and France had agreed a mutual assistance pact with Poland and that Italy would remain neutral, he decided to delay it. Britain desperately tried to negotiate with Hitler in an attempt to stop the attack, but he demanded that Poland send a plenipotentiary to Berlin to discuss the handover of Danzig and the Polish Corridor to Germany as well as to agree to safeguard the German minority in Poland. The Poles refused to comply with this request, and, on the evening of 31 August, Germany declared that it considered its proposals rejected.

Much of what we know about Hitler's plans to go to war in the west comes from a series of documents known as the Führer's directives (*Führerbefehle*). These were instructions and strategic plans issued personally by Hitler himself to his senior commanders. They were absolutely binding and took precedence over all other laws. They covered a wide range of subjects, from detailed direction of military units to the governance of occupied territories and their populations. There were fifty-two directives issued in total, which should not be confused with the so-called Führer's orders, issued later in the war.

On 3 April Hitler issued a directive concerning war preparations through Field Marshal Wilhelm Keitel, the chief of the high command of Germany's armed forces. Attached to it was a document containing details of Case White (*Fall Weiss*), the projected attack on Poland. During the months that followed a series of supplementary instructions were issued by the high command, until finally, on 31 August, preparations were complete and Hitler could issue directive number one, which read:

Since the situation on Germany's eastern frontier has become intolerable and all political possibilities of peaceful settlement have been exhausted, I have decided upon a solution by force.

The attack on Poland will be undertaken in accordance with the preparations made for Case White, with such variations as may be necessitated by the buildup of the Army which is now virtually complete.

The allocation of tanks and the purpose of the operation remain unchanged.

Date of attack: 1st September, 1939.

This time also applies to operations at Gdynia, in the Bay Of Danzig, and at the Dirschau Bridge.

In the west it is important to leave the responsibility for opening hostilities unmistakably to England and France. Minor violations of the frontier will be dealt with, for the time being, purely as local incidents.

The assurances of neutrality given by us to Holland, Belgium, Luxembourg, and Switzerland are to be meticulously observed.

The western frontier of Germany will not be crossed by land at any point without my explicit orders.

This applies also to all acts of warfare at sea or to acts which might be regarded as such.

The defensive activity of the Air Force will be restricted for the time being to the firm repulse of enemy air attacks on the frontiers of the Reich. In taking action against individual aircraft or small formations, care will be taken to respect the frontiers of neutral countries as far as possible. Only if considerable forces of French or British bombers are employed against German territory across neutral areas will the Air Force be permitted to go into defensive action over neutral soil.

It is particularly important that any infringement of the neutrality of other States by our western enemies be immediately reported to the High Command of The Armed Forces.

Should England and France open hostilities against Germany, it will be the duty of the Armed Forces operating in the west, while conserving their strength as much as possible, to maintain conditions for the successful conclusion of operations against Poland. Within these limits enemy forces and war potential will be damaged as much as possible. The right to order offensive operations is reserved absolutely to me.

The Army will occupy the West Wall and will take steps to secure it from being outflanked in the north, through the violation by the western powers of Belgian or Dutch territory. Should French forces invade Luxembourg the bridges on the frontier may be blown up.

The Navy will operate against merchant shipping, with England as the focal point. In order to increase the effect, the declaration of danger zones may be expected. The Naval High Command will report on the areas which it is desirable to classify as danger zones and on their extent. The text of a public declaration in this matter is to be drawn up in collaboration with the Foreign Office and to be submitted to me for approval through the High Command of The Armed Forces.

The Baltic Sea is to be secured against enemy intrusion. The Commander-in-chief of The Navy will decide whether the entrances to the Baltic Sea should be mined for this purpose.

The Air Force is, first of all, to prevent action by the French and English Air Forces against the German Army and German territory.

In operations against England, the task of the Air Force is to take measures to dislocate English imports, the armaments industry, and the transport of troops to France. Any favourable opportunity of an effective attack on concentrated units of the English Navy, particularly on battleships or aircraft carriers, will be exploited. The decision regarding attacks on London is reserved to me.

Attacks on the English homeland are to be prepared, bearing in mind that inconclusive results with insufficient forces are to be avoided in all circumstances.

As determined by the document, Hitler ordered the assault on Poland to begin on 1 September 1939, and troops from Germany and the Slovak Republic subsequently crossed the border on that date. Two days later, on 3 September, France and Great Britain, followed by the Dominions of the British Commonwealth, declared war on Germany.

3

DEPLOYMENT OF THE BEF

Immediately after war was declared Britain began to send troops to the Continent, specially designated in advance for such a circumstance. This army was called the British Expeditionary Force (BEF). It had been created in 1938 to enable Britain to respond quickly in the event of war with Germany. The first ships left Southampton on 9 September 1939, and by March the following year 316,000 men had been transported. They were mainly deployed along the border between France and Belgium in the north-east section of the country, and when compared to the troops available to Germany, this force now seems wholly inadequate.

When Hitler came to total power in 1934 he also became commander-in-chief of the armed forces. Acting on his own initiative, his defence minister, Werner von Blomberg, had the armed forces adopt Nazi symbols on their uniforms and arranged for all military personnel to take the Hitler oath, a statement of personal loyalty to the Führer. This oath read: 'I swear by God this sacred oath that to the leader of the German empire and people, Adolf Hitler, supreme commander of the armed forces, I shall render unconditional obedience and that as a brave soldier I shall at all times be prepared to give my life for this oath.'

Hitler wasted no time in rebuilding his armed forces, announcing both rearmament and conscription in March 1935. Under the terms of the Treaty of Versailles, Germany was permitted to have a standing army of around 100,000 men, which was intended solely for the purpose of internal security. Hitler decreed that a quantity of conscripts equal to this number would be called up and trained each year. The *Reichswehr* of the Weimar Republic was officially renamed the *Wehrmacht* on 21 May 1935. The word *Wehrmacht* meant 'defence force' and would encompass all of Germany's fighting men. It consisted of the *Heer* (army), the *Kriegsmarine* (navy) and the *Luftwaffe* (air force).

When Hitler formally announced the existence of the *Wehrmacht*, it already included thirty-six divisions and as such contravened the Treaty of Versailles in no uncertain terms. In December 1935, General Ludwig Beck, chief of German general staff, added forty-eight tank battalions to the rearmament plan; tanks were also restricted by the treaty.

The *Wehrmacht's* arsenal received a large boost as a consequence of the occupation of Czechoslovakia. In a speech delivered in the Reichstag, Hitler stressed that by occupying Czechoslovakia, Germany gained sufficient weaponry to arm about half of the then *Wehrmacht*. This included over 2,000 field cannon, nearly 500 tanks, 500 anti-aircraft artillery pieces, 43,000 machine guns, and over 1,000,000 rifles. As well as these the Nazis had acquired huge quantities of bullets and artillery shells.

In spite of the alarming situation in Germany, Britain's army remained fully professional at first with a Territorial Army representing its reserves. However a move to mobilise an armed force began in 1936, when plans to expand the existing Territorial Army were put in place after a report was given to the House of Commons on 12 March of that year by Duff Cooper, the Secretary of State for War, in which he pointed out that in future warfare the use of enemy aircraft flying from anywhere on the Continent would put Britain on the front line. In that same report conscription in the United Kingdom was discussed. It was realised that if there were a war with Germany at that point, there would not be enough time to expand the army to satisfactory levels.

In March 1937, the British regular army stood at roughly 121,000 at home and 89,000 overseas, with 716 tanks, many of which were of First World War vintage. In a speech by Cooper's successor, Leslie

Hore-Belisha, on 10 March 1938, the number was given as 500,000. Recruiting for the Army accounted for around 60,000 men a year, but it remained short of 1,200 officers and 22,000 other ranks even under peacetime manning.

In November 1938 the British prime minister Neville Chamberlain and foreign minister Lord Halifax went to Paris where talks about the formation of the BEF were concluded with Édouard Daladier, the French prime minster. Although this force would help to defend the French border, its principal objective was to safeguard Great Britain and keep the wolves away from her own doors.

Even after an agreement had been struck with the French, Chamberlain appears to have been a little evasive about the subject. When questions were asked about the outcome of these talks in the House of Commons on 28 November, he asserted that there was no commitment to send an expeditionary force to France at that time. In reality the troops required for such an expedition were already being ear-marked under the watchful eye of General Sir John Dill, general officer commanding Aldershot Command; however, when the war did eventually break out and the first troops left Southampton bound for Europe, it would not be Sir John Dill who would lead them but General Lord Gort.

John Vereker, 6th Viscount of Gort, was born in 1886 of Anglo-Irish aristocratic descent. After schooling at Harrow, he immediately joined the Army. After training to become an officer at the Royal Military Academy at Sandhurst, he joined the Grenadier Guards. During the First World War he had a highly decorated career: he was mentioned in despatches on nine occasions, won the Military Cross, the Distinguished Service Order, and was awarded the Victoria Cross for outstanding bravery in September 1918. Between the wars his illustrious career continued. He became commander of the Guards Brigade in 1930 and commander of the Staff College in 1936. In 1937 he was promoted to the rank of full general. With his exemplary record, he was seen as the ideal candidate to become commander-in-chief of the British Expeditionary Force.

On arriving in France Lord Gort and his troops were in theory under the command of the French, as General Alphonse Georges has been appointed commander-in-chief of Allied forces on the north-east front by French supreme commander General Maurice Gamelin. However he was also a commander in his own right and could make independent decisions if he thought they were in the British interest. His orders from London basically stated: 'If any order given by him [General Georges] appears to you to imperil the British field force it is agreed between the British and French governments that you should be at liberty to appeal to the British government before executing that order.'

Other key figures in BEF command included Lieutenant General Sir Henry Royds Pownall, who was chief of staff; Major General Philip Neame VC, deputy chief of staff, responsible for operations and staff duties; Lieutenant General Sir Wellesley Douglas Studholme Brownrigg, adjutant general; Lieutenant General Wilfred Gordon Lindsell, quartermaster general; Major General S. R. Watson, in command of the Royal Artillery; and Major General Ridley Pakenham-Walsh, who was head of the Royal Engineers.

The main ports initially used by the BEF were Cherbourg, Brest, Nantes and Saint-Nazaire. Once movement had been established through these and the feared attacks on the troop ships by the Luftwaffe failed to materialise, the force also began to use Le Havre, Dieppe, Boulogne-sur-Mer and Calais. Major General Philip de Fonblanque, who was in charge of logistics and lines of communication, had his headquarters in Le Mans, where there was an important railway junction. Dieppe was the main medical base of the BEF and Le Havre the principal supply and ordnance source. From Saint-Saens to Buchy, north-east of Rouen, lay the BEF ammunition depot, and infantry, machine gun and base depots were at Rouen, Évreux and L'Epinay. A main railway line linking bases from Normandy to the Belgian border ran through Rouen, Abbeville and Amiens. Brigadier Archibald Beauman was responsible for base security and guarding army camps and airfields under construction.

The first deployment of the BEF had been successfully transported to France by 11 October 1939. Leslie Hore-Belisha reported to Parliament that 158,000 men had been ferried across the Channel within five weeks of the commencement of hostilities. Convoys from Southampton had averaged three crossings each night and the BEF had been moved intact without a single casualty to any of its personnel. By 19 October, the force had also received 25,000 vehicles, which completed the first deployment.

The vast majority of British troops were positioned along the border between France and Belgium from Bailleul in the west to Maulde in the east. One division, called Saar Force, was dispatched to the Maginot Line to serve alongside the French 3rd Army. At that time Belgium and the Netherlands remained neutral, so no Allied troops were positioned within their borders.

As Belgium had suffered greatly during the First World War, there was little appetite within the country to involve itself in any potential European conflict, so in October 1936 King Leopold III announced that his country would remain neutral in the event of another war in Europe. To this end the Belgian government tried to extract itself from various Allied alliances. For instance, it left the Locarno Treaty and repudiated a defence pact it had made with France in 1920. Accordingly in 1937 it also negotiated with Nazi Germany, who guaranteed to recognise its neutrality.

During this period, and in spite of its neutrality, Belgium began to construct and modernise its fortifications around the country, particularly those in the north towards the border with Germany. These defences included the Koningshooikt–Wavre Line (K-W Line), which was also known as the Dyle Line because of its proximity to the River Dyle. It was built between September 1939 and May 1940 and consisted of a network of bunkers and barricades between the village of Koningshooikt near Antwerp and the city of Wavre. The barricades were mainly comprised of Cointet-elements, which were pieces of heavy steel fencing about three metres wide and two metres high mounted on concrete rollers and used as mobile anti-tank obstacles; the elements were connected together with steel cables. There were also things like concrete ditches filled with water and other steel constructions designed to repulse armoured vehicles. In 1940 the Belgian army numbered between 600,000 and 650,000 men, so in theory if the country was invaded it was considered capable of defending its own territory – initially, in any case.

As for the Netherlands, their government was convinced that their country would not be able to withstand an invasion from a major foreign power, so they spent very little on defence and instead hoped that their neutrality would save them from attack. The government did however begin to work on plans for the defence of the country as a precaution against invasion. This included the New Dutch Waterline, an area to the east of Amsterdam that would be flooded, and, from 1939, fortified positions including the Grebbe and Peel-Raam Lines that protected the key cities of Dordrecht, Utrecht, Haarlem and Amsterdam.

As well as consisting of units of the British army, the BEF included two Royal Air Force (RAF) formations. The first of these was the Advanced Air Striking Force, commanded by Air Vice-Marshal Patrick Playfair. Their job was to work alongside the French army patrolling the border with Germany. The second formation was the Air Component of the BEF itself, which was commanded by Air Vice-Marshal Charles Blount and was initially based in the Pas-de-Calais. It had two functions, the first of which was to operate in support of the British land forces as they took up their positions along the Belgian frontier. Their secondary task was to patrol over convoys plying through the English Channel in case they drew the unwelcome attention of the enemy.

In April 1939 Leslie Hore-Belisha persuaded Neville Chamberlain's Cabinet to introduce a limited form of conscription with the passing of the Military Training Act the following month. Single men between twenty and twenty-two years of age were liable for the call up; they were to be known as 'militiamen' to distinguish them from the regular army or territorials. The intention was for the first intake to undergo six months of basic training before joining the active reserve. They would then be recalled for short training periods and attend an annual camp. However when the war began, in September 1939, the Military Training Act was overtaken by the National Service (Armed Forces) Act and the first intake was absorbed immediately by the Army. This act imposed a liability for conscription of all men aged between eighteen and forty-one except those who were deemed to be in reserved occupations or were rejected for medical reasons.

Over the next six months, troops, materiel and vehicles continued to arrive in France, and by March 1940 the BEF had doubled in size to 316,000 men. Among these troops was a young soldier called Thomas William (Bill) Ward, who was one of Leslie Hore-Belisha's conscripted militiamen. He gives us a vivid insight of how quickly soldiers were gathered, trained and subsequently sent to the front.

Bill was born in 1918 and in 1935 had become a cadet in the Merchant Navy Service. Because of this experience he had hoped to join the Royal Navy when the war began. However it was not to be and he was called up by the Army, serving with the King's Own Yorkshire Light Infantry. Bill was also very artistic and in the evenings had attended Sheffield College of Arts, hoping one day to put his artistic talents to good use. For Bill, as with many young men, life and personal aspirations were about to be put on hold for the next six years as they were expected to do their duty for king and country. Bill Ward wrote:

I was called up in Sheffield and sent to the local barracks, which was a decorative medieval looking building. I wanted to join the Royal Navy as I had made a voyage as an apprentice on a Houlder Brothers ship the *Dunster Grange*. I was patted on the shoulder and told I was in line for a commission in the RN.

After a few weeks I received an official letter directing me to Wakefield with a 3rd class railway ticket, where I was to join the KOYLI. I could not imagine what those initials stood for, so I went out and met a neighbour on the main road, who had been a soldier during the last war. In asking what branch of the Navy it was he burst out laughing and told me, it was not the Navy but the Army and a unit that ran, not marched, and carried its rifles like walking sticks: The King's Own Yorkshire Light Infantry. He advised me to go and get a haircut, which I did. That was a bit of good advice I shall never regret.

The bright and cheeky Sheffield boys had no respect for the red sashed sergeant who came to meet us at Wakefield train station, and gathered us all together. He took the teasing in good heart. When the bus ran into a modern barracks I got out and stood in amazement beside a huge flat parade ground, where we watched a very young bugler march out and play a call! It was Strensal Barracks near York. We had been transported there in a fleet of coaches from Wakefield Station. It had been a rowdy journey during which the staff sergeant took some ribbing.

Suddenly there was a loud bellow in my ear. A lance corporal wanted to know if I had fallen asleep. The crowd of recruits with whom I had travelled had marched off to the quarter masters store in a corner of the parade ground and I was being urged to catch up. It wasn't long before I was shuffling off in a pair of heavy leather ammunition boots trying to catch up with my companions, with the leather boot laces dangling from my hands.

We arrived at a Militia Spider, a very new wooden and strong cuprinol-smelling group of huts. We were allocated beds on which I was glad to dump my armful of clothing and bedding and follow instructions to the dining hall with my mess tins.

Sunday came and we still had only one mess tin each, so after our first course, the remnants of that course was scraped out on to the centre of the table, to form a ridge of potatoes and gristly meat. My middle class upbringing withheld me, but I soon saw the advantage of doing likewise, when down between the rows of seats came orderlies with big oval dixies and a large spoon. In the dixies was a rather blue rice pudding which went slap on the centre of our mess tin. During that week I acquired an enamel plate and mug, so meal times became more civilised. The long tables were not such a horror, and perhaps my more civilised eating equipment, or the vigorous thumping around the parade ground improved my appetite.

We had a few hectic weeks taking delivery of mortars, Bren gun carriers and equipment, and we looked like soldiers, even though we didn't feel like the real thing. I had been promoted to lance corporal and had a beautiful dark green stripe on a white stripe.

Embarkation leave went brilliantly, then it was back to Wakefield and the hectic scramble to acquire all our kit. There was no anxiety as we were a twenty year old militia unit, untrained, and the war had not properly started. We felt safe. Little did we know!

The railway station at Dewsbury was black that night. I had to get my section of seven men into a compartment, complete with their packs, to which were strapped steel helmets, and each carried a 9lb rifle. They were just seven black oval heads, amongst 800 other black oval heads. Miraculously, 800 men embarked. A few well informed girls had appeared from somewhere and down the platform a small group of Scottish bag pipers played plaintively, 'Will ye no come back again'. They had come from a unit stationed locally.

The compartment was hot and stuffy and every time the train pulled up sharply a pack and steel helmet fell off the rack with a thump and a sharp grunt from a militia boy. By morning we were in Southampton. Our Brigade No 138 was made up of one battalion of KOYLI, one of York and Lancaster Regiment and a third of the Lincolnshire Regiment. There we all were, being bundled out of the trains which had pulled up on the dockside and shuffling untidily over the dock to board three cross channel steamers. Somehow we all managed to get on board our respective ships. It was fresh and clean in the morning sea air, after the stuffy hot journey. Down below decks, tables were lined up with tea and thick cheese sandwiches for us all.

The Channel crossing with two destroyers escorting was tremendously exciting and our pals in the other ships were within waving distance all the way. We were fed again, this time on thick jam sandwiches as we got into Cherbourg. What a super little French town is Cherbourg, and what a picturesque harbour. Trains came alongside the piers, but there were no passenger trucks like in England, just cattle trucks boldly labelled 'Huit chevals' and '40 hommes'. Not having any horses it was just a platoon to each wagon. We had no idea where we were going. I sat with my legs hanging out of the wagon door, and we cheered every French girl that passed by - and they cheered back! Motorcyclists came alongside when we stopped at crossings. Later, we were told they were Germans. Certainly our parents heard from Lord Haw Haw's broadcast that evening that the 46 Infantry Division had landed in France and that 138 Brigade were entrained. Well, it wasn't difficult for the enemy to discover who we were, as so many soldiers leaned out chatting to everyone who could talk in English. We came to halt about tea time just beyond a station called, I think Caen, and disembarked. We marched off to a ready-made camp of Nissen huts. Here we were tasked with making a siding for an ammunition dump. There were big orchards to clear: it seemed such a shame. Our enthusiastic subalterns soon learned to use dynamite under the roots and we cleared the trees, burning them.

Bill was just one of the 316,000 British troops who arrived in France between September 1939 and March 1940. By May 1940 the BEF order of battle consisted of eight infantry divisions incorporated within three corps (a corps being a battlefield formation usually composed of two or more divisions). These were I Corps, II Corps and III Corps. I Corps, commanded by Lieutenant General Michael Barker, was made up of the 1st Infantry Division (Major General Harold Alexander), the 2nd Infantry Division (Major General H. C. Lloyd) and the 48th (South Midland) Infantry Division (Major General Augustus Thorne). II Corps, under Lieutenant General Alan Brooke, comprised the 3rd Infantry Division (Major General Bernard Law Montgomery), the 4th Infantry Division (Major General Dudley Graham Johnson VC) and the 50th (Northumbrian) Motor Infantry Division (Major General Giffard Le Quesne Martel). III Corps, led by Lieutenant General Sir R. F. Adam, involved the 42nd (East Lancashire) Infantry Division (Major General William George Holmes) and the 44th (Home Counties) Infantry Division (Major General Edmund Archibald Osborne).

There was also one division allocated to Saar Force, the 51st (Highland) Infantry Division, commanded by Major General Victor Morven Fortune. There was also the 5th Infantry Division under Major General Harold Franklyn, which acted independently as part of Lord Gort's headquarters troops along with the 1st Army Tank Brigade and the 1st Light Armoured Reconnaissance Brigade. Finally, there were three divisions undergoing training or performing labour duties: the 12th (Eastern) Infantry Division (Major General Roderic Loraine Petre), the 23rd (Northumbrian) Infantry Division

(Major General A. E. Herbert) and the 46th (West Riding) Infantry Division (Major General H. O. Curtis). Bill Ward, whose story we will return to later, was serving with the 46th in the 2/4th Battalion, King's Own Yorkshire Light Infantry. Although this was technically an infantry battalion, its militiamen had very little military training and were employed as pioneers, mainly doing construction and other labour tasks.

Finally there was the BEF Air Component and the Advanced Air Striking Force of the RAF. There is a full list of corps and other divisional units that served with the initial BEF formations, excluding Royal Artillery, Royal Engineers and Royal Corps of Signals, in Appendix I.

4

THE PHONEY WAR

In the months that followed the declaration of war and the deployment of the BEF to France, very little happened in Western Europe and the British military contingent was not involved in action. The generals of course expected an attack at any moment, but nothing transpired and each day became a waiting game. The truth was that a large part of the *Wehrmacht* was deployed on the Polish front so Hitler probably could not have launched a successful attack in the West at that time anyway.

This period of relative inactivity in France, which would last until May 1940, has become known as the 'Phoney War'. This term was allegedly first used by an American senator named William Borah, who in September 1939 commented on the lack of action in France when he stated, 'There is something phoney about this war.' Winston Churchill, who at that time was First Lord of the Admiralty, initially referred to the same period as the 'twilight war'; it first appeared in British newspapers as 'phoney' in January 1940. The French referred to this period as the '*drôle de guerre*', which meant 'funny' or 'strange' war. The Germans, on the other hand, termed it the '*sitzkrieg*', or 'sitting war', a play on the word blitzkrieg.

It was not only on the western front that the British expected a German attack to take place, as it was widely believed that Britain itself would be subjected to an aerial onslaught. In fear of cities being bombed by the *Luftwaffe*, the British government had drawn up plans to evacuate school children and some other categories of civilians from what were considered to be endangered zones. The plan was to move evacuees from these areas to places considered to be safe, such as the West Country, Wales and Yorkshire. The first evacuation scheme got under way on 1 September 1939, and within four days more than 1,300,000 people had been relocated from London alone, with other large cities also complying. Children left their families heading for the unknown, carrying little more than their gas mask and a suitcase. However, so little happened in the coming weeks that most of these children soon returned home.

In retrospect, and on reading Hitler's directive number two, which was issued on 3 September, it is clear that the Führer hoped that Great Britain and France would commence hostilities in the West, which would thus make them the aggressors on the diplomatic stage. The relevant paragraphs read:

A) In respect of England

Navy: Offensive action may now begin. In carrying out the war against merchant shipping, submarines also, for the time being, will observe prize regulations. Intensified measures leading to the declaration of danger zones will be prepared. I shall decide when these measures shall become effective.

The entrances to the Baltic Sea will be mined without infringing neutral territorial waters.

In the North Sea the blockade measures envisaged for defensive purposes and for the attacks on England will be carried out.

Air Force: Attacks upon English naval forces at naval bases or on the high seas (including the English Channel), and on definitely identified troop transports, will only be made in the event of English air attacks on similar targets and where there are particularly good prospects of success. This applies also to action by the Fleet Air Arm.

These limitations do not apply to operations in the German Bight, in the western mined areas, or during actions directly supporting naval operations.

I reserve to myself the decision about attacks on the English homeland and on merchant shipping.

B) In respect of France

Army: The opening hostilities in the west will be left to the enemy. Commander-in-chief Army will decide on the reinforcement of our forces in the west from such reserves as are still available.

Navy: Offensive action against France will only be permitted if the enemy has first opened hostilities. In that case the same instructions apply to France as have been laid down for England.

Air Force: Offensive action against France will only be undertaken after French attacks on German territory. The guiding principle must be not to provoke the initiation of aerial warfare by any action on the part of Germany.

In general the employment of the Air Force in the west will be governed by the need to preserve its fighting strength after the defeat of Poland for decisive action against the western powers.

To assume that nothing entirely happened during this period would be wrong as a number of incidents of note did take place. One of these happened at 9:00 a.m. on 3 September, the opening day of the war itself, when a German U-boat attacked and sank the British passenger ship the SS *Athenia* as it plied its way to Canada. After this the British government was left in no doubt that Germany was prepared to sink civilian as well as military vessels.

The German commander Fritz-Julius Lemp later claimed that he believed the *Athenia* was a naval boat as it was sailing in a zigzag manner and in the poor light he could not differentiate between a liner and a naval vessel. Of the 1,418 passengers and crew aboard the ship, 115 died. Fifty-four of the dead were Canadians and twenty-eight were US citizens, which led to German fears that the incident could force America to enter the war on the side of the Allies.

During the opening weeks of the war the French army was slightly more involved militarily than the British. On 7 September, in accordance with their alliance with Poland, France began the Saar Offensive with an advance from the Maginot Line cutting through the German-occupied Saarland.

The Maginot Line was a formidable series of concrete fortifications, tank obstacles and heavily protected gun installations that the French had constructed on their side of its borders with Switzerland, Germany and Luxembourg during the 1930s. It was named after the French minister of war, André Maginot, who had been largely responsible for its construction through lobbying the government for the necessary funding. However, the line did not extend all the way to the English Channel because the French did not want to offend Belgium, given its policy of neutrality. This would prove to be a huge mistake.

The line was built as a response to France's experience in the First World War, a static affair that saw armies dug in with little advance or movement for long periods of time. The fortifications were considered to be impervious to most forms of attack, including artillery and tank fire as well as bombing from the air. The French hoped that these fortifications would give their army the time it needed to mobilise in the event of an attack and move it to the required areas. The Maginot Line was highly praised by French military and civil leaders who genuinely believed that its existence would prevent any further invasions of their country from the east.

By the time of the Saar Offensive, France had mobilised ninety-eight divisions, including 2,500 tanks. On the opening day of the offensive eleven divisions of the 2nd Army Group advanced across the border towards the thinly manned Siegfried Line, the German equivalent of the Maginot Line.

An original Siegfried Line was built by the Germans in the First World War in northern France, but in the 1930s a new defensive wall was constructed directly opposite the Maginot Line. It stretched more than 390 miles and featured more than 18,000 bunkers, tunnels and tank traps. This network of defensive structures stretched from Kleve in the north, on the border with Holland, to the town of Weil am Rhein in the south, near the border with Switzerland. It was planned in 1936 and built between 1938 and 1940.

The strategy behind the Saar Offensive was for French forces to take control of the area between the French border and the Siegfried Line, while at the same time probing and testing the German defences. Having occupied this area, the plan was then to commence a full-scale thrust through the heart of Germany, scheduled to begin on 16 September.

The French divisions advanced along a twenty-mile front near the city of Saarbrücken, the capital of Saarland, where they encountered very little opposition from the German defenders. In a five-mile thrust they captured about twelve villages and towns, completely unopposed. Four Renault R35 light infantry support tanks were destroyed in a minefield to the north of Bliesbruck.

On 10 September there was a small German counter-attack on the village of Apach, which they successfully retook. However, the French forces regrouped and reclaimed the village a few hours later. On 12 September, the 32nd Infantry Regiment seized the German town of Brenschelbach, while at the border between the three countries of France, Germany and Luxembourg, the Schengen Bridge across the River Mosel was destroyed thus denying the Nazis an important crossing point. The half-hearted Saar Offensive came to an abrupt halt when the French reached the Warndt Forest, an area of territory that had been extensively mined by the Germans.

On 12 September, the Anglo-French Supreme War Council, sometimes referred to simply as the Supreme War Council (SWC), gathered for the first time at Abbeville in France. Established to oversee joint military strategy at the start of the war, at its inaugural session Britain was represented by the prime minister, Neville Chamberlain, and Lord Chatfield, who was his minister for coordination of defence; the French delegation was headed by their prime minister, Édouard Daladier, and General Maurice Gamelin, supreme commander of the French armed forces.

It was decided at this meeting to bring an immediate halt to all offensive actions, and as a result General Gamelin ordered his troops to stop about a half a mile short of the German positions along the Siegfried Line. Poland was not notified of this decision and instead Gamelin informed Marshal Edward Rydz-Śmigly, the commander-in-chief of the Polish armed forces, that half of the French divisions were still fighting the enemy. He also claimed that the French advance had forced the *Wehrmacht* to withdraw at least six divisions from Poland, which was probably only partially true. The following day, the commander of the French military mission to Poland, General Louis Faury, informed the Polish chief of staff, General Waclaw Stachiewicz, that the planned major offensive on the western front had to be postponed.

While all of this was going on, the war in Poland continued. On 17 September the Soviet army invaded the country from the east, while in the west the Polish army held out in Warsaw against the Germans until 27 September when they officially surrendered; small groups of resistance fighters held out in the city until 6 October. Then, the invasion complete, Poland was divided up between Germany and the Soviet Union, with Lithuania and Slovakia also receiving small areas. The Poles established an underground state with an underground army and continued to fight alongside the Allies on many fronts.

After the fall of Poland Hitler still hoped that he could prevent further military action in western Europe. On 6 October he made a public peace overture to Britain and France but insisted that the future of Poland was to be determined exclusively by Germany and the Soviet Union. Chamberlain rejected this on 12 October, saying 'past experience has shown that no reliance can be placed upon the promises of the present German government'.

From 16 to 17 October, the German army, now reinforced with troops returning from the Polish campaign, conducted a counter-offensive in the west that retook all the territory they had previously lost to the French. By then General Gamelin had ordered all his divisions to retreat back to their barracks along the Maginot Line from where they had started the offensive a month earlier, having lost around 2,000 men. The Germans are thought to have lost 196 soldiers, plus 114 missing and 356 wounded; they further reported that eleven of their aircraft had been shot down.

After the Saar Offensive the Phoney War continued in earnest for the French as well as the British. For the British troops along the Maginot Line, the inactivity was coupled with a belief that the fortifications in which they were installed formed an unbreakable barrier. Morale was very high among British troops both here and along the border with Belgium, a situation helped in part by visits from entertainers like George Formby, who memorably painted a picture of a Tommy's life in his song 'Imagine Me in the Maginot Line', which included the lines:

> Now imagine me in the Maginot Line
> Sitting on a mine in the Maginot Line
> Now it's turned out nice again
> The Army life is fine
> French girls make a fuss of me
> I'm not French as you can see
> But I know what they mean when they say *'oui, oui'*
> Down on the Maginot Line

At the war's outset George Formby had volunteered to join the army but was turned down because he had flat feet. To do his bit he joined the Home Guard in Blackpool but also began to give his aforementioned concerts to entertain the troops. He was the first major star to visit the BEF in France and had a tremendous welcome wherever he went. A number of newsreels show George performing to the troops in March 1940 and they all included the above song, which proved a big hit with the soldiers.

Away from France the war manifested on several other fronts. On 14 October, for instance, the British battleship HMS *Royal Oak* was anchored at Scapa Flow in Orkney when she was torpedoed by a German submarine. Of the 1,234 men and boys aboard the ship, 833 were killed or died later of their wounds. Royal Navy chiefs were convinced that the base at Scapa Flow was impregnable to submarine attack and totally safe for their ships while at anchor there. In Germany this daring raid made an immediate hero out of the U-boat's commander, Günther Prien, who became the first German submariner to be awarded the Knight's Cross of the Iron Cross. Many people in Britain first learned about the loss of the *Royal Oak* from the radio broadcasts of the Nazi propagandist William Joyce, better known as Lord Haw-Haw, as previously mentioned by Bill Ward.

In actual fact the nickname Lord Haw-Haw applied to a number of people who broadcast Nazi propaganda on the British airwaves at the time. The first of these was Wolf Mittler, a German journalist who spoke with a flawless English accent that he had picked up from his mother, who had been born in Ireland to German parents. However the nickname is most commonly deployed while describing Joyce, who replaced Mittler in 1939. Joyce was American-born but raised in Ireland. While a teenager he became an informant for the British forces by giving them details of Irish Republican Army (IRA) members during the Irish War of Independence. He later moved to England, where he became a senior member of the British Union of Fascists, but after being tipped off that he was going to be interned, in August 1939 he fled to Germany where he found like-minded people. Joyce would go on to become the main German broadcaster in English for most of the war and became a naturalised German citizen. He had a peculiar hybrid accent that was almost of the conventional upper-class variety, and people soon began to mimic his distinctive pronunciation of the famous phrase with which he began all his broadcasts: 'Germany calling, Germany calling.'

On 16 October the Germans also began to carry out aerial attacks on military targets on the British mainland, when they attacked ships of the Royal Navy based at Rosyth in the Firth of Forth. This resulted in the first two enemy aircraft being shot down over mainland Britain, both of which crashed in the sea. They were downed by Supermarine Spitfires, the aircraft that would play such an important role in the air defence of Britain a year later during the Battle of Britain.

During the Phoney War, the Royal Air Force was itself engaged in raids over Germany. However, it was not bombs that were dropped but propaganda leaflets. Sir Kingsley Wood, Secretary of State for Air, called them 'truth raids' which served to inform the German populace about the evils of Nazi Germany and to show their leaders just how vulnerable their country was to potential bombing raids – if they could drop leaflets over Germany, they could just as easily drop bombs.

In the naval war Britain would soon have its first victory over the Germans but far away from the fields of France in the South Atlantic Ocean in what is known as the Battle of the River Plate in December 1939. This would prove to be the first major naval battle of the Second World War and, remarkably, the only episode of the entire conflict to take place in South America. The British Admiralty had sent out various battle groups to search for a German pocket battleship called the *Admiral Graf Spee* that had been commerce raiding since the start of hostilities and attacking the cargo ships on which Britain depended. One of these groups of three vessels was made up of the Royal Navy cruisers, HMS *Exeter*, HMS *Ajax*, and a New Zealand ship HMS *Achilles*. They discovered their quarry off the estuary of the River Plate close to the coast of Argentina and Uruguay in South America and went in for the kill.

In the battle that followed, *Exeter* was severely damaged and was forced to retire, while *Ajax* and *Achilles* both suffered moderate damage. However the damage inflicted to the German ship was critical: her fuel system had been crippled. *Ajax* and *Achilles* shadowed the *Graf Spee* until she entered the port of Montevideo, the capital city of neutral Uruguay. Here her crew hoped to make urgent repairs, but her captain, Hans Langsdorff, was told that his stay could not be extended beyond seventy-two hours. Rather than confront the overwhelmingly superior force that the British had led him to believe was awaiting him on his departure, he scuttled his damaged ship. So as 1939 came to a close, Britain ended the first year of the war with a victory, albeit far away from the western front.

In mid-February 1940, another interesting incident occurred subsequent to the hunt for the *Graf Spee* that would bring the action much closer to events in Europe. It involved a German vessel called the *Altmark*, which was used as a supply ship for the scuttled battleship. As a naval auxiliary ship, while attempting to return home she could legally claim freedom from search by foreign forces. However, she was believed to have a large number of British merchant sailors on board as prisoners taken from ships sunk by the *Graf Spee*. If these men did get to Germany, it would have been good propaganda for the Nazis at a very early stage in the war.

On 16 February 1940 the British 4th Destroyer Flotilla intercepted the *Altmark* off the south coast of Norway, which was a neutral country. Two Norwegian warships were escorting the German vessel and warned the British ships not to interfere with her as she passed through their waters. The commander of the 4th Flotilla, Captain Philip Vian, received orders from Winston Churchill at the Admiralty to board the *Altmark,* even though she had taken refuge in neutral seas. An offer was put to the *Altmark*'s captain that she could proceed to the Norwegian port of Bergen under escort and once there undergo a search. However, when the destroyer HMS *Cossack* tried to pull alongside the much larger German craft, the supply ship attempted to ram her. In doing so the *Altmark* ran aground and British sailors rushed aboard her and freed the 299 merchant sailors who had been held in the cargo hold. Afterwards the *Altmark* was refloated at high tide and continued to Germany without her prize, infuriating Hitler and annoying the Norwegians who felt their neutrality had been violated by the British.

To keep themselves occupied, the British soldiers on the western front would send out reconnaissance patrols to find out what the enemy was up to. These would sometimes encounter German patrols engaged in similar duties. They would observe each other but rarely clash. The first battle fatality among the ranks of the BEF was a twenty-seven-year-old corporal from the 1st Battalion, King's Shropshire Light Infantry called Thomas William Priday, a pre-war regular who was attached to the 3rd Infantry Brigade of the 1st Infantry Division, based at the small village of Luttange. He was killed on 9 December 1939 when his patrol set off a booby trap and was subsequently fired upon by friendly forces. An official report noted:

> Report received of first casualties (1 killed 4 wounded) of 3 Inf Bde on the SAAR Front – this had been caused by a patrol leader losing his way in the dark and walking into one of our own booby traps. The ambush party unfortunately fired into the ensuing melee.

If any part of the British contingent was likely to exchange shots with the enemy first, it would undoubtedly have been the Royal Air Force. The following account makes us appreciate just how slow things were to happen. Among the RAF squadrons who went to France with the Air Component was No. 1 Squadron, equipped with Hawker Hurricanes, in which Billy Drake was serving. The squadron established itself at Cherbourg-Octeville on 9 September 1939 to cover the arrival of the BEF. Then, on 9 October, after the BEF had completed its disembarkation the squadron moved to their designated permanent base at the village of Vassincourt in the Lorraine region, where their duty was to provide fighter support and defence for the aircraft and airfields of the RAF's Advanced Air Striking Force. Billy

Drake recalled the situation in France at that time and the system, or lack of it, which was used to intercept enemy aircraft:

At the beginning of the war we were one of four squadrons that were sent to France to look after the Expeditionary Force. We had no organisation looking after us as we did in England during the Battle of Britain, telling us what or what not to do. In France we had no radar and no Observer Corps. The French themselves had no concept of how to operate their Air Force and therefore our only contact with the Germans was to see contrails flying over us, at which we would take off, intercept them where possible, and do whatever we could.

It was not until 19 April 1940 that Billy Drake actually met the enemy himself for the first time, more than seven months after his arrival. On this occasion several pilots were scrambled after a contrail was spotted in the sky, which actually turned out to be a Spitfire on a photo-reconnaissance mission. However, whilst in the air they spotted some Messerschmitt Bf 109s of the *Luftwaffe* and took pursuit. In his logbook he noted: 'I Me 109 shot down in Germany and perhaps 1 other.' Talking about this occasion, he said:

There was an occasion where I caught up with a 109 but he saw me and just stuck his nose down and went back to his base as fast as possible. I followed him and we crossed the Rhine. He obviously knew the area well and when I looked up from him I suddenly saw we were flying towards high-tension cables. We dived underneath them and eventually he pulled up, which was his fatal mistake, because as he pulled up he lost speed and I was able to get close behind him, close enough to shoot him down in flames.

So as the spring of 1940 continued, signs of enemy activity were seemingly on the increase, but when the Nazis did eventually begin their attack in the west it would not be in France or Belgium as expected: it would be in Denmark and Norway.

5

OPERATION *WESERÜBUNG*

In February 1940 the Soviet Union and Germany agreed on a trade deal in which the Soviets would receive military and industrial equipment in exchange for raw materials. Germany also imported a lot of its iron ore from Sweden but the sea channels the shipments crossed were within the waters of neutral Norway. In order to safeguard these supply lines, Germany invaded both Denmark and Norway on the morning of 9 April in Operation *Weserübung*. Denmark quickly capitulated but Norway was to put up staunch resistance.

The occupation of Denmark, its small neighbour to the north, was not initially one of Germany's aims, but the decision to invade was taken in a bid to dominate Norwegian waters before the Allies had the opportunity to do so themselves. When planning for the invasion began, military chiefs did not at first see the necessity to occupy the entire country as all they required were selected areas from where the *Luftwaffe* could operate over the Baltic and North seas. In particular they considered that the Danish airport at Aalborg in the north of Jutland would be crucial to their domination of the area. As late as February 1940 there was still no definite plan to occupy the country in its entirety until Hitler took it upon himself to authorise its total seizure. His official line to the people of Denmark was that he was doing it to protect them from an invasion by the British and French.

Interestingly, a great many German speakers had traditionally lived in Denmark, so the two neighbours had much in common. The area most heavily populated by German-speaking Danes was naturally around the border region in the former Duchy of Schleswig, which had historically belonged to both countries at different times. Similar to the Saarland, under the terms of the Treaty of Versailles they had been promised a plebiscite in 1920 to decide for themselves whether or not they wished to remain in Denmark or unite with Germany. In this instance the vote had gone in favour of remaining with Denmark, but Hitler nevertheless was certain that the Nazis would find a great deal of support from within this neutral nation.

Denmark was a constitutional monarchy ruled over by King Christian X; its prime minister at the time was Thorvald Stauning. Their ambassador to Germany, Herluf Zahle, who coincidentally had been the president of the League of Nations from 1928 to 1929, was convinced before the event that Germany was planning an attack and issued a warning, which his government chose to ignore. The Danish army's intelligence office was also convinced that an assault was imminent, but again this was disregarded and no preparations were made to resist an invasion force.

In due course the warnings proved correct, and at 4:15 a.m. on 9 April light German forces, without any armoured vehicles, crossed the border in a coordinated operation, while at the capital city of Copenhagen, which straddles the islands of Zealand and Amager, ships began to disembark further troops. They were also quick to establish control in the central island of Funen. Simultaneously German aircraft flew across the border and began to drop propaganda leaflets encouraging the Danish forces and population to accept the occupation peacefully and without the need for bloodshed. They claimed that Germany's occupation of Denmark was in order to protect it from the Allies.

The invasion was so swift that the Danish government did not have time to declare war on Germany and individual commanders in the field had to make their own decisions about whether to resist or not. Poorly equipped units of the Danish army in various parts of the country did put up some resistance, most notably the Royal Guard in Copenhagen, but their situation was hopeless. The Danish army was tiny compared to that of the aggressor and its equipment obsolete. It has been suggested that this was partially as a result of a pre-war policy of trying to avoid antagonising neighbouring Germany by supplying the army with modern equipment. Whatever the reason, the suddenness of the assault made any attempt to defend the country impossible and in total sixteen Danish soldiers died during the occupation.

Denmark's landscape was ideal for the German forces to operate in as it was predominantly flat, so it was quickly appreciated that a thrust from Schleswig-Holstein, the northernmost of Germany's states and which lay on the other side of the border, would have seen the country quickly overrun with tanks. On realising that resistance to armoured units would be futile and could only result in further loss of life, the Danish government surrendered 'under protest' after only two hours, hoping to secure an advantageous agreement with the Nazis.

Due to the cooperation of the Danish government, Germany claimed it would continue to recognise the country's neutrality as well as respect its sovereignty and territorial integrity. Compared to some of the other countries it would later occupy, Germany took a lenient stance as it had no particular strategic or ideological interests in the region: they simply wanted to safeguard their iron ore supply routes and prevent the Allies taking the initiative in the area. For this reason they were happy to let the Danes run their own domestic affairs, whom they considered to be fellow Aryans. Also, Hitler being the great propagandist that he was, saw this as a publicity vehicle. He thus proclaimed Denmark to be 'a model protectorate' and announced to the watching world that it would illustrate how a Europe controlled by the Nazis could look and function.

Because of these factors, Denmark enjoyed a very favourable relationship with Nazi Germany. Its government remained largely unaltered with the king retaining his role as head of state. Its parliament was able to function almost exactly as it always had done and the Germans took little interest in their internal policy making. The police and judicial system also remained largely in Danish hands. The prime minister, Thorvald Stauning, was a Social Democrat who before the war was strongly opposed to the Nazi Party and deeply concerned about the prospects for Europe under Nazism. Nonetheless, his party would continue to pursue a strategy of cooperation, hoping to maintain democracy and home control for as long as possible. There were many issues that had to be worked out with their occupiers in the months that followed the invasion in an attempt to meet the occupier's demands, but ultimately and with some compromises the two nations established a working relationship.

The main target of Operation *Weserübung* was, of course, Norway and here the battle would rage more furiously. The Nazis were well aware that Norwegian territorial waters were absolutely vital to Germany, not only for the transport of Sweden's iron ore to the blast furnaces at home but to help break the Allied blockade against their shoreline.

Hitler also knew that he would have to move quickly to stop Britain from taking a similar course of action in the Baltic. He had already witnessed how the British had ignored Norway's neutrality during the *Altmark* incident and feared that if they took control of Norwegian waters they would almost certainly be able to stop Germany's own navy from leaving its bases, as well as disrupting their vital supply lines.

The German plan, as standard, was to act as quickly and decisively as possible before her enemies had time to react. Their attack on Norway would be largely seaborne, yet Hitler was well aware that the Royal Navy was far superior to the *Kriegsmarine* in every category of ship except arguably its submarines, so the operation would have to be executed with total surprise, denying the British time to intervene.

Virtually the entire German navy would be employed in this venture, which would see troops landed all along the Norwegian coast from Oslo in the south to Narvik in the north. This was a huge gamble because even if all the troops did manage to get ashore, there was a chance that if the British acted quickly enough they could be in a position to cut the Germans off and inflict catastrophic damage to their limited fleet. However Hitler had total faith in the ability of the *Luftwaffe* to keep the British at bay. For this operation X. Fliegerkorps (10th Air Corps) commanded by General der Flieger Hans Geisler would be deployed, consisting of some 400 bombers, principally Junkers Ju 88s, based in northern Germany whose crews had been specially trained in maritime operations.

Fortuitously for the British, at the same time as Germany was planning Operation *Weserübung*, they were embarking on their own operation in the area, directed at containing the German navy within the Baltic and preventing its access to the high seas. It would do this by heavily mining the shipping channels. As a coincidence, the two operations went ahead almost simultaneously, which meant that as the German invasion fleet set sail there was already a strong British force arriving on the scene.

The Royal Navy commenced minelaying on 8 April but it was disrupted by the breaking news of major German fleet movements around the port of Bremerhaven. The Admiralty consequently diverted its full strength to deal with the threat. The following day Nazi troops began to land at various locations along the coast of Norway – but things did not go entirely to plan.

A German task group entered the Oslofjord on the night of 8 April led by the heavy cruiser and flagship of the fleet, the *Blücher*, and made its way towards the Norwegian capital of Oslo. On board and in command of the fleet was Konteradmiral Oskar Kummetz. On an island in the middle of the fjord was the Oscarsborg Fortress. Because the attack was a surprise, Colonel Birger Eriksen, the commander of the fortress, did not know whether the approaching ships were German or British; in order to keep the attack secret Germany had not declared war on Norway.

Eriksen was in a dilemma as a result of his country's neutrality: he did not know whether or not his battery could legally open fire. Then, as the ships passed another fortress further down the fjord, a series of warning shots were fired from it. The German ships continued on regardless and, at 4:21 a.m. when they had reached a range of approximately 1,800 metres, Eriksen gave the order to fire, declaring: 'Either I will be decorated, or I will be court-martialed!'

The two eleven-inch guns at the fortress opened up, smashing shells against the *Blücher* and causing massive damage to it. One shell entered a magazine, causing several explosions and setting the ship ablaze, while a second one disabled her electrical supply. Further damage was incurred a few minutes later by another shore battery commanded by Captain Andreas Anderssen, which employed antiquated torpedoes that had not been reliably tested. Luckily however both torpedoes detonated and subsequently sank the cruiser. From the 800 crew and 1,500 invasion troops on board the *Blücher* intended for the occupation of Oslo, only around 200 survived. The ship was also transporting the forces needed to control the political apparatus in Norway after the invasion.

Because of this situation, the rest of the ships in the task group landed their troops some fifty miles away from Oslo. Nevertheless, the capture of the city was only delayed by a few hours, as it was taken by German paratroopers later that day – in fact the very first airborne troops ever used in warfare. These men at first captured the airfield before marching triumphantly through the streets of the capital. At the same time another group of paratroopers captured the airfield at Stavanger in the west of the country. This delay proved long enough for the Norwegian royal family, headed by King Haakon VII, and his government to effect their escape. This was a huge disappointment for the Germans, who had hoped to capture the king and his ministers in one fell swoop and make them sign a document of surrender.

Elsewhere around the Norwegian coast other naval battles raged between the Royal Navy and the *Kriegsmarine*. In one incident the *Blücher*'s sister ship, *Admiral Hipper*, was damaged when she was rammed by the British destroyer HMS *Glowworm*, which sank shortly afterwards, taking more than 100 of her crew with her. The *Admiral Hipper*, which had picked up the British survivors, was still able to participate in the capture of the city of Trondheim despite being damaged.

The *Glowworm* was commanded by Lieutenant-Commander Gerard Roope, who drowned in the course of trying to rescue survivors and was posthumously awarded the very first Victoria Cross of the Second World War, Britain's highest decoration for valour in the face of the enemy. The citation, which did not appear in *The London Gazette* until after the war, read:

The King has been graciously pleased to approve the award of the Victoria Cross for valour to the late Lieutenant-Commander Gerard Broadmead Roope, Royal Navy. On 8 April, 1940, HMS *Glowworm* was proceeding alone in heavy weather towards a rendezvous in West Fjord, when she met and engaged two enemy destroyers, scoring at least one hit on them. The enemy broke off the action and headed north, to lead the *Glowworm* on to his supporting forces. The Commanding Officer, whilst correctly appreciating the intentions of the enemy, at once gave chase. The German heavy cruiser, *Admiral Hipper,* was sighted closing the *Glowworm* at high speed and an enemy report was sent which was received by HMS *Renown.* Because of the heavy sea, the *Glowworm* could not shadow the enemy and the Commanding Officer therefore decided to attack with torpedoes and then to close in order to inflict as much damage as possible. Five torpedoes were fired and later the remaining five, but without success. The *Glowworm* was badly hit; one gun was out of action and her speed was much reduced, but with the other three guns still firing she closed and rammed the *Admiral Hipper.* As the *Glowworm* drew away, she opened fire again and scored one hit at a range of 400 yards. The *Glowworm*, badly stove in forward and riddled with enemy fire, heeled over to starboard, and the Commanding Officer gave the order to abandon her. Shortly afterwards she capsized and sank. The *Admiral Hipper* hove to for at least an hour picking up survivors but the loss of life was heavy, only thirty-one out of the *Glowworm's* complement of 149 being saved. Full information concerning this action has only recently been received and the Victoria Cross is bestowed in recognition of the great valour of the Commanding Officer who, after fighting off a superior force of destroyers, sought out and reported a powerful enemy unit, and then fought his ship to the end against overwhelming odds, finally ramming the enemy with supreme coolness and skill.

In another encounter the German light cruiser *Karlsruhe* led the assault on the city of Kristiansand, but when she arrived at the fjord in which the municipality nestled, heavy fog obscured her view. As a result they had to wait until the next morning to begin the attack. As *Karlsruhe* eventually entered the fjord, on 9 April, she came under heavy fire from the Norwegian coastal guns. The cruiser subsequently turned to bring her full broadside to bear and for about two hours took part in an artillery duel with the shore battery, until heavy fog again covered the port causing both sides to cease fire. The Norwegians surrendered an hour later and the German ships were given free range to land the invasion troops they ferried.

Having accomplished her task, the *Karlsruhe* left Kristiansand with three torpedo boats to escort her; but the British submarine HMS *Truant* was waiting outside the fjord. When her crew spotted the German ships emerging, she fired a spread of torpedoes. Two of these hit the cruiser and the resulting explosions punched large holes in her hull allowing thousands of tons of water to flood the ship. The flooding disabled her engines and electricity generators, which consequently cut off power to the pumps that were trying to deal with the rising water. With the pumps shut off, there was no hope of saving the vessel, and her commander, Captain Friedrich Rieve, issued the order to abandon ship two hours after the attack. One of the torpedo boats escorting her, the *Greif,* rescued her crew and then fired two torpedoes at the ship to ensure that she sank and to prevent her from being boarded by the British.

Another ship, the *Königsberg*, was damaged by Norwegian shore batteries while transporting 600 troops to Bergen and was later attacked by British naval dive-bombers to become the first major warship to be sunk by aircraft. After reaching her objective she transferred some of the soldiers to smaller vessels and then entered the port at high speed in an attempt to disgorge the rest of the infantrymen. A coastal battery at Kvarven Fort, strategically located by the main shipping channel leading to Bergen, opened fire and scored three direct hits that caused severe flooding and fires in her boiler rooms.

Adrift and without power, the *Königsberg* had to drop anchor; she was going to need major repairs done before being capable of sailing home. The rest of her group returned to Germany, leaving her stranded and alone in the harbour. Then, on the evening of 9 April, she was attacked by British bombers, with no effect. The following morning the British launched a further raid against her using sixteen Blackburn Skua dive-bombers of the British Fleet Air Arm based at the Royal Naval Air Station at Hatston in Orkney.

The Skuas attacked in three groups at around 7:20 a.m., catching the ship's crew completely off guard. She was hit by at least five bombs, causing her to take on a heavy list almost immediately.

The captain ordered the crew to abandon ship, and as it took almost three hours for the ship to completely capsize and sink, it gave the crew enough time to evacuate most of the dead and wounded. They also had time to remove a significant amount of ammunition and equipment from the stricken cruiser. Amazingly only eighteen men were killed in the attack.

Meanwhile at Narvik in the far north of Norway, ten German destroyers were able to get all their troops ashore, managing to sink two Norwegian coast defence vessels in the process. The senior British officer in the area was Vice Admiral William Jock Whitworth of HMS *Renown*. In order to deal with these German vessels, the Admiralty sent him a single flotilla on 10 April consisting of five destroyers, HMS *Hardy*, HMS *Havock*, HMS *Hostile,* HMS *Hotspur* and HMS *Hunter*. This would certainly not be enough to help him mount a successful counter-offensive.

These five ships, commanded by Captain Bernard Armitage Warburton-Lee from aboard the *Hardy*, made a surprise attack on German destroyers and merchant ships in Narvik Harbour during a blinding snowstorm. They sank two of the German destroyers and damaged three others. This attack was almost immediately followed by an engagement with five more German destroyers, during which Captain Warburton-Lee was mortally wounded when a shell hit *Hardy*'s bridge. For his exploits in this engagement he was posthumously awarded the Victoria Cross and was the first recipient to be noted in *The London Gazette* during the Second World War. The citation read:

For gallantry, enterprise and daring in command of the force engaged in the First Battle of Narvik, on 10 April, 1940. On being ordered to carry out an attack on Narvik, Captain Warburton-Lee learned that the enemy was holding the place in much greater force than had been thought. He signalled to the Admiralty that six German destroyers and one submarine were there, that the channel might be mined, and that he intended to attack at dawn. The Admiralty replied that he alone could judge whether to attack, and that whatever decision he made would have full support. Captain Warburton-Lee led his flotilla of five destroyers up the fjord in heavy snow-storms, arriving off Narvik just after daybreak. He took the enemy completely by surprise and made three successful attacks on warships and merchantmen in the harbour. As the flotilla withdrew, five enemy destroyers of superior gun power were encountered and engaged. The captain was mortally wounded by a shell which hit the bridge of HMS *Hardy*. His last signal was 'Continue to engage the enemy.'

Three days after this engagement, Vice Admiral Whitworth arrived with another flotilla consisting of HMS *Warspite* and nine accompanying destroyers: now he had the tools to do the job. The force subsequently engaged and annihilated the rest of the German flotilla – but not before the enemy had established a foothold in several parts of the country.

During Operation *Weserübung* the *Kriegsmarine* had suffered badly at the hands of the Royal Navy but at least most of the troops needed for the invasion had been successfully landed. The Allies needed to act quickly if they were to mount a counter-offensive, and they decided to centre their efforts around Trondheim with a two-pronged pincer attack from Namsos in the north and Åndalsnes in the south. Acting on the advice of their military chiefs, both Neville Chamberlain and Paul Reynaud, who had replaced Édouard Daladier as the prime minister of France on 21 March, agreed that in retaking Trondheim their forces would be able to link up with the Norwegian army and block the Germans at one of the narrowest parts of the country.

It was decided that Namsos was the most suitable spot to land the troops and supplies assigned to the northern pincer because its harbour and approaches were ice-free all year round and possessed three good wharves, two made of wood and one of stone, which were suitable for docking small warships and transports. From here, Trondheim was forty miles to the south by road.

On 14 April a small party of Royal Marines was landed in Namsos under the command of Captain W. F. Edds and took up positions in the hills around the town to give cover to the main force when it arrived. The following day the force commander, Lieutenant General Sir Adrian Carton de Wiart VC, arrived in the harbour aboard a Short

Sunderland flying boat, which drew the attention of X. Fliegerkorps, whose aircraft machine gunned it as it landed. Regrettably, at this point no Allied aircraft were available to provide protection against the *Luftwaffe*.

Because of his lack of air support, de Wiart decided to divert the large and slow troopships ferrying his men of the 146th Infantry Brigade 100 miles to the north, where they were transferred on to fast destroyers so that they could enter Namsos more speedily and hopefully before the *Luftwaffe* could inflict too much damage. Unfortunately, within the first hour of transferring the troops on to the destroyers, German bombers descended on the scene. With the transfer only partially completed, the British naval commander Vice Admiral Layton ordered the destroyers to sail to Namsos immediately, taking whatever troops and equipment they had managed to get on board with them. This amounted to thirty-six officers and 1,208 other ranks, which finally arrived in Namsos on 16 April.

Once ashore General de Wiart wasted no time in setting up his headquarters and sending troops to guard the bridge over the nearby fjord, which was essential for moving his force south. He sent other men to occupy the village of Bangsund to the south of the bridge. He also sent 300 troops due east to the area of Grong, which was along a second and less direct route to Trondheim. Here they linked up with small numbers of Norwegian troops under the command of Colonel Ole Getz. Smaller groups again were also sent beyond Bangsund in an attempt to reach the head of Trondheimsfjord, the large body of water on which along its southern shore sat the city.

Most of the remaining troops were still aboard the troopship RMS *Empress of Australia*, 100 miles to the north. Vice Admiral Layton decided that taking his destroyers back to Namsos again was far too risky, so instead he transferred the men on to a Polish transport ship, the MS *Chrobry*, which duly arrived in Namsos just before sunrise on 17 April. However, in the rush to get away before any German bombers arrived, the soldiers landed without much of their kit.

Two battalions of French troops, of the 5th Alpine Chasseurs Demi-Brigade, landed on 19 April under heavy air attack. One of the transports conveying the French was too long to enter the harbour and returned to the United Kingdom without landing many of the French supplies, leaving the troops without straps for their skis or the mules they were hoping to use for transport in the mountains. However in total some 6,000 Allied troops did manage to get ashore. To the south the 148th Infantry Brigade had meanwhile landed at Åndalsnes under the command of Brigadier Harold de Riemer Morgan.

By 21 April some of the British forces had advanced as far south as the hamlet of Verdal, about halfway to Trondheim, where they observed a German gunboat in the fjord accompanied by two armed trawlers and a destroyer: their first sight of the enemy. After the invasion, the Germans had roughly 1,800 troops in the Trondheim area, some in the city and some protecting the railway to Sweden. They had also captured the airfield at Værnes, now Trondheim's international airport, which enabled them to fly extra troops in daily; by 19 April they had around 5,000 men available in the area.

When British Royal Engineers reached Verdal, a crucial bridge here was being defended against German attackers by a force of around eighty Norwegian soldiers. The majority of the British force was still a little further back, but in an attempt to outflank them the Germans landed forces from the boats on the fjord at several points behind them. The Norwegians and Royal Engineers evacuated the bridge and withdrew to join the main Allied force.

As the situation developed the advantage was certainly with the Germans. They were well equipped and had both air support and the support of naval gunfire. Heavy fighting occurred around the small village of Vist until the Germans outflanked the British positions by going around them on skis through the deep snow. The Luftwaffe also attacked and destroyed the British forward base at Steinkjer, causing the loss of much of their supplies. The bombing destroyed 242 houses in the town, which left more than 1,800 Norwegian civilians homeless. Luckily none were killed.

German bombers also made a concerted attack on Namsos itself, destroying most of the wood-constructed houses, as well as the railway terminal, a church, the French headquarters and the two wooden wharves. The third wharf, built of stone, was damaged but survived. There was only one Allied ship in the area during the attack, the anti-submarine trawler HMS *Rutlandshire*. She was attacked by fourteen bombers and badly damaged. The ship was beached and the survivors were machine gunned in the water. None were killed and only two injured, and they were later rescued by the destroyer HMS *Nubian*.

With no air support of their own, the Royal Navy ships supporting the Allied operation suffered badly; the slow anti-submarine sloops and trawlers in particular were very vulnerable to air attack. On 30 April, the sloop HMS *Bittern* was sunk by Junkers Ju 87 dive-bombers off Namsos. On 1 May, three British anti-submarine trawlers at the entrance to the Namsenfjorden were destroyed by aircraft. HMT *Arab* evacuated the crew of one of these, HMS *St Goran*. From 28 April to 2 May, *Arab* endured thirty-one separate air attacks herself and her captain, Lieutenant Richard Been Stannard, Royal Naval Reserve, received the Victoria Cross for his actions during those five days. The citation published in *The London Gazette*, on 16 August 1940, read:

The King has been graciously pleased to approve the grant of the Victoria Cross to Lieutenant Richard Been Stannard, RNR, HMT *Arab*, for outstanding valour and devotion to duty at Namsos. When enemy bombing attacks had set on fire many tons of hand grenades on Namsos wharf, with no shore water supply available, Lieutenant Stannard ran *Arab's* bows against the wharf and held her there. Sending all but two of his crew aft, he then endeavoured for two hours to extinguish the fire with hoses from the forecastle. He persisted in this work till he had to give up the attempt as hopeless.

After helping other ships against air attacks, he placed his own damaged vessel under shelter of a cliff, landed his crew and those of two other trawlers, and established an armed camp. Here those off duty could rest while he attacked enemy aircraft which approached by day, and kept anti-submarine watch during the night.

When another trawler near-by was hit and set on fire by a bomb, he, with two others, boarded *Arab* and moved her 100 yards before the other vessel blew up. Finally, when leaving the fjord, he was attacked by a German bomber which ordered him to steer east or be sunk. He held on his course, reserved his fire till the enemy was within 800 yards, and then brought the aircraft down.

Throughout a period of five days *Arab* was subjected to thirty-one bombing attacks and the camp and Lewis gun positions ashore were repeatedly machine-gunned and bombed; yet the defensive position was so well planned that only one man was wounded.

Lieutenant Stannard ultimately brought his damaged ship back to an English port. His continuous gallantry in the presence of the enemy was magnificent, and his enterprise and resource not only caused losses to the Germans but saved his ship and many lives.

During the action on the Namsos front, the Norwegians had no aircraft in the area whatsoever, and the only Allied air presence to counter the *Luftwaffe* was during the first British landings, when a brief patrol was mounted well offshore by several obsolete Gloster Gladiator biplanes operating from the aircraft carrier HMS *Glorious*, which managed to shoot down three Nazi bombers. Eighteen Gladiators of No. 263 Squadron (RAF), from the *Glorious*, had been sent to operate from a frozen Lake near the village of Lesjaskog, but these were too far south to help at Namsos. This lack of air support was probably the biggest failing of the entire campaign in Norway.

The situation was hopeless, and on 28 April General de Wiart received orders to evacuate his troops. The following day a convoy consisting of three British destroyers and one French destroyer left Scapa Flow under the command of Lord Louis Mountbatten on board HMS *Kelly*. A larger naval force, under the command of Admiral John Cunningham, followed at a distance to protect them against attack by German battlecruisers. That evening on reaching their rendezvous point, which was about forty nautical miles from Namsos, they encountered thick fog and the plan to evacuate the troops that night was cancelled until the fog lifted.

On land the situation was becoming critical as German troops were closing in on the British rearguard in the hills outside the town. Mountbatten was not prepared to wait, and on 2 May he took his ships towards the harbour by moving among the fog. This was an

extremely dangerous undertaking on such a rocky coast. Outside
the harbour the fog had cleared, and before them they could see
Namsos in flames and swarms of German bombers diving around.
Mountbatten knew it would be suicidal to proceed so he ordered his
ships to hide back in the fog and wait further along the shore.

The next day, 3 May, the fog had still not lifted, but Admiral
Cunningham knew that time was running out to reach the Allied troops
before the better equipped and supplied Germans arrived. He ordered
the heavy cruiser HMS *York*, five destroyers and three transports to
get inside the harbour as quickly as possible, using the rest of his fleet
as a screen; Mountbatten led this force on board HMS *Kelly*. When
they rounded the last bend of the fjord they could see Namsos still
burning. At this point, Mountbatten did not know if the Allied troops
would be at the wharf or whether the Germans had taken the town.
As he closed in, miraculously amid the blazing buildings he could see
Carton de Wiart with approximately 5,500 British and French troops
lined up on the wharf, waiting to get off.

The evacuation began at 22:30 with the transports pulling up to
the damaged wharf and taking off the first of the men. These were
followed by the destroyers, who rescued the other soldiers and
ferried them to the *York*. The last of the convoy, the destroyer HMS
Afridi, waited for the men of the British rearguard, who were holding
the Germans back during the evacuation. A tricky disengagement
followed and a rush for the ship ensued. There was no time to destroy
supplies left on the wharves so the *Afridi* shelled the equipment as she
pulled away from Namsos, at 2:20 a.m. on 4 May.

As the convoy began its journey back to Scapa Flow, reconnaissance
aircraft of X. Fliegerkorps appeared over them at first light. Soon
bombers were overhead and they attacked continuously throughout
the day. During one attack the French destroyer *Bison* was hit in the
forward magazine and exploded, with 136 killed. Some of the other
destroyers turned back to pick up survivors who were being machine
gunned in the water. After picking up some of the survivors the
Afridi was herself struck by two bombs and capsized, with the loss of
around 100 men including some of the rearguard who had held the
Germans back and the wounded from the *Bison*. The convoy finally
reached Scapa Flow on 5 May.

While all of this had been going on a similar situation was occurring at the southern end of the pincer at Åndalsnes, where the 148th Infantry Brigade had suffered heavy losses fighting the Germans to the north of Lillehammer. Though they were later relieved by the 15th Infantry Brigade, by 27 April all the Allied troops in this area had also been extracted.

Even after this disaster, the Allies still hoped that northern Norway might be held in order to deny the Germans their supplies of iron ore. The Germans had occupied Narvik with a mixed force of mountain troops reinforced by the crews of the destroyers that had landed them, and with a parachute battalion dropped in from the air. The Allies sent a force made up of British, French, Norwegian and Polish troops. For the first time in the campaign the Allied troops were provided with air cover: one squadron of Gladiators and one of Hurricanes, flown from HMS *Glorious*. This force succeeded in retaking Narvik on 28 May.

In the end this first Allied victory counted for nothing, as far away in the Low Countries the Germans had launched another front; it was decided not to send any further troops to help Norway, and those already there were given orders to evacuate.

The evacuation was marred by the loss of HMS *Glorious*, which with an escort of two destroyers was returning ahead of the rest of the fleet carrying ten evacuated Hurricane fighter aircraft and nine pilots, as well as the commanding officer of No. 46 Squadron. Unfortunately she was spotted and sunk by the German battlecruiser *Scharnhorst*, and only two of the pilots who had fought in Norway survived. These were Flight Lieutenant Patrick Jameson and the CO, Squadron Leader Kenneth Cross, who were rescued three days later from rafts by the crew of a trawler from the Faroe Islands. During this attack the *Scharnhorst* was itself torpedoed and seriously damaged by one of the escorting destroyers, HMS *Acasta*.

The remaining pilots and ground crew of the squadron were evacuated on board other ships, including the SS *Arandora Star*. These included Pilot Officer John Fraser Drummond and Sergeant Pilot Stanley Andrew, who were both later killed during the Battle of Britain. Drummond was awarded the DFC for his service in Scandinavia. His citation read:

During operations in Norway this officer shot down two enemy aircraft and seriously damaged a further three. On one occasion, as pilot of one of two Hurricanes which attacked four Heinkel He 111s, he damaged one of the enemy aircraft and then engaged two of the others. Despite heavy return fire, P/O Drummond pressed home his attack, silenced the rear guns of both aircraft, and compelled the Heinkels to break off the engagement.

By the end of the campaign in Norway the *Kriegsmarine* had suffered greatly and now had only three cruisers and four destroyers operational. This was certainly not a force that would be capable of dominating the English Channel or giving cover to a cross-Channel invasion force; in one way the Norwegian campaign was undoubtedly a factor that helped to save Britain a few months later after the fall of France.

The campaign in Norway had gone so badly that it led to a vote of no confidence in the Conservative prime minister Neville Chamberlain, which ultimately led to his resignation. Ironically, Winston Churchill, the First Lord of the Admiralty, was the favourite to replace him, even though his department had been responsible for many of the mistakes that were made at Namsos and elsewhere. Churchill, who was known for his military leadership qualities, was appointed British prime minister on 10 May, forming an all-party coalition that quickly won popular support throughout Great Britain.

6

FALL GELB VERSUS
THE DYLE PLAN

10 May 1940, the day Winston Churchill became prime minister of Great Britain, was monumental for a number of reasons. That same day the British occupied the North Atlantic territories of Iceland, Greenland and the Faroe Islands in an effort to prevent the Germans seizing them first. More importantly, however, it was the date on which the Germans launched their long expected attack on France, by simultaneously invading the neutral nations of Belgium, the Netherlands and Luxembourg, collectively known as the Low Countries.

Hitler's plan and promise to the German people was to establish a Third Reich, or empire, that would last for a thousand years. He intended this to be the successor to both the Holy Roman Empire and the German Empire formed by Otto von Bismarck in 1871, after he cleverly engineered a series of wars that united the German states, with himself as the inaugural chancellor.

Hitler's new Reich would largely be built by expanding Germany's borders to the east and taking territories from people who the Nazis deemed less racially pure than themselves. At its centre would be a great new capital city called Germania, which Hitler envisaged to be the centre of the civilised world. This would entail the almost total redevelopment of Berlin.

In order to build his Third Reich, Hitler was aware that Germany would probably have to go to war with the Soviet Union in the east and the Allied powers of France and Great Britain in the west, unless of course he could avoid the latter through negotiations. His goal was always to try and avoid fighting this war on both fronts simultaneously. His invasion of Poland and the declaration of war on Germany by the Allies had given the situation in the west the most urgency, yet his directives dating from this period still hoped to avoid hostilities before he was ready. On 9 September, one week after the start of the war, directive number three stated:

1. Operations against the Polish Army and Air Force will continue with the necessary forces until it is safe to assume that the Poles are no longer capable of establishing a continuous front which can tie down German forces.

2. Should it be clear that some part of the Eastern Army and of the Air Force are no longer necessary for the completion of this task and for the pacification of occupied territories, arrangements are to be made to transfer these forces to the west.

   As the Polish Air Force becomes progressively weaker, further air defence units may be made available for use against our western enemies.

3. Even after the half-hearted opening of hostilities by England, at sea and in the air, and by France, on the land and in the air, my personal approval must be obtained:

   (a) For any crossing of the German land frontier in the west.
   (b) For all flights beyond the western frontier of Germany, unless they are necessary to meet heavy enemy air attacks.
   (c) For air attacks against England.

   The Air Force is, however, free to operate in the German Bight and in the western mined areas, and in immediate support of naval action at sea.

Hitler suspected that once military action began the French would ignore the neutrality of the Low Countries and occupy them in order to secure a direct route through the heart of Germany. He was also mindful that in occupying them, Allied aircraft would be considerably closer to the Ruhr, which would be vital for the Nazi war industry. To prevent this from occurring he began to formalise plans to invade these countries himself. By directive number six, issued on 9 October, his language was at last turning to the offensive:

1. Should it become evident in the near future that England, and, under her influence, France also, are not disposed to bring the war to an end, I have decided, without further loss of time, to go over to the offensive.
2. Any further delay will not only entail the end of Belgian and perhaps of Dutch neutrality, to the advantage of the Allies; it will also increasingly strengthen the military power of the enemy, reduce the confidence of neutral nations in Germany's final victory, and make it more difficult to bring Italy into the war on our side as a full ally.
3. I therefore issue the following orders for the further conduct of military operations:

    (a) An offensive will be planned on the northern flank of the western front, through Luxembourg, Belgium, and Holland. This offensive must be launched at the earliest possible moment and in greatest possible strength.
    (b) The purpose of this offensive will be to defeat as much as possible of the French Army and of the forces of the Allies fighting on their side, and at the same time to win as much territory as possible in Holland, Belgium, and Northern France, to serve as a base for the successful prosecution of the air and sea war against England and as a wide protective area for the economically vital Ruhr Basin.
    (c) The time of the attack will depend upon the readiness for action of the armoured and motorised units involved. These units are to be made ready with all speed. It will depend also upon the weather conditions obtaining and foreseeable at the time.

4. The Air Force will prevent attacks by the Anglo French Air Forces on our Army and will give all necessary direct support to its advance. It is also important to prevent the establishment of Anglo French air bases and the landing of British forces in Belgium and Holland.

5. The Navy will do everything possible, while this offensive is in progress, to afford direct or indirect support to the operations of the Army and the Air Force.

6. Apart from these preparations for the beginning of the offensive in the west according to plan, the Army and Air Force must be ready, at all times, in increasing strength, to meet an Anglo French invasion of Belgium, immediately and as far forward as possible on Belgian soil, and to occupy the largest possible area of Holland in the direction of the west coast.

7. These preparations will be camouflaged in such a way that they appear merely to be precautionary measures made necessary by the threatening increase in the strength of the French and English forces on the frontiers between France and Luxembourg and Belgium.

8. I request Commanders In Chief to submit to me their detailed plans based on this directive at the earliest moment and to keep me constantly informed of progress through the High Command of the Armed Forces.

In planning the attack in the west, it seems that Hitler was very optimistic about Germany's ability to win a quick campaign, although his military chiefs of staff found his demands unrealistic. For a start, a considerable proportion of their forces were still being deployed in Poland. Various types of vehicles, including tanks and half-tracks, would need either repair or general servicing before they would be ready to participate in a new campaign. Statistics collected during the war estimated that German casualties in Poland were 10,570 killed in action, although a study conducted in 2000 by the German Armed Forces Military History Research Office revised that figure to around 15,000. They also lost 674 tanks and 564 aircraft, so it was not quite the walk over that history might suggest.

In the first instance Hitler proposed beginning the invasion in the west on 25 October 1939. However, after his chiefs of staff convinced him that this would not be possible to achieve in such a short time, he amended the start date to 12 November. The commander-in-chief of the army, General Heinrich Walther von Brauchitsch, was in the unenviable position of having to inform the Führer that this was still a totally unrealistic deadline.

Brauchitsch was one of several senior military figures who given the opportunity might have made an attempt to overthrow Hitler in 1939. By early November of that year, together with Franz Halder, the chief of the general staff, he had begun to consider ousting Hitler, especially after he fixed 'X-Day', the invasion of France, as 12 November. Both officers were convinced that the invasion was doomed to failure.

The members of the army general staff prepared a special memorandum that advised against launching an attack on the Western powers that year. Brauchitsch reluctantly agreed to read this document to Hitler, and he did so in a meeting on 5 November. He attempted to persuade him to put off X-Day by claiming that morale in the army was extremely low, a statement that enraged Hitler, who accused the general staff and Brauchitsch himself of disloyalty, cowardice, sabotage and defeatism. In response, the general proffered his resignation.

Following this meeting, Brauchitsch returned to army headquarters at Zossen, where both he and Halder agreed that overthrowing Hitler was simply not feasible at that time. Hitler on the other hand followed the gathering by calling a meeting of his general staff in which he ranted that he would 'smash the West within a year'. Interestingly, though, Hitler refused to accept the general's resignation and announced that X-Day would be postponed until further notice. Brauchitsch agreed to continue working for the Führer; after all, Hitler's compromise over the invasion schedule had largely alleviated both his and Halder's primary motivation for their covert plot to overthrow him.

However, Hitler's promise of postponement did not last very long. After both the British and the French rejected his latest offer of peace, on 12 October, he ordered his chief of staff to draw up a campaign plan with all due haste. The plans for the campaign in the Low Countries were codenamed *Fall Gelb*, or Case Yellow, or to give them their full title *Aufmarschanweisung No. 1, Fall Gelb, Deployment Instruction No. 1, Case Yellow*. Franz Halder presented the first draft to the Führer on 19 October, who was not overly enthusiastic about their detail.

Halder's initial plan was based on Germany's strategy during the First World War, a long, protracted affair beginning with an advance through Belgium, pushing the Allied armies back to the River Somme. Halder's plan has been compared to the Schlieffen Plan, which was the thinking behind the German invasion of France and Belgium in August 1914, conceived by Field Marshal Alfred von Schlieffen, chief of the imperial German general staff. At its heart was the strategy of Germany fighting the war on two fronts at the same time. This was exactly what Hitler had hoped to avoid. He was hoping to defeat the Allies in the west as quickly as possible, before an invasion of Russian-held territories could be implemented.

Most disappointing for the Führer was Halder's estimate that in the initial campaign he would expect to lose anywhere up to half a million men, and further that if the plan proved a success and a protracted war followed, Germany would not be in a position to consider subsequent operations in France until their strength had recovered sufficiently, which he estimated would be 1942 at the earliest.

Hitler was not happy with the plans whatsoever, making the suggestion to his generals that if they took the initiative and attacked the Allies as soon as possible, catching them completely unaware and unprepared, then they might secure a quick and easy victory in spite of their own shortfalls and lack of preparation.

What occurred next was a series of postponements as both Hitler and his staff tried to iron out the plans so that they were more workable. The main obstacle during these negotiations was the Führer's lack of understanding of how poorly prepared his own army was for a successful campaign at that time, especially because of their losses in Poland, particularly in terms of vehicles. This resulted in Halder presenting a revised plan to the Führer on 29 October, *No. 2, Fall Gelb, (No. 2, Case Yellow)*. In this revised plan the main thrust of the proposed attack would still be through central Belgium but there would be secondary attacks on the flanks, including one through the Netherlands.

Hitler was still uneasy with Halder's plans, and luckily for him he was not alone. His main ally was General Gerd von Rundstedt, the commander of Army Group A. For the plan to work, it would be his troops that would have to encircle and destroy the main body of Allied forces. The plan pinpointed the town of Sedan in northern France as the best place to achieve this. Sedan was just across the border from Belgium to the south of the River Meuse and was situated inside the sector that Rundstedt's army group would attack.

Rundstedt was also concerned by the fact that Halder's plan did not adhere to the classic principles that had guided German strategy since the nineteenth century. This was known as *Bewegungskrieg*, or 'manoeuvre warfare', and it advocated defeating the enemy by incapacitating their ability to make decisions through shock and disruption. Rundstedt consulted his own chief of staff, Lieutenant General Erich von Manstein, and together they agreed that an alternative operational plan had to be arranged that would reflect these basic ideas. It would primarily increase the strength of Army Group A at the expense of Army Group B, which was located to the north under the command of General Fedor von Bock, who would not have such a crucial role during the initial thrust.

Manstein was therefore given the task of drawing up the alternative plans that would consequently favour Rundstedt's army group. While in the process of formulating these he held informal discussions with Lieutenant General Heinz Guderian, who had commanded the *Wehrmacht*'s elite armoured formation, XIX Panzer Corps, in Poland. Initially Manstein's proposal worked on the assumption that the Allied armies would cross the Belgian border from the Sedan area once hostilities began. If the Germans could therefore flood through the Ardennes Forest to the south of them, they would then be able to move north, attacking and encircling the enemy from the rear. Then, and probably influenced by the input of General Guderian, the plans altered quite dramatically.

It was envisaged that the *Panzerwaffe*, which was the main armoured force of the army, would first concentrate on seizing the area around Sedan. Then, without waiting for the infantry divisions to catch them up they would press on independently and instead of turning north would bypass the enemy in Belgium and continue west through northern France. This shock tactic would punch a hole through the Allied lines all the way to the English Channel, which if executed quickly enough could lead to a total collapse in the enemy's command structure and communications base. This might also avoid the high numbers of battle casualties that would be caused by using tanks and infantry in the conventional sense.

Implementing such a plan would be a huge gamble as it would mean that the armoured units would have to work without infantry support for much of the time, something which had not been tried before. Then there was the question of the terrain. The Ardennes presented a rugged landscape of steep valleys, meandering rivers and dense forest. Could an army get through this natural obstacle quickly enough to surprise the enemy? If they could, it would certainly catch the Allies where they were vulnerable and least expecting an attack. On the other hand, the armoured spearhead as well as their accompanying infantry could get bogged down and draw attention to themselves, giving the Allies time to react.

When Manstein's alternative plan was complete, Rundstedt offered its first memorandum to Halder and the rest of the general staff for consideration on 31 October. They were immediately skeptical that such an operation could work and discarded it. However, this initial draft was supported by General Guderian, who had experienced the ground in question during the First World War and was of the opinion that it would work. Manstein, who recognised that the plan was unorthodox, carefully played down the strategic role of the armoured units as he knew this would cause a negative reaction from the generals. He also avoided giving Guderian's name as having had any influence. Six further drafts followed between then and 12 January, each more radical than the previous one. All of these were rejected by German army headquarters and none of them were ever brought to the attention of Hitler.

Ignoring the concerns of Rundstedt and one or two others, the general staff ploughed ahead with *No. 2, Fall Gelb*, which was scheduled to begin on 17 January. However an incident took place on 10 January that arguably altered the planning again, an event which has become known as the Mechelen Incident (or Affair).

The plans for invasion were so top secret that very few people had access to them, but one of those who did was one Major Helmuth

Reinberger of the *Luftwaffe*. He was responsible for organising the supplies for VII Flieger Division, a formation tasked with landing paratroopers behind the Belgian lines at Namur on X-Day. He was ordered to take his copy of the plans in person to Cologne and give them to the chiefs of staff of *Luftflotte* 2 (Air Fleet 2), from where they were due to be handed over from General Hellmuth Felmy to General Albert Kesselring two days later.

It was forbidden to ferry top secret documents by air, so Reinberger initially intended taking them by train from Münster. But he then changed his mind, and flew from Loddenheide airfield in a Messerschmitt Bf 108B Taifun, piloted by his friend Major Erich Hoenmanns, the base commander, who in point of fact did not know that Reinberger was carrying the plans; the Bf 108B was normally used as a reconnaissance aircraft.

During this ill-fated flight Hoenmanns, who was flying using visual rules only, became disorientated in a heavy snow storm and completely missed the airfield at Cologne. He decided that if he headed west he would be able to pick up the River Rhine and get his bearings from there. Unfortunately when he arrived over the river it was frozen solid and covered by a carpet of dense snow, so he failed to see it and flew on. When he did eventually stumble across a large watercourse that he assumed to be the Rhine, it was in fact the River Meuse, the border between the Netherlands and Belgium.

What happened next is uncertain, but for some reason the aircraft stalled and Hoenmanns had to make a forced landing in a field. His aircraft was very badly damaged but its two occupants survived. Thinking they were still in Germany, Reinberger did not have time to destroy the documents before they were apprehended by Belgian security forces, who took them to a border post near Mechelen-aan-de-Maas, now called Maasmechelen. Here they were interrogated by Captain Arthur Rodrique. At one point Reinberger tried to kill himself by taking Rodrique's pistol, as he knew that if he returned to Germany he would face the death sentence for allowing the top secret plans to be captured by the enemy.

Soon the plans were in the hands of the Belgian intelligence services, who initially could not ascertain whether they were genuine or part of an elaborate hoax. Nevertheless they had to assume the plans were real and that the proposed invasion was imminent, so details of the plans were quickly circulated to civil and military leaders in France, Great Britain, the Netherlands and Luxembourg. Whilst some governments discarded them as being a deception, the French in particular took them seriously and immediately began to move their troops towards the Belgian border with the intention of deploying them inside their neighbour's territory. However the Belgian's still hoped to keep their neutrality and their border guards refused to let the French cross, much to the annoyance of General Gamelin.

The Nazis were quickly alerted to the movement of the French troops and soon realised what had happened and that the plans had been compromised. Hitler was furious. His initial reaction was to launch the invasion immediately before the Allies had time to react to the captured information. The general staff persuaded him otherwise, especially after the weather took a turn for the worse, and the invasion was postponed again. This time Hitler demanded that a new plan should be drawn up.

In the meantime Halder had arranged for Erich von Manstein to be relieved from his job as Army Group A's chief of staff. He was given command of an army corps in Prussia, where hopefully both he and his plans would be forgotten forever. Unhappy with this situation, some of Manstein's staff brought his case to the direct attention of Hitler, who as it transpired had himself, without any knowledge of Manstein's plan, suggested an attack through the Ardennes focusing on Sedan but had been talked out of the idea as being irresponsible. On 2 February, Manstein's plan was finally put before him.

After Hitler had studied this novel scheme for some time, he called a meeting on 17 February attended by Manstein, General Rudolf Schmundt, the chief of personnel of the army, and General Alfred Jodl, the chief of operations at German armed forces high command. After listening to what Manstein had to say and being suitably impressed, he agreed to adopt the plan in its entirety.

Even at this stage Halder remained hostile towards the idea of tanks being used independently without infantry support; when he issued the first draft of the new plan, on 24 February, he had completely removed this element from it, much to the annoyance of General Guderian. However for some reason, which still remains a mystery, he then completely changed his opinion and advocated the independence of the armoured divisions. Most of the general staff remained steadfastly against the idea and began to criticise Halder in the same manner that he had opposed Manstein when he first suggested the plan. Because of this change of heart, Halder earned the nickname the 'gravedigger of the Panzer force'.

No. 4, Fall Gelb, the final plans for the invasion of France and the Low Countries, had now been finalised. There were still many objectors, but ultimately their opinions were ignored. The main concern was that it would be dangerous to concentrate all of the advance forces in a position where they could not be supplied adequately. If the Allies did not react as predicted, they themselves would be cut off with their supply route severed and the offensive would end in disaster. Halder argued that the new plan was Germany's only real hope of securing total victory, which was Hitler's belief also. It was an incredible gamble to take, but without a brave and audacious plan the alternative would almost certainly be defeat. On the other hand, if *No. 4, Fall Gelb* worked, the *Wehrmacht* would quickly encircle the Allied armies in Belgium and find itself on the coast of the English Channel. Surely victory would then only be a matter of time.

While the Germans had been formalising their battle plans, the Allies were also considering theirs, the codename for which was the Dyle Plan, or D Plan for short. The responsibility for all Allied strategy was given exclusively to the French. The British appreciated that the BEF was only a small part of the overall Allied force and, as the fighting would largely take place in France and the Low Countries, they were happy to go along with the French strategic proposals.

In drawing up their plans the French tried to engineer a situation in which the fighting would not reach their own soil, and they hoped to contain the enemy well to the north-east, in Belgium. This plan was conceived by General Gamelin and took its name from the River Dyle that flows through the centre of Belgium from the port of Antwerp, where the Belgians had conveniently built the K-W Line.

When the time was right, the idea of the plan was for the Allies to cross the Belgian border and advance to the River Dyle and take up positions in the fortifications there. Here they would hope to halt the advance of the *Wehrmacht*'s Army Group B, which they believed would be the main force assembled against them; in reality, and according to the Manstein Plan, the main thrust would actually come in the south towards Sedan by Army Group A. However the French were oblivious to this fact and had in any case ruled out the possibility of an army being able to penetrate the dense woodlands of the Ardennes without being detected. Moreover, below the Ardennes was the Maginot Line, which they believed to be unassailable, so there was absolutely no likelihood of an attack coming there – or so they thought. In fact, Gamelin was so confident of this plan and of the Germans movements that he made no preparations to extricate Allied forces from Belgium if they were encircled by troops arriving from the south; he simply did not consider this a possibility.

All of this was made difficult by the fact that Belgium had proclaimed itself neutral in October 1936. In fact, Gamelin's first plan was far more respectful towards Belgium's position of neutrality. This plan, entitled *Escaut*, or *E Plan*, was based on a series of defended positions and fortifications along the France–Belgian border rather than within Belgium itself.

In the months before the invasion the Belgians had made the decision to build a network of bunkers and anti-tank defences along the River Dyle as part of their precautions against invasion. They had also built similar fortifications in an area known as the Gembloux Gap. Gamelin saw the advantage of this and decided that if an attack did come in the northern sector he could quickly move his armies to the River Dyle and Gembloux Gap, where they could entrench themselves in the defensive positions already established by the Belgians.

The Allies did not know it at the time but adopting the Dyle Plan would prove a massive error and would conform to exactly what the Germans hoped they would do. Ultimately it would prove to be one of the decisive factors contributing to the Allied defeat in the Battle of France. When Hitler was later told that the Allies had advanced to the River Dyle, he reportedly said, 'I could have wept for joy, they had fallen into the trap.'

The Dyle Plan did have its critics, most notably General Gaston Billotte, the commander-in-chief of France's 1st Army Group, and General Alphonse Joseph Georges, commander-in-chief of the

North-East Front. Georges in particular was worried that Gamelin was too certain that the German main effort would take place in Belgium and the Netherlands. He even had a premonition that an attack in the Low Countries could be a diversion with the main assault coming further south. If it did, the Allies would be starved of the necessary resources to react.

Because of their position next to Germany, the Belgians themselves were able to gather intelligence about Nazi troop movements. They quickly became aware of the situation when German forces started to concentrate along their frontier. As far as they were concerned this could only mean one thing: the Germans were planning to move through the heavily forested Ardennes. If this did happen and the Allies meanwhile advanced to the River Dyle, they could see how the Germans would be able to isolate the Allied field armies in Belgium and north-eastern France from the rest of their forces. They also anticipated that the Germans would try to land airborne and glider forces behind the Allied lines. These warnings were offered to the French and British, who decided to treat them as pure fantasy and ignored them.

It was not only the Belgians who had their doubts about the Dyle Plan and where exactly the offensive would come. In March 1940, Swiss intelligence detected six or seven Panzer divisions on the Germany–Luxembourg–Belgium border; motorised divisions were also later detected building up in the area. French intelligence further observed through aerial reconnaissance that the Germans were constructing pontoon bridges over the River Our on the Luxembourg–German border. The French military attaché in the Swiss capital, Bern, subsequently warned his government that the centre of the German attack would come at Sedan sometime between 8 and 10 May. This report was dated 30 April. Other neutral sources also provided intelligence, including the Vatican. Then, perhaps most telling of all, a French pilot sighted a German armoured column, estimated at some 100 kilometres in length, moving towards the Luxembourg border inside Germany. Gamelin received all of these reports, considered them and then roundly rejected them. Had he taken notice of these warnings and not pressed so assuredly ahead with the Dyle Plan, things might have turned out very differently.

7

OPPOSING FORCES

By the time of the start of the *Fall Gelb* operation the German armed forces stood at around the 6,000,000 mark. These were divided between approximately 4,000,000 serving in the army, 1,000,000 in the air force, and 180,000 in the navy. On 10 May 1940, when operations in the west began, almost half of this total was already being deployed in Poland, Denmark and Norway, which left approximately 3,000,000 men available for the new offensive.

In preparation for the offensive three army groups had been positioned inside Germany close to the borders of the Low Countries and France, forming a battle line that stretched from the area around Essen in the north to Strasbourg in the south. Army Group B covered the northern sector with Army Group A taking the middle section and Army Group C the southern area.

Army Group A, commanded by General Gerd von Rundstedt, would carry out the decisive movement of the campaign to cut through the Ardennes Forest, capture the area around Sedan and cut off the Allied troops in Belgium, before punching on to the coast. The success of the whole plan depended on them. Similarly, it was here that the operation would fail if Manstein's planning had got it wrong.

The manoeuvre that Army Group A would execute is sometimes referred to as a 'sickle cut'. In point of fact it was Winston Churchill who coined this phrase while attempting to describe how it had worked. The term was never used in any official capacity when talking or writing about the operation, however.

Army Group A comprised three complete armies: the 4th Army, commanded by General Günther von Kluge; the 12th Army, under General Wilhelm List; and the 16th Army, under General Ernst Busch. Crucially, it also included Panzer Group Kleist, the armoured spearhead commanded by General Paul Ludwig Ewald von Kleist.

Army Group B was commanded by General Fedor von Bock. Their job would be to advance through the Low Countries and lure the northern units of the Allied armies over the border through Belgium and away from the main attack in the Ardennes. As well as giving Army Group A a better chance of reaching the Channel, it would also trap the Allied troops positioned in the area in a pocket. The group consisted of the 6th Army, commanded by General Walther von Reichenau, and the 18th Army, under General Georg von Küchler.

Army Group C was to take up the most southerly aspect of the attack, commanded by General Wilhelm Ritter von Leeb. Their task was to prevent the Allies from making a flanking movement from the east and to launch small attacks against the Maginot Line and the upper Rhine. Again this would keep considerable numbers of Allied troops occupied and away from the central sector of the attack. The group was made up of the 1st Army, under General Erwin von Witzleben, and the 7th Army, commanded by General Friedrich Dollmann. A list of all the divisions within Army Groups A, B and C, together with the names of senior commanders, can be found in Appendix II.

As well as German troops the Axis forces included two Italian armies, which would serve in the Alpine border region between France and Italy. In total these two armies, commanded by Prince General Umberto di Savoia, numbered about 312,000 troops. The 1st Italian Army, under General Pietro Pintor, comprised 2nd Corps (General Francesco Bettini), 3rd Corps (General Mario Arisio), and 15th Corps (General Gastone Gambara). The 4th Italian Army, commanded by General Alfredo Guzzoni, was made up of 1st Corps (General Carlo Vecchiarelli), 4th Corps (General Camillo Mercalli) and the Alpine Corps (General Luigi Negri).

Because of their successes in the early days of the war, there persists a historical myth that the Nazi army of 1940 was a well-trained professional body of men with outstanding technology: the reality was slightly different. Although Hitler had reintroduced conscription in 1935, at least 45 per cent of his forces were over forty years old. Half of them probably had no more than just a few weeks basic training and were certainly not combat ready in any sense, nor was the average infantry soldier as well equipped as those in the Allied armies.

The officer class on the other hand was of a very high quality, as although Germany was forbidden to have a general staff between the wars, the army continued to conduct their typical roles under the disguised name of *Truppenamt*, which meant 'Troop Office'. This pretence was deemed necessary in order for Germany to be seen to be meeting the requirements of the Treaty of Versailles. It completely revised German tactical and strategic thinking, and during this period some of the *Wehrmacht*'s future leaders, such as Heinz Guderian, were first able to formulate the battle doctrines that would work so effectively a few years later. In addition to this, in October 1934 many of the officers who had been forced to retire at the close of the First World War were recalled; those who were no longer considered fit for combat duties were given administrative jobs, releasing others for front-line service.

According to Versailles the Germans were only permitted to have thirty-three officers in a divisional headquarters but, surprisingly, they decided themselves that thirty would be enough. This was in stark contrast to other contemporary armies: the Americans for instance had seventy-nine. What this showed was that Germany was creating an army that would be attack-minded, with its officers able to make their own battlefield decisions without consulting their superiors first. In contrast, Allied officers would have to pass everything upwards through the chain of command before a decision could be taken. This made German officers much more effective in the field at every level from battalion strength down to platoons.

Oddly the treaty had placed no limitations on the number of non-commissioned officers (NCOs) that a division could have. This gave the army the opportunity to train almost everyone to NCO standards, and by 1922 over 50 per cent of those serving were already a *gefreiter* (lance corporal) or above. What this meant in practice was that when the army began to mobilise, although the basic soldier had little training, he had high-quality, professional leaders. It also meant that the best of the NCOs could be trained to do junior officer roles such as platoon commanders.

All of this had two effects, the first being that when the Germans did rearm they could quickly promote these NCOs to officers as the army expanded. Secondly it created a culture of wider leadership below the level of officer. This suited the *Wehrmacht*'s philosophy of *bewegungskrieg*, the war of movement, where the use of personal judgment and reactive decision making were vital.

The *Wehrmacht* also had a fourth service working alongside the army called the Waffen SS, in which there were approximately 100,000 men. These were in a sense the descendants of the pre-war Brownshirts, the uniformed thugs who had helped Hitler rise to power. Now they had become the armed wing of the Nazi Party. The term SS stood for *Schutzstaffel*, or 'protective squadron'. This new military-styled organisation was mainly drawn from the Aryan stock of Nazi Germany itself, although it also included volunteers and some conscripts from both occupied and unoccupied lands seen as racially pure. They had a reputation of being fanatical and ruthless, and were later associated with many battlefield atrocities.

Although the SS would serve alongside the regular army, they were never actually part of it and retained their own command structure and to a certain degree their own authority. After the war, Hitler's plan was to continue to use them as the party's armed wing and from their ranks form an elite police force that would help to implement Nazi rule and justice. Before the war, the group was controlled by the SS *Führungshauptamt* (SS operational command office) under Reichsführer-SS Heinrich Himmler. However upon mobilisation its tactical control was given to the supreme command of the armed forces (*Oberkommando der Wehrmacht*). Hitler was particularly proud of these men and had total faith in their loyalty to the cause.

One area where the Wehrmacht was well behind the Allies was in terms of its being motorised, having around 120,000 vehicles in total; most of their logistical support was still provided by horse-drawn wagons. The French alone by comparison had around 300,000 vehicles.

To succeed *Fall Gelb* would be heavily reliant on the part played by the Panzer divisions, but the Germans were considerably outnumbered in tanks, having somewhere around 2,500 according to various sources, compared to the 5,800 fielded by the French alone. Nor at that time did they have a heavy combat tank that could compete in firepower and armour with the French Char B1, which was among the most formidable machines of its day, armed with a 47 mm gun in the turret and a larger 75 mm howitzer in the hull. The Char B1 would prove to be very effective when used in direct combat against German tanks. In one instance, on 16 May, a Char B1 single-handedly destroyed thirteen German tanks from an ambush position while taking 140 hits and surviving. However its sluggish speed and high fuel consumption made it unsuitable for a war of movement in which German vehicles were faster and more mechanically sound. There were also not enough of them, with only around 300 available for the battle. After the Fall of France, 161 of these giants were captured by the Germans, who modified and used them for training purposes either as flamethrowers or self-propelled guns.

The two main tanks used by the *Wehrmacht* in the west in May 1940 were the Panzer I and Panzer II, a remarkable enough force considering that, according to the Treaty of Versailles, Germany was prohibited from designing and manufacturing armoured vehicles of any sort. However, as early as 1926 a number of German companies, including Daimler-Benz and Rheinmetall, were producing prototype armoured vehicles; to conceal their real purpose they were codenamed *großtraktors*, or 'large tractors'.

In 1931 Major General Oswald Lutz was appointed the inspector of motor transport in the German army, with Heinz Guderian as his chief of staff: both men continued to champion the creation of a German armoured force that would be kept secret from the Allies. When Hitler came to power in 1934, he happily sanctioned their ambitions.

In 1933 specifications for an armoured vehicle had been issued to the leading German motor companies – Rheinmetall, Krupp, Henschel, MAN and Daimler Benz. Their designers were also able to cooperate with the Swedish Landsverk Company, which was making armoured cars at the time. Krupp's design, dubbed the *Krupp-Traktor*, was eventually selected. It was inspired by the British Carden Lloyd Mk VI Tankette, two of which had been secretly acquired from the Russians, who had based their own T-27 tankette on them. This would ultimately and through many variants lead to the creation of the Panzer I.

In order to get around other restrictions forced on the country by the Treaty of Versailles, the Russians had allowed the Germans to use a secret tank training school at Kazan in the Soviet Union, known as the Kama Tank School, where they trained officers and crew in tank warfare and used the facility to help develop their own vehicles. The school operated from 1929 to 1933 after which the Germans closed it and trained its tank force at home. Similar schools were established in the Soviet Union for German pilots and officers training in gas warfare.

Because of the circumstances surrounding its creation the Panzer I was not really designed as a combat vehicle but rather to help train tank crews in modern battle techniques. Nevertheless it did see combat during the Spanish Civil War, where, although poorly armed with just two 7.92 mm machine guns, its experiences on the Iberian Peninsula provided the *Wehrmacht* with vital lessons in tank warfare.

Guderian continued to press for better and heavier tanks, which would later become the Panzer III and Panzer IV. However with the war approaching and the development of these falling behind, the Panzer II was ordered as a stop gap. Most Panzer IIs were armed with a single 2 cm KwK 30 L/55 cannon, similar to an anti-aircraft gun, capable of firing at a rate of 600 rounds per minute. It also had a 7.92 mm machine gun mounted coaxially with the main gun. Together with the Panzer I, the II would provide the main weapons of the German tank forces during the invasions of both Poland and France, but they were both a long way short of the formidable beasts that Germany would develop later in the war, culminating with the Tiger II – better known by its nickname 'King Tiger'.

One huge advantage that German tank crews did have over their numerically superior French counterparts was wireless, which turned out to be crucial in the days ahead. All German tanks and most other military vehicles were equipped with Telefunken radios developed in the late 1930s, which enabled them to communicate at different levels. They could receive orders at a moment's notice from their command vehicle and even talk between themselves in the heat of battle.

Radio gave the Panzer divisions the ability to respond quickly in battle as the situation rapidly changed around them. If a tactic had been implemented and suddenly found not to be achieving its aim, orders could be sent to each tank commander simultaneously to change it, and to react without the enemy realising what was occurring. Whether an individual or a squadron of tanks, communication allowed units to follow new orders instantaneously, while on a grander scale it could be used to coordinate formations and bring them together for mass firepower in attack or defence. There is no doubt that Panzer commanders regarded their radio as a crucial part of their equipment, second only to their weaponry. Training in battlefield communications was seen as being equally important as gunnery practice.

French tanks might have been superior to the Germans in their firepower but without radios it was hard to control them in groups, so they sometimes marauded independently. The French had spent very little of their defence budget between the wars on developing radio communications. Its army still largely used field telephones and couriers to pass messages on the battlefield; often their only means of communication was by word of mouth. This made the French slow to react to battlefield situations and gave the Germans the decisive edge.

Another thing that made the German's tanks much more efficient, particularly in the newer Panzers, was that they were designed for a crew of five men, each with a dedicated job to do. Crews consisted of a commander, driver, mechanic, gun aimer and gun loader. The French had smaller crews and the commander himself also acted as the loader of the main gun, so while he was doing this secondary task he was distracted from his primary functions of observation and directing the tank in battle. Again, this slowed the French tanks down considerably. Having a well-trained team of individuals for each task made the German crews a much tighter combat unit and much more effective.

A further groundbreaking use of radio which had been developed between the wars by various armies, including the British, saw light aircraft used to spot for artillery. Aircraft could fly over enemy lines and report their coordinates back to a command centre, from where the fire of the guns could be laid directly on to the enemy positions. Equipped with their Telefunken radios, Panzer commanders had almost the same advantage and facilitated communication between the tanks and the *Luftwaffe*.

Some Panzer divisions had a group of tactical air control troops attached to them called the *Fliegerleittruppen*. These groups had their own fleet of specially equipped vehicles, variants of the standard Sd.Kfz. 251 half-track armoured fighting vehicle. As more of these vehicles became available more tanks consequently would benefit from their service. Certainly all of the Panzer divisions in General Guderian's corps that would make the initial thrust to the English Channel could call on this support. It is claimed that during this phase of the battle Guderian's troops would never have to wait for more than twenty minutes for an aircraft to attack a target using the coordinates given by a tank crew in the front line.

The *Luftwaffe* allocated VIII Fliegerkorps (8th Air Corps), under General Wolfram Freiherr von Richthofen, to work in support of the invasion. Among its armada were a number of Junkers Ju 87s, or 'Panzer Stukas' as they became known, which were dedicated to working with the tanks. On average one of these aircraft could arrive over the target within half an hour from receipt of orders. Again, all of this just helped to give the Germans the upper hand.

During the Phoney War V Fliegerkorps (5th Air Corps) had been allotted the task of patrolling the borders to keep enemy aircraft in check and gain air superiority, in other words making sure their own aircraft dominated the sky. They did this from airfields close to the borders of the Low Countries. Meanwhile Richthofen established his own headquarters at Koblenz in October 1939, from where his corps steadily rose in strength from forty-six *staffels* (squadrons) to fifty-nine.

Richthofen, who was the cousin of the famous First World War fighter ace Baron Manfred von Richthofen, was given the task of supporting both Army Group B in the Netherlands and Army

Group A through Belgium, most particularly General Kleist's Panzer troops (Army Group A) and General Reichenau's 6th Army (Army Group B). To do this he based his *geschwaders* (groups) at airfields around Düsseldorf and Cologne. The corps assumed the specialist identity of a ground-attack formation. After the launch of *Fall Gelb* and as soon as a breakthrough had occurred, V Fliegerkorps would vacate their airfields near the borders in favour of VIII Fliegerkorps, as the requirement changed from one of gaining air superiority to providing effective air support for the army.

By 9 May Richthofen's air armada consisted of approximately 5,100 combat aircraft, 487 transport planes and fifty gliders. The combined Allied total was only 2,935 aircraft, about half the number of the German force. VIII Fliegerkorps employed small numbers of all the main German aircraft types of the day, such as the Dornier Do 17, Junkers Ju 88 and Heinkel He 111. However, their two main aircraft were the Junkers Ju 87, used to attack enemy positions on the ground, and the Messerschmitt Bf 109, used for fighter cover to keep enemy aircraft away from the advancing troops.

The Junkers Ju 87, more commonly known as the 'Stuka', which is shortened from *Sturzkampfflugzeug* and meaning 'dive-attack' aircraft, was manufactured by Junkers Flugzeug und Motorenwerke of Dessau. It was used in dive-bombing and ground attack roles in which it was lethal to its enemy if left unchallenged. It was fitted with a siren that emitted an ear-piercing scream as it dropped out of the sky in a near vertical dive, a sound that terrified anyone below. However, for all of this, it was extremely vulnerable to Allied fighters and anti-aircraft guns. It was powered by a Junkers Jumo 211DA engine, but only had a maximum speed of 232 mph and cruising speed of 175 mph which left it floundering against the Hawker Hurricanes the British had deployed to the Continent. In fact it fared so badly over England in the summer of 1940 that it had to be withdrawn from daylight operations.

The Messerschmitt Bf 109, on the other hand, was an outstanding fighter aircraft of the time. It was designed by Willi Messerschmitt and manufactured by Messerschmitt A G of Augsburg. The Bf 109 was powered by a Daimler-Benz DB 601A engine and had a maximum speed of 354 mph. Only the Supermarine Spitfire could match its speed, though unfortunately these were not used in France as fighter aircraft. It was armed with two 20 mm cannon in the wings with sixty rounds per cannon, and two 7.9 mm machine guns firing between the blades of the propeller with 1,000 rounds per gun. The prototype first flew in September 1935 – ironically, it was powered by a British Rolls-Royce Kestrel engine.

Although there were no Spitfires deployed in France for fighter duties, the Hawker Hurricane, which the British did use, was certainly equal to the Me 109 in some areas despite being deficient in others. Billy Drake faced these aircraft in France while flying Hurricanes and notes:

> We realised that the 109 had certain characteristics that were superior to us and the only method we had of combating their superiority was to out-turn them. If we tried to climb with them or dive away from them we were sitting ducks. Provided we saw them in time we could evade them.

Paul Farnes had also flown Hurricanes in France with No. 501 Squadron and agrees that the Me 109 was faster while the Hurricane was more manoeuvrable. The Hurricane pilot also had the advantage of protective armour as there was a fifteen and a half inch steel plate behind his seat:

> The 109 was considerably faster, but the Hurricane was more manoeuvrable and could take a hell of a lot of punishment. And of course we were shielded from the back with a steel plate, but the 109 wasn't. They did eventually get armour but to start with they didn't, so if you got a burst at a 109 from behind, you were liable to do a lot of damage. As well as not having the armour plating protection, they just couldn't take the punishment that our Hurricanes took.

Whilst in some regards the Germans were outnumbered and outgunned by the Allies and in others the opposite was the case, they still managed to pull off an astonishing victory. If this analysis has offered a few technical clues as to why this might have happened, it cannot give a definitive explanation. Another factor that cannot be disregarded was the Führer himself. As supreme commander of the armed forces he was often impulsive and inclined to take risks on the grandest of scales. In the early days of the war it appears that his gambles sometimes paid off.

Earlier we learnt how between the start of the war in September 1939 and March 1940 around 316,000 troops of the British Expeditionary Force had arrived in northern France to serve alongside the French army. This had been an ongoing process throughout the Phoney War and further troops would later join them.

As soon as the Germans started to attack, the BEF, then under Lord Gort, was ordered to take part in General Gamelin's plan to cross the Belgian border and move up to the River Dyle and occupy the fortifications along the K-W Line. It was here that the Allies planned to stop the enemy's advance and establish the same type of entrenched warfare that had epitomised the tactics of both sides during the First World War, even though this slow, dogged campaign of attrition was quite alien to German military philosophy. Assuming the Belgian forces stood their ground and put up a strong defence along their own border, the Allies estimated that it would take the Germans roughly two to three weeks to move their army the sixty-two miles to the right bank of the river. In fact it would take them only four days.

Similar to the Germans, in preparation for the approaching battle the French forces were made up of three army groups. The 1st Army Group, commanded by General Gaston-Henri Billotte, was given the vital job of guarding France's north-east frontier and executing General Gamelin's plan of entering the Low Countries if and when they were invaded by the Germans. The group was composed of four complete armies: 1st Army (General Georges Maurice Jean Blanchard), 2nd Army (General Charles Huntziger), 7th Army (General Henri Giraud), and the 9th Army (General André Georges Corap); it also included most of the BEF under Lord Gort and some Belgian forces. Billotte would remain commander-in-chief of the 1st Army Group until his death in a car crash on 23 May 1940, and would be succeeded by General Blanchard.

Once the order was given for the BEF to advance to the River Dyle they would cross the border and position themselves to the right of the Belgian army between Leuven and Wavre. The French 7th Army would go furthest north to hold the line on the River Scheldt linking up with Dutch forces. The French 1st Army would defend the Gembloux Gap between Wavre and Namur, while the French 9th Army would cover the Meuse sector between Namur and the area to the north of Sedan. General Gamelin was convinced that the spearhead of the German attack would come through the Gembloux Gap as this was the most lightly fortified point along the whole series of stop lines that protected Holland, Belgium and France. It was also flat country, ideal for tanks to operate in.

After the advance to the north had been executed, this would leave only the 2nd French Army in France itself, entrenched around Sedan to form the rear. The 2nd Army was given low priority in almost everything from manning to anti-aircraft guns and anti-tank weapons. They consisted of five divisions, two of which were composed of poorly trained and poorly equipped reservists, many in their thirties or forties, as well as one division of Senegalese colonial troops.

French high command remained adamant that the German attack would be conducted from the north down through the Low Countries. They were still convinced that the Ardennes was impassable to tanks, even though their own intelligence services and those of the Belgian army had warned them that long columns of armour had been spotted travelling towards the German side of the forest. War games in 1937 and 1938 had also quite clearly indicated that a mechanised army could penetrate the Ardennes. The commander of the 9th Army, General Corap, made his feelings quite clear, saying that he believed it was 'idiocy' to think that they could not. Despite this, it seems that General Gamelin ignored all the evidence; it simply did not fall in line with his strategy. Because of this the 2nd Army had been tasked with defending a considerably larger front than their available manpower allowed. Little did they know that this undermanned and ill-equipped force would soon come face-to-face with the elite Panzer troops of the *Wehrmacht*.

The other two army groups were both based further south to guard sections of the Maginot Line. The 2nd Army Group, under General André-Gaston Prételat, was responsible for manning the bulk of the fortified line from Montmédy to south of Strasbourg. It comprised three armies: 3rd Army (General Charles Condé), 4th Army (General Édouard-Jean Réquin), and the 5th Army (General Victor Bourret).

The 2nd Army Group also included the British troops in the sector, the 51st (Highland) Infantry Division commanded by Major General Victor Fortune, which had been mobilised in August 1939. They had departed from Southampton in mid-January and disembarked at Le Havre. On 22 April it was completely detached from the rest of the BEF to come under the command of the French 3rd Army as the Saar Force and was stationed at the Ouvrage Hackenberg fortress on the Maginot Line.

Finally there was the 3rd Army Group, under General Antoine-Marie-Benoît Besson, which was responsible for manning the southern end of the Maginot Line and the River Rhine. It had just the one army, the 8th, commanded by General Jeanny-Jules-Marcel Garchery.

In preparation for war the French had mobilised almost one third of the entire male population of the country between the ages of twenty and forty-five. This brought the strength of their armed forces to around the 5,000,000 mark. Of these, around 2,240,000 served with units in the north. The British contributed thirteen divisions to this force. It was hoped that once the invasion began, the armies of Holland, with around 400,000 men, and Belgium, with 650,000, would quickly join the fight. In fact when the Belgians did take up arms, King Leopold III took personal command of the army with Lieutenant General Édouard van den Bergen as his chief of staff. There were two further Polish divisions serving with the Allies, under the overall command of General Władysław Sikorski: the 1st Grenadier Division, under General Boleslaw Bronislaw Duch, attached to the 2nd Army Group; and 2nd Infantry Fusiliers Division, commanded by Brigadier General Bronislaw Prugar-Ketling, attached to the 3rd Army Group.

The success of the Dyle Plan would largely depend on the Allied armies being able to hold the line against the onslaught of what they envisaged would be infantry supported by tanks. The main way of doing this would be with the use of artillery firing from entrenched positions along the K-W Line. The French had 10,700 guns, the British 1,280, the Belgians 1,338, and the Dutch 656. This gave the Allies a total of around 14,000 artillery pieces – 45 per cent more than the Germans. The French would also deploy most of their tanks as static guns.

As we learnt in the last chapter, the French army was much more motorised than its opponent in terms of the numbers of vehicles it had, but this did not necessarily make it more mobile. The Germans still relied heavily on horses to carry out numerous tasks, even in some instances pulling field guns. However, tanks would hold the key to the battle. In total the French possessed around 5,800 tanks; the British, Dutch and Belgians had relatively little armour of any consequence between them.

The French had planned for a defensive war and built tanks accordingly, to be dug in behind the Maginot Line or wherever they wished to try and stem the enemy's advance. Infantry tanks were consequently designed to be very heavily armoured with powerful guns, some of which, like the Char B1 mentioned earlier, were very effective against the German machines when used in this way.

Another tank in service at the start of the offensive was the Renault FT, which was of pre-war vintage. These were slowly being replaced by the Renault R35 as the standard light infantry tank in service in the French army. However, not enough had been produced by May 1940 and the French military lacked crews trained to fight in them, so eight battalions using the FT had to be kept operational. At the outbreak of war only 975 R35s had been delivered out of a total order for 2,300.

The French also had the SOMUA S35 medium tank, armed with a 47 mm SA 35 gun. Around 700 of these had been ordered but only 430 had been issued to the army by June 1940. Of these, about 288 were in front-line service at the beginning of the Battle of France.

Many of the failings of the French tank force were more to do with strategy and tactics rather than technology and design. They were deployed to expect a long, sluggish affair, similar to the trench warfare of 1914–1918. The Germans on the other hand were planning their war of movement, a concept quite alien to the French military planners. The battle doctrine employed by the French military was a slow-paced, deliberate operation in conformity with rigorous planning, in which the use of tanks was severely hindered. Tanks were assigned to infantry divisions to provide support for them, whereas in the German army the thinking was progressively becoming the opposite: infantry should be used to support the armour. This strategic (mis)conception prevented the French tanks from being a strong independent operational force; because of this they were unable to respond quickly to a German assault characterised by rapid movement and combined-arms.

The British contributed several types of tank to the battle as well as other armoured vehicles, but, again, these proved simply inadequate. Their main tank force during the build-up to events was the 1st Army Tank Brigade, which comprised the 4th Battalion Royal Tank Regiment and the 7th Battalion Royal Tank Regiment, equipped mainly with Matilda I (A11) and Matilda II (A12) infantry tanks. British tanks however were hindered by the same doctrine as the French: they were not designed for speed as they had to work at the same pace as the infantry units, which of course would be attacking on foot.

The British infantry tank came about as a result of a general staff requirement for a tank that could directly support an infantry attack, armed only with a heavy machine gun and needing to go no faster than a man walking. Because of their slow speed, they were able to carry heavy armour capable of sustaining attacks from standard anti-tank weapons.

The job of designing an infantry support tank was given to Sir John Carden at Vickers-Armstrong Ltd in 1935. The specification was for an inexpensive vehicle that could be manufactured using only components that were already commercially available. This resulted in a small two-man vehicle, with a low hull and a turret fitted with a single heavy machine gun, either a Vickers .303 machine gun or a larger Vickers .50 machine gun. Designed for quick delivery as well as low cost, the vehicle used stock parts from other sources: it had a Ford V8 engine, a Fordson gearbox, a steering mechanism similar to the one used in Vickers light tanks and suspension adapted from the Mk IV Dragon artillery tractor.

The crew consisted of two people, the commander and the driver. However, and again similar to the French, the commander had several functions. As well as directing the driver and operating the wireless, he had to load and fire the machine gun. Making matters worse, as there was no room in the commander's turret for the wireless, it was placed in the hull and the commander had to duck down inside to operate it. The driver's position was equally cramped and the turret could not be traversed forwards while the driver's hatch was open. The top speed was 8 mph, although the general staff considered that sufficient for the job in hand. The tank was apparently named 'Matilda' by General Hugh Elles, Master-General of the Ordnance at the time, because of its diminutive size and duck-like shape.

As well as the Matilda I (A11), the 7th Battalion Royal Tank Regiment also had twenty-three of the larger Matilda II (A12), also known as the Matilda Senior. This was some improvement, weighing more than twice as much as its predecessor and armed with a QF 2-pounder (40 mm) tank gun; it also had a 7.92 mm Besa machine gun as its secondary armament. It had a crew of four: the commander, gunner, loader and driver. In reality, when facing the Germans the machine gun became its principal weapon as for some unexplained reason there were no shells for the 2-pounder guns available.

There were other tanks in France in 1940 employed by divisional cavalry units, which were old cavalry regiments that had been converted to armour for reconnaissance duties. The main tank here was the Vickers-Armstrong Light Tank Mk VI, which had been used between the wars to police far corners of the empire, particularly India. It had a crew of three: the commander, gunner and driver. The commander doubled as the radio operator; thankfully there was room in the turret for his wireless. It was armed with a Vickers .50 machine gun with coaxial 15 mm and 7.92 mm Besa machine guns.

When the Mk VI was first produced, in 1936, the general staff considered it to be better than any light tank produced by any other country at that time. When the British government began its rearmament process in 1937, the Mk VI was the only tank with which the War Office was ready to proceed with manufacturing. The development of a medium tank for the army had met with severe problems, largely due to spiraling costs, and models only existed as prototypes. As a result of this, when the Second World War began the vast majority of the tanks available to the BEF were Mark VI variants.

In May 1940 the BEF's armoured element would be considerably strengthened with the arrival of the first units of the 1st Armoured

Division, equipped with 257 tanks, a large number of which were aforementioned Mk VI variants. They were reinforced with numerous other armoured vehicles such as scout cars and Bren gun carriers – but would it be enough?

It would be fair to say that in operational terms the French did not seem to give much consideration to using tanks as offensive weapons. In the 1930s Colonel Charles de Gaulle, who at that time was on the staff at the École Militaire (French Military College), had tried to convince French high command that they needed to form special armoured divisions supported by aircraft and infantry. He believed that modern battlefields would be tank dominated and fast paced: trench warfare was now obsolete. However nobody listened, as at the time French high command was focused on maintaining broad and continuous fronts as it had done in the First World War. Training in the army was also focused on a static war, with the majority of personnel only trained to man fortifications such as the Maginot Line. When the attack did finally come, the French had no understanding of it and lacked any tactics as to how to deal with its speed and directness.

An even more pressing threat was the *Luftwaffe*, which outnumbered the Allies quite considerably. The French air force (*Armée de l'air*) had 1,562 aircraft, supplemented by the RAF. In the main German aircraft were much more modern and efficient than those of the Allies, especially the Messerschmitt Bf 109. The Allies unfortunately had many obsolete models that were simply no match for them, though the French Dewoitine D.520, the Curtiss P-36 Hawk and the British Hawker Hurricane were notable exceptions.

The D.520 was designed in response to a 1936 demand from the French air force for a fast modern fighter with a good climbing speed, armed with a 20 mm cannon. The D.520 was not as fast as the Bf 109 but it certainly had better manoeuvrability and could hold its own against it in a dogfight. The downside was that by May 1940 only thirty-six of these superb machines had been delivered to front-line squadrons.

The French also flew the US-built Curtiss P-36 Hawk (also known as the Curtiss Hawk Model 75), which would perform well against the Bf 109. Its prototype first flew in May 1935; the French put in an order for 300 aircraft. However negotiations with the Americans were drawn-out, mainly due to the cost of the fighters, which was double that of the alternatives the French government was considering at the time. However the pressure of continuing German rearmament persuaded France to purchase 100 aircraft and 173 engines.

The first Hawk arrived in France in December 1938 and entered service in March 1939. After the first few example aircraft were supplied, they were delivered in pieces and assembled in France. It was officially designated as the Curtiss H75-C1 (and in fact the name 'Hawk' was not used by the French). The aircraft was powered by a Pratt & Whitney R-1830 engine and it had instruments specially calibrated for the metric system for the French. It was armed with four 7.5 mm FN-Browning machine guns; later models had six. A total of 316 H75s were delivered to France before the German occupation. On 20 September 1939 Sergeant André-Armand Legrand, flying one of these imported machines with the French Groupe de Chasse 2/5 La Fayette, was credited with the first French air victory of the Second World War on the western front when he shot down a Messerschmitt Bf 109E.

Pilots within the air component of the BEF were blessed with the Hawker Hurricane, which was also a match for the Bf 109. Between 10 and 20 May, the Hurricane squadrons in France would shoot down an estimated 350 enemy aircraft. In the same period only seventy-five Hurricanes were destroyed in action by the enemy, although a further 120 were lost on the ground to bombing or strafing.

The Hurricane was designed by Sydney Camm and developed by Hawker Aircraft Limited of Kingston upon Thames. The prototype K5083 first flew on 6 November 1935 at Hawker's facility at Brooklands at Weybridge, in Surrey, which was originally built as a motor racing circuit in 1907. Motor racing gave way to aviation, and the Hurricane was among the aircraft that were tested and built here, although they did not start coming off the production line until 1937.

The Hurricane Mark I had a maximum speed of 320 mph with a wooden propeller or 325 mph with a three-bladed metal one. It had a cruising speed of 230 mph and a service ceiling of 34,000 feet, and was powered by either a Rolls-Royce Merlin II or III engine. The

Hurricane Mark II on the other hand had a Merlin XX engine, which made it about 20 miles per hour faster and gave it a higher service ceiling. Both aircraft normally carried eight Browning .303 machine guns in the wings. The fuselage of the Mark II was strengthened so that wings carrying heavier armaments could be fitted. Future variants could carry twelve machine guns, or four 20 mm Hispano-Suiza cannon.

According to several veterans, one important advantage that the Hurricane had over the German fighters, or indeed even over the Spitfire, was its sturdiness. Paul Farnes, a pilot sergeant with No. 501 Squadron during the battle, describes some of his experiences when flying a Hurricane:

> The Hurricane could take quite a lot of punishment. On one occasion I had run out of ammunition, but as there were still 109s about I went into a steep dive. I remember looking at the clock. I had got up to something like 450 mph, when all of a sudden there was a terrific buffeting of the aircraft. I thought I had been shot up. I tried to open the hood but I couldn't, as it was stuck. Eventually I got out of the dive and landed at the nearest airfield. On landing we found that I hadn't been shot up, but that the fuselage had been battered in. I didn't know it at the time but I had reached the Hurricane's Mach number. In those days none of our aircraft could reach the speed of sound and when you got to what was called its Mach number, the aircraft more or less became uncontrollable. The Mach number is a percentage of the speed of sound. I think the Hurricane had a Mach number of something like 8.4. It's the sort of thing one wouldn't normally do, and couldn't do in straight and level flight – you would have to be in a very steep dive.

The Allies certainly had aircraft that could compete with the German machines. They also had the means to deal with the *Luftwaffe* on the ground in terms of anti-aircraft guns, although again nowhere near enough to deal with the massed threat. The French army kept an arsenal of around 2,000 of all types, with the 25 mm anti-aircraft gun being the most abundant.

The BEF had ten regiments of QF 3.7 inch guns, then the most advanced heavy anti-aircraft weapon in the world. They also had seven and a half regiments of Bofors 40 mm guns, with either three or four batteries per regiment. This represented roughly 300 heavy and 350 light anti-aircraft guns.

What is clear is that in terms of manpower and machines, neither side had an out and out advantage at the outset; the Germans were strong in some areas, while the French and British were stronger in others. The battle would almost certainly be decided on tactics.

8

INVASION OF THE LOW COUNTRIES

On the morning of Friday 10 May 1940 the waiting was finally over as the *Wehrmacht* launched *Fall Gelb*, the long anticipated invasion of the Low Countries. Elements of Army Group A began their advance towards the Ardennes via Luxembourg, while at the same time Army Group B began its feint by crossing the Dutch and Belgian borders. Hitler watched on with baited breath to see how the Allies would react, waiting to see whether they would take the bait and move their forces north to face the invaders.

Luxembourg, similar to the other Low Countries, was a neutral power. Its policy of neutrality went back to 1867 with the passing of the Treaty of London. As a condition of this treaty it did not have an army as such, although it did maintain the tiny Luxembourgish Volunteer Corps. In 1940 this was made up of thirteen officers looking after two companies of men, one consisting of 425 volunteer soldiers and the other of 255 armed gendarmes.

When the war began in September 1939 Luxembourg found itself in a very precarious position, sitting as it did on the borders of Germany, France and Belgium. Its position of neutrality and limited armed forces meant that both the Germans and the Allies could easily occupy its territory if they considered it would benefit them militarily. The French had fortified their side of the border with a section of the Maginot Line.

There is little doubt that public opinion in Luxembourg was firmly on the side of the Allies but their government had been careful not to antagonise the Nazis. A good illustration of this stance was the fact that their popular English-language radio station, Radio Luxembourg, was taken off-air in September amid fears that it might offend the Germans.

Luxembourg at the time was a form of constitutional monarchy known as a grand duchy. The head of state was Charlotte, Grand Duchess of Luxembourg, the second daughter of Grand Duke William IV and his wife, Marie Anne of Portugal. When William died he had been succeeded by his eldest daughter, Marie-Adélaïde, but she had abdicated in 1919 amidst an atmosphere of post-war revolution. A referendum was subsequently held to decide on a new constitution in which nearly 80 per cent of the people voted to keep a grand ducal monarchy with Charlotte as its head of state as she expressed no political preference. Of course, as with other European states at the end of the First World War, the power of the monarch was severely curtailed and the real authority lay with the prime minister, Pierre Dupong.

In the case of an invasion it was quite clear that Luxembourg would be unable to defend itself. However, in the spring of 1940 as hostilities became increasingly likely, a decision was taken to build some basic fortifications along the borders with both France and particularly Germany. These were known as the Schuster Line, named after the man charged with their construction, Joseph Schuster. The line mainly consisted of concrete blocks, with iron gates established at all the bridges on the border with Germany; the nation's border was almost entirely made up of stretches of the rivers Our, Sauer and Moselle. There were also blockades on some of the roads leading to both France and Germany. A series of radio outposts were established along the German border that could send messages to the nearest volunteer corps barracks in the event of an incursion.

It was obvious that these obstacles would not be able to prevent a modern army from invading, but they could stall them. Their official purpose, in actual fact, was to slow down the progress of the invaders to give the government time to take whatever actions were needed; ultimately this might entail the evacuation of the royal family and the government itself. The barricades also helped to calm the population down, who were rightly concerned about the tanks gathering on the other side of their eastern frontier.

Many German nationals lived in Luxembourg and there were numerous Nazi sympathisers among the local population. In an attempt to make the invasion go as smoothly as possible, German high command issued instructions to their supporters living inside the duchy as to the actions they should take at the start of operations. On the evening of 9 May the grand ducal government acquired a copy of this document and alarm bells started to ring.

Security was immediately tightened, border posts were put on full alert and the police were mobilised and deployed to defend public buildings; they were also given the task of arresting suspected members of a Nazi fifth column. German soldiers dressed as civilians and supported by Nazis inside the country with local knowledge tried to sabotage the radio posts and destroy the barricades along the border. The police got wind of the situation and were able to stop them in their tracks.

Members of the German legation in the country were detained for questioning. Allegedly they had been using legation cars to distribute subversive material and organise the activities of the fifth columnists. However, as they still had diplomatic immunity the police had no choice but to release them again.

It was now evident that something was about to happen, especially after German troops were thought to be on the move on the other side of the rivers. Consequently all of the iron gates along the Schuster Line were ordered to be closed on 10 May at 3:15 a.m. Several bridges were also destroyed. In order to provide them with better protection, members of the royal family were evacuated from their residence in Colmar-Berg to the grand ducal palace in Luxembourg City.

The German invasion began at 4:35 a.m. as the Panzer troops of General Guderian's XIX Corps descended on the border crossings. The force was made up of the 1st Panzer Division, commanded by Major General Friedrich Kirchner, the 2nd Panzer Division, under Major General Rudolf Veiel, and the 10th Panzer Division, under Major General Ferdinand Schaal. They encountered very little resistance and the iron gates of the Schuster Line made no impact whatsoever. They were simply torn down, and ramps were built over the concrete blocks so that the tanks could drive over the top of them. In other cases they were simply blown up by German engineers.

The only guards at the border to meet the the Panzers' advance were soldiers of the Luxembourgish Volunteer Corps who had volunteered for guard duty that night. The rest of the corps made the shrewd decision to stay in their barracks. Outside of this small force, the reception the Germans found at the bridges was made up of customs officials and some gendarmes. The radio outposts were quickly taken and the border secured.

Amidst the confusion, Pierre Dupong and his foreign minister, Joseph Bech, tried to contact the German ambassador, first at the legation building in Luxembourg City and then at his private residence. They were abruptly informed that he was not at home. The majority of the government, including Dupong and Bech, then decided to evacuate the capital, and at 6:30 a.m. they set off in a motorcade for the town of Esch near the French border. Unfortunately upon arrival they found the place overrun with German soldiers who had landed earlier in Fieseler Fi 136 Storch liaison aircraft with the orders to hold the area until the arrival of Guderian's main force. It is claimed that in the disarray a police officer approached the soldiers and asked them to leave and was promptly arrested himself. As the government's motorcade finally approached Esch they spotted a German roadblock ahead and decided to try and avoid capture by taking a lengthy detour through the countryside.

While all of this was going on the royal family had themselves been advised to escape the city. A group consisting of the Grand Duchess Charlotte, her husband Prince Félix and her mother, the Dowager Grand Duchess Marie Anne, along with other ministers and staff headed for the village of Redange close to the border with Belgium. Another group including Hereditary Grand Duke Jean, the son of Charlotte and Félix, also headed independently for Esch.

At around 8:00 a.m. Dupong and his group finally reached and crossed the French border near Longlaville, at a position where the three countries of Luxembourg, France and Belgium meet. They were later joined by the parties of both Grand Duchess Charlotte and the Hereditary Grand Duke. His party had apparently been stopped by the Germans at a roadblock but the chauffer had driven straight through; they had not looked back until they reached France.

Luxembourg City was occupied before midday, and although the police made a token attempt at resisting, their situation was hopeless, most being taken prisoner. In the limited resistance that did occur, six policemen and one soldier of the Volunteer Corps were wounded.

How seriously General Gamelin took the invasion of Luxembourg is hard to tell. He probably thought this was a diversion, aimed at drawing the Allied forces away from Army Group B, which he still believed would instigate the main attack further north. After all, the Germans had little reason to attack through Luxembourg, as to do so they would have to face the impossible terrain of the Ardennes, while if they turned south they would come up against the impregnable Maginot Line.

However a decision was made to send French forces across the border to try and ascertain the strength and disposition of the enemy. These forces consisted of elements of the 3rd Light Cavalry (3 DLC or 3 Division Légère de Cavalerie), commanded by General Robert Petiet. They were supported by the 1st Spahi Brigade; the Spahis were light cavalry regiments recruited primarily from the indigenous populations of Algeria, Tunisia and Morocco. Still using horses, they were considered by the French to be the best way to operate in the rugged Ardennes. This force also included the 2nd company of the 5th Armoured Battalion (5 BCC or 5 Bataillon de Chars de Combat). This small army crossed the southern border, and after conducting a probe of the German forces they later returned to their original positions behind the Maginot Line. In the meantime both French and British aircraft had carried out a limited bombing of the German troops.

By the evening of 10 May most of the country was in German hands. Huge numbers of civilians fled before the advancing Panzers, mostly trying to escape to France or Belgium. In due course, Pierre Dupong and most of his government found their way to Canada, while Grand Duchess Charlotte chose to exile herself in London from where she became an important symbol to the people of Luxembourg during the days ahead. As for Hereditary Grand Duke Jean, he would later join the British Army.

The German invasion of Luxembourg was over in a day, but further north, as Army Group B launched its feint offensive in the Netherlands and Belgium, things did not go quite as smoothly as they had hoped. This diversion was designed to lure the Allied armies in the north of France away from General Rundstedt's Army Group A as it proceeded through the Ardennes. The ruse worked and General Gamelin immediately sent his 1st Army Group over the Belgian border in accordance with the Dyle Plan. This force included the BEF, which was to make its way up to the K-W Line where they would entrench and wait for the German army to arrive. The French 7th Army had the furthest to go as they were tasked with crossing the Dutch border and supporting the troops of that country.

The invasions of Holland and Belgium were in fact more than just a diversion. Army Group B had every intention of defeating the armies of these two countries and establishing Nazi occupations. At this stage in the war these countries were considered of particular importance, as from here the *Luftwaffe* would be able to launch attacks against England and shipping in the English Channel. Here General Fedor von Bock encountered a slight dilemma, though: in the original planning for *Fall Gelb*, his army group was given priority as it was here that the main assault was originally intended, yet after the adoption of Erich von Manstein's plan, Army Group B had been stripped of many of its troops and armour to reinforce General Rundstedt's group. That said, Hitler and high command still expected him to achieve all of his objectives with the forces at his disposal.

Although in late 1939 the German government had issued a guarantee to the Netherlands to respect their neutrality, the Dutch military had begun to slowly mobilise. By the spring of 1940 it was considered to be at full strength but poorly trained and equipped. Spending on defence had not been a priority for the Dutch between the wars, and the infantry soldiers of the Netherlands Royal Army were largely equipped with pre-First World War equipment. The army consisted of a small professional cadre of 1,500 officers and 6,500 other ranks. These were responsible for maintaining the military establishment and for the training of the annual intake of 60,000 conscripts, who were obligated to serve eleven months' national service. At the time of mobilisation, the home army including reserves numbered between 300,000 and 400,000 men of all ranks. Holland did possess an overseas army policing its colonies but this would have no bearing on the situation at home.

The home army comprised four corps, each responsible for a geographical area of the country centered respectively on Amsterdam, Arnhem, Breda and Amersfoort. Each of these corps were made up of two infantry divisions, one or two heavy artillery regiments, one independent artillery battalion, and a signals and reconnaissance battalion. In addition to these was a light brigade with an armoured car squadron, cyclist regiment, two hussar regiments and one horse artillery regiment; there was also an anti-aircraft brigade.

The most obvious deficiency in the Dutch forces was its shortage of armour, having just one platoon of five British-made Carden Lloyd Mark VI tankettes. There were also two squadrons of armoured cars, each with a dozen Landsverk M36 or M38 vehicles from Sweden; another dozen Dutch-made DAF M39 armoured cars were in the process of being introduced.

Dutch artillery ranged from obsolete German Krupp guns of various calibres to modern 10.5 cm Bofors howitzers from Sweden. Their anti-tank force consisted mostly of around 400 Bohler 4.7 cm L/39 guns from Austria and another 300 pieces from various other manufacturers. Most of these weapons were horse-drawn. One hundred and twenty modern anti-tank weapons had been ordered from Germany but strangely these had not been delivered by the time of the invasion.

The Dutch air force, the *Militaire Luchtvaartafdeling* (ML), which was part of the army rather than an independent service like the RAF, had an estimated fleet of 155 aircraft. Most of these were manufactured in Holland by Fokker or Koolhoven. Out of this air armada only 125 aircraft were operational at the time, seventy-four of which were outdated biplanes. Another forty operational aircraft served with the marine air service and there were a similar number of reserve and training aircraft that could be called on if required.

The Dutch government was another constitutional monarchy, headed by Queen Wilhelmina. Her prime minister in May 1940 was Dirk Jan de Geer. They had hoped that their neutrality would be enough to prevent the Germans from invading as they had always enjoyed good relations with their neighbour. However, several reliable sources had pre-warned them that their neutrality was about to be violated by the Nazis. This intelligence led to the mobilisation of Dutch forces in April 1940.

Prior to the invasion the country's armed forces were totally unprepared for battle, but Holland would not be easy to conquer in a conventional war. About a quarter of the country, particularly in the west, is below sea level and had been reclaimed from the water by an extensive network of dunes, dykes and dams. In the seventeenth century, the Dutch Republic had devised an effective defence system, called the Holland Water Line, which could protect all major cities in the west by flooding parts of the countryside around them. In the early nineteenth century this line was extended to the east beyond Utrecht and fortifications were added. This new position was called the New Holland Water Line, and in 1940 pillboxes were further added to include machine guns. If the Germans did advance through Holland from the east, large areas could be flooded to help delay their progress.

The area to the west of the New Holland Water Line became known as Fortress Holland. To the north-east it was bordered by Lake IJssel and to the south it was protected by a series of rivers that ran almost parallel to one another. This entire landscape functioned as a huge national redoubt, behind which an army could hold out for a prolonged period of time, possibly even months. This would give the Allies plenty of time to send reinforcements.

From September 1939 another main defence line was constructed further to the east that ran down the country from the shore of Lake IJssel in the north near Amersfoort to the Belgian border in the south. This barrier was made up of the Grebbe Line in the north, built on the orders of the commander of the field army, Lieutenant General Jan Joseph Godfried Baron van Voorst tot Voorst, and the Peel-Raam Line in the south, ordered by the commander-in-chief of the Dutch army, General Izaak Herman Reijnders. In front of this main defence line there were also stretches of the Rivers IJssel and Maas, and at each of these stop lines hundreds of pillboxes armed with machine guns had been built. All of this, it was hoped, would delay the Germans long enough for French help to arrive.

The 4th and 2nd Belgian Army Corps would be positioned along the Grebbe Line with the 3rd Army Corps dug in behind the Peel-Raam Line. The light division would provide cover to the southern flank, while the 1st Army Corps would protect the Fortress Holland area.

General Reijnders' plan was for the army to hold the Grebbe and Peel-Raam lines for as long as possible and then to fall back to Fortress Holland. However the government considered this plan too risky and, unable to reach a compromise, on 5 February 1940 Reijnders resigned and was quickly replaced by General Henri Gerard Winkelman. Together with the government and the army chiefs of staff, Winkelman eventually decided that the Grebbe Line alone would be the main defence line where the decisive battle would take place. This would also be the best place to inaugurate a counter-attack in the event that the Germans faltered.

All of these defence lines would be a huge help in stopping an infantry and armour attack but the Dutch government was well aware that the *Wehrmacht* posed another threat, as they had used airborne troops in Denmark and Norway with great effect. Consequently the Dutch became worried about the possibility that they too could fall foul to a similar assault. In order to repulse enemy airborne forces, troops were positioned at the main ports and airbases, such as The Hague's airfield at Ypenburg and the Rotterdam airbase of Waalhaven. These were reinforced by additional anti-aircraft guns, two tankettes and twelve of the twenty-four operational armoured cars. Their fears proved correct as the Germans set in motion a daring plan, which if successful would defeat the Dutch without having to face any of the land fortifications across the country. What happened next became known as the Battle for The Hague.

The German plan was to surprise the Dutch and hopefully capture the head of the army, General Winkelman, the government and possibly even the queen. The idea was to fly over Holland and out across the North Sea to make it appear that they were attacking England. They would then turn back over land to bomb strategic positions around the country's administrative centre, The Hague, before offloading airborne forces. These troops would cut off all the roads leading to The Hague so that nobody could enter or leave.

In the early hours of 10 May the *Luftwaffe* began the operation and flew past The Hague and out across the sea as planned. However, instead of tricking the defenders, by the time the aircraft had circled back to approach the city again, they were on high alert. At around 6:00 a.m. the airfield at Ypenburg to the south-east of the city was bombed and immediately afterwards German transport aircraft dropped the 1st Battalion of the 2. *Fallschirmjäger* (Parachute) *Division* around the area. This was one element of the 7th *Flieger Division* commanded by General Kurt Student. Many of these missed the airfield and landed in fields nearby.

The Dutch defenders put up stiff resistance from their positions along the perimeter of the airfield, and when Junkers Ju 52 transport aircraft arrived bringing reinforcements from the 22nd *Luftlande* (Air Landing) *Division*, they were met with heavy machine gun fire. This left the airfeld littered with bodies and burned-out aircraft. The Germans eventually regrouped and gained a foothold. Further transports, unable to land on the airfield, made desperate landings on the main road that led from The Hague to Rotterdam, where they offloaded further reinforcements of the 22nd *Luftlande*. Despite heavy German casualties and a runway blocked by wrecked planes, Ypenburg finally fell to the attackers.

While all of this was taking place, another group of paratroopers landed around Ockenburg airfield to the south-west of The Hague. Here the defence was much weaker than at Ypenburg as the airbase was only protected by a total of ninety-six men, mostly raw recruits. Even so, they managed to inflict considerable casualties on the airlanding troops. However in spite of their valiant efforts, after two hours of fierce fighting, Ockenburg airfield was secured at around 8:00 a.m., although similar to Ypenburg the runway was left blocked with burning transport aircraft.

Having finally secured these two positions, German units began advancing towards The Hague. On the way they encountered stubborn resistance from a sundry group of defenders, including represenatives of army labour units and even the Royal Military Band. This tenacious defence stalled the Germans long enough for Dutch infantry to arrive on the scene, and by 10:00 am. the German advance had been halted and the Dutch were poised to mount a counter-attack.

To the north of the city another group of paratroopers had seized a partially constructed airfield at Valkenburg. Here the resistance was not as great and the initial bombing caused many casualties among the defenders. When the Ju 52 transport aircraft arrived, the attackers were able to quickly disembark and overrun the Dutch positions. However, because the surface of the runway was unfinished, most of the aircraft were wrecked on landing and unable to take off again. Consequently, when the next wave of aircraft arrived they were unable to land and had to abort the attempt, although a few chose to land on the beach to the west. Other aircraft, those either unable to land at the airfields or which for some reason had become lost, made landings on the beach at the Hook of Holland and elsewhere along the coast.

The soldiers that did manage to secure the airfield at Valkenburg next attempted to push south towards The Hague. However without reinforcements they were unable to make any influence on the main battle taking place to the south.

Although the German airborne troops had succeeded in capturing all three of the airfields they had been tasked with taking, they had failed in their main objective of isolating The Hague and forcing the Dutch to surrender. Because of this the Dutch army was able to launch its counter-attack, which began at Ypenburg. Here the Dutch Grenadier Guards fought their way back to the airfield to take up positions from where they could launch artillery attacks against the German defenders, who were eventually left with no choice but to surrender.

At Ockenburg, four Fokker T.V heavy bombers of the Dutch air force bombed the German positions, after which troops stormed the airfield. The defenders retreated and many were captured. However, some of the Nazi soldiers escaped to nearby woods and would later make their way towards Rotterdam to join in the fighting there. By the end of the day Dutch forces had retaken all three of the captured airfields.

For the Germans, the attempt to take The Hague was a disaster. It is thought that around 400 were killed, 700 wounded and 1,745 taken prisoner. Many of these were immediately shipped to prisoner-of-war camps in England. They also lost 182 transport aircraft, mainly

Ju 52s. However it had been at a very heavy price to the Dutch, who had suffered 515 killed in action.

Elsewhere in the Netherlands the Germans had been much more successful. They had breached the Grebbe Line and penetrated Fortress Holland by bypassing the New Water Line from the south. The French 7th Army had been unable to reach the area in time to make any impact, and the queen and her ministers had escaped to London to establish a government in exile.

After failure in The Hague, the Germans focussed their efforts on Rotterdam, the country's largest port. By 13 May General Georg von Küchler's 18th Army had captured all the important bridges around the city and considerable forces were poised to attack, including more of General Student's airborne forces and the 9th Panzer Division, commanded by General Alfred Ritter von Hubicki. They also included the 1st SS Panzer Division *Leibstandarte SS Adolf Hitler*, a motorised regiment of the Waffen SS attached to the 18th Army. They would earn the dubious reputation of accidentally shooting General Student in the head in Rotterdam, a wound from which he survived.

On the morning of 14 May, Hitler issued directive number eleven, which gives some idea of how he thought operations were going in Holland after the first four days. It included the following:

> The progress of the offensive to date shows that the enemy has failed to appreciate in time the basic idea of our operations. He continues to throw strong forces against the line Namur-Antwerp and appears to be neglecting the sector facing Army Group A.
>
> On the northern flank the Dutch Army has shown itself capable of a stronger resistance than had been supposed. For political and military reasons, this resistance must be broken quickly. It is the task of the Army, by moving strong forces from the south in conjunction with an attack against the eastern front, to bring about the speedy fall of Fortress Holland.

What occurred next came as a devastating blow to the Dutch and marked the beginning of the end. In command of Rotterdam's defenders was Colonel Pieter Scharroo, who attempted to coordinate the recapture of strategic positions such as the Willemsbrug Bridge, one of the port's key river crossings. On 14 May, General Küchler planned a combined assault on the city, using tanks of the 9th Panzer Division supported by flame throwers, the SS troops and combat engineers. In the first instance, the airborne troops were to make an amphibious crossing of the River Nieuwe Maas upstream of the Dutch positions and then make a flanking attack on them; the attack was to be preceded by an artillery bombardment. General Küchler had also sent a request to the *Luftwaffe* asking for a group of Junkers Ju 87 dive-bombers of *Luftflotte* 2 to make a precision attack against Scharroos's defences before his assault. What he actually got were Heinkel He 111 heavy bombers, who proceeded to carpet-bomb the city in what is called the Rotterdam Blitz.

The start of the raid was originally set for 13:20. Küchler sent Colonel Scharroo an ultimatum, threatening that the city would be destroyed if he did not surrender. Scharroo refused, and Küchler postponed the attack until 16:20 in order for the Dutch to consider a second ultimatum. However, before this revised request even reached the Dutch, around ninety He 111 bombers of *Kampfgeschwader* 54 appeared over the city. They proceeded to unleash 1,150 fifty-kilogram bombs and 158 massive 250-kilogram bombs. Most of these fell either in the historic city centre or in residential areas. The result, aided by the wind, was a firestorm that lasted for several days and devoured large quantities of buildings. About one square mile of the city was flattened with an estimated 25,000 homes, twenty-four churches, 2,320 shops, 775 warehouses and sixty-two schools destroyed. The exact number of civilians who perished is not known but is thought to have been around 850. Luckily, many people had evacuated the city in the previous days due to the ongoing fighting, which helps to explain the remarkably low number of fatalities.

The Dutch armed forces had no way of stopping these types of attacks. Their tiny air force had already been virtually annihilated and most of their anti-aircraft guns had been positioned to protect The Hague. So when the Germans sent them another ultimatum threatening to bomb the city of Utrecht, they finally gave in. The document of surrender was signed by General Winkelman on behalf of the Dutch and General Küchler for the Germans at the village of Rijsoord on 15 May.

At the same time that Army Group B was attacking Holland, it was also commencing the invasion of Belgium, the second area involved in the strategic feint, where the 6th Army under General Walther von Reichenau was the principal antagonist. The first serious obstacle they faced was the heavily defended Albert Canal, which stretched through the north-east of the country near the Dutch border from Antwerp in the west to Liège in the east. Their main route of approach was blocked by the formidable Fort Eben-Emael, one of the largest and most modern forts of its type in the world. It was constructed between 1931 and 1935 and considered to be impregnable. The way it was positioned at the junction of the canal and the River Meuse allowed it to control the movement of anything trying to cross this part of the country. This was a major problem for the depleted Army Group B and it would have to be neutralised if Reichenau was to keep to his schedule.

In the early hours of 10 May, a force of seventy-eight paratroopers from the 7th Flieger Division, led by First Lieutenant Rudolf Witzig, landed precariously on top of the fort in DFS 230 gliders laden with high explosives with the intention of disabling it. Although the attackers were unable to get inside the fort itself, they were able to destroy most of its armaments from outside; the following day, with the arrival of reinforcements, the garrison of 650 men surrendered. Apparently, the Germans had planned the capture of the fort well in advance and in preparation had practiced assaulting a full-scale mockup of its exterior.

The Germans lost only six of their assault team while managing to keep all the defenders pinned down until they were relieved. After this extraordinary feat, Hitler personally decorated all those who had taken part. Fort Eben-Emael was regarded as the linchpin of Belgium's border defences, so this represented a devastating blow from which their army would find it hard to recover.

As well as taking the fort, German paratroopers also quickly seized most of the bridges over the canal, and although the Belgians did attempt to retake them, their attacks were broken up by dive-bombing from the *Luftwaffe*. In a state of shock and disbelief that their defences had been so quickly breached, Belgian Supreme Command, which was headed by King Leopold III himself, gave the order to retreat to the K-W Line where the BEF and the 1st French Army were still entrenching.

The Allies had seriously believed that the Belgians would hold out along the border for several weeks, which would give them time to prepare their defences, particularly at the Gembloux Gap where General Gamelin had pinpointed the weak spot and where the spearhead of the invasion would come. This seemed to be confirmed when General Erich Hoepner's XVI Corps, including the 3rd Panzer Division and the 4th Panzer Division, began to roll across all the captured bridges on the Albert Canal and to move in the direction of the Gembloux Gap.

The French desperately needed time to establish their positions, so in order to delay the Germans as long as possible General Georges Blanchard, the commander of the 1st Army, sent out the 2nd DLM and the 3rd DLM under General René Prioux to engage the German tanks at Hannut, to the east of Gembloux, and give him sufficient time to dig in.

The ensuing Battle of Hannut took place between 12 and 13 May and was the largest tank battle that had ever been fought up until that point, with approximately 1,500 armoured vehicles taking part. The French disabled some 160 Panzers during the fighting, while losing 121 of their own tanks, ninety-one Hotchkiss H35s and thirty SOMUA S35s. Ultimately the French withdrew and the Germans managed to recover many of their disabled machines, some of which were soon back in the front line. In total the Germans lost twenty tanks of the 3rd Panzer Division and twenty-nine belonging to the 4th Panzer Division.

Although General Reichenau had achieved his primary objective of diverting the French 1st Army away from Sedan, he had failed in his second task, the destruction of the French forces pitted against him. However on 14 May he attempted to break the French line again by leading a frontal assault against the Gembloux Gap. His attempt was repelled by the 1st Moroccan Infantry Division, costing the 4th Panzer Division another forty-two tanks, twenty-six of which were irreparable.

At this point General Gamelin probably thought that the Dyle Plan had proved to be the correct course of action to take and that the Germans were being held at the K-W Line. That was all about to change because of events taking place to the south.

Although up until this point in the war a number of Victoria Crosses had gone to recipients serving in the Royal Navy, none had been awarded to the Army. The first would go to twenty-five-year-old Second Lieutenant Richard Annand, who found himself on the River Dyle at Gastuche in Belgium on 15 May with the 2nd Battalion, The Durham Light Infantry. The entry in *The London Gazette* announcing his award appeared on 23 August 1940 and read as follows:

> For most conspicuous gallantry on the 15th–16th May 1940, when the platoon under his command was on the south side of the River Dyle, astride a blown bridge. During the night a strong attack was beaten off, but about 11am the enemy again launched a violent attack and pushed forward a bridging party into the sunken bottom of the river. Second Lieutenant Annand attacked this party, but when ammunition ran out he went forward himself over open ground, with total disregard for enemy mortar and machine-gun fire. Reaching the top of the bridge, he drove out the party below, inflicting over twenty casualties with hand grenades. Having been wounded he rejoined his platoon, had his wound dressed, and then carried on in command.
>
> Richard Annand's platoon sergeant said later, 'Mr Annand came to me at platoon headquarters and asked for a box of grenades as they could hear Jerry trying to repair the bridge. Off he went and he sure must have given them a lovely time because it wasn't a great while before he was back for more.'
>
> During the evening another attack was launched and again Second Lieutenant Annand went forward with hand grenades and inflicted heavy casualties on the enemy. When the order to withdraw was received, he withdrew his platoon, but learning on the way back that his batman was wounded and had been left behind, he returned at once to the former position and brought him back in a wheelbarrow, before losing consciousness as the result of wounds.

9

BATTLE FOR THE SKIES

In the early hours of 10 May the waiting was finally over as the Germans launched their blitzkrieg through Luxembourg, Holland and Belgium. By deploying aircraft, tanks and airborne troops in their combined attack they soon had the upper hand. In the last chapter we saw how the armed forces of these three countries had attempted to stem the tide and how the French had gone to their aid. The British Expeditionary Force was only a small part of this effort and, apart from those serving on the Maginot Line, the main body of British troops had accompanied the French 1st Army Group as it crossed the Belgian border and moved up to the K-W Line, which it would help to strengthen between Leuven and Wavre.

It would take time for the British to dig in and prepare their positions to withstand repeated attacks. Although the BEF would come face-to-face with the enemy much earlier than anticipated, the RAF contingent would battle them from day one.

When the RAF first arrived on the Continent in September 1939 they comprised the Advanced Air Striking Force (AASF) and the Air Component of the BEF. In January 1940 both of these were taken under the wing of a new RAF command, called British Air Forces in France (BAFF), which was established under the leadership of Air Marshal Arthur Barratt to provide unified control of all RAF units based in France. By May 1940 the Advanced Air Striking Force comprised eight Fairey Battle light bomber squadrons (Nos 12, 88, 103, 105, 142, 150, 218 and 226); two Bristol Blenheim medium bomber squadrons (Nos 114 and 139); and two Hawker Hurricane fighter squadrons (Nos 1 and 73). The Air Component was made up of five Westland Lysander squadrons for tactical reconnaissance and photographic survey missions (Nos 2, 4, 13, 16, and 26); four Bristol Blenheim squadrons for strategic reconnaissance (Nos 18, 53, 57 and 59); and four Hawker Hurricane fighter squadrons (Nos 85, 87, 607 and 615).

In this chapter we read the accounts of some of those who served with the RAF in France or supported operations from England. Much of the following is borrowed from my book *Voices from the Battle of Britain,* which also covered the period of the Battle of France. Billy Drake for example, who was serving with No. 1 Squadron in the Advanced Air Striking Force from an airfield at Vassincourt, recalled that for those on the front line the German attack was not as sudden or came as such a big a surprise as history often suggests:

> At the beginning of May we certainly heard a lot of noise going on at night and realised that maybe the Phoney War had come to an end and that something was about to happen. The first thing we were told as we got out at five o'clock one morning was that we were to move from our present base to another airfield at Berry-au-Bac, near Reims, which we did. From there we went on patrols or did whatever we were told to do and we were fairly busy. During the first two days we were flying anything from three to five trips a day which was quite exhausting.

During this period Drake shot down a number of enemy aircraft, the first engagement occurring on 10 May itself when he and Pilot Officer Peter 'Boy' Mould shared in the shooting down of a Heinkel He 111. He would later claim three Dornier Do 17s confirmed and a fourth unconfirmed before himself being shot down three days later.

In the face of the sudden German onslaught British reinforcements were already on their way, among them No. 501 Squadron, which flew from Tangmere in Sussex to Bétheniville in France on 10 May to join the Advanced Air Striking Force. Tony Ancrum was a member of the squadron's ground crew and recalled how the personnel flew out aboard an Imperial Airways Ensign and two Bristol Bombay troop carriers. However their arrival was marred with a tragedy that must have shaken their spirits to the core:

The one outstanding and poignant memory that stays with me constantly is this: on the morning of 10 May 1940 members of the squadron chosen to go to France were assembled and loading onto two Bombay troop carriers. I was among those loaded onto the first Bombay. However, at the last moment we were all instructed to disembark and load onto the second one. We took off and landed safely at the airfield at Bétheniville. After disembarking we were told to start digging trenches. Shortly thereafter we heard and watched the second Bombay with officers, further ground crew and reserve pilots approaching. As we watched it coming in, at about 300 feet, it literally fell out of the sky. As to why it crashed in such a dramatic manner I do not know. I have heard many theories but never the official one.

Among the four dead and twelve injured in the crash was the squadron's adjutant, Flying Officer Alister Percy. In the moments before the crash the aircraft had approached with a high nose-up attitude. The captain abandoned the approach and went around again. However, the same thing happened and this time the aircraft stalled. One of the survivors later reported that the most likely cause of the accident was an incorrect distribution of passengers and cargo. Hurricane pilot Paul Farnes was due to fly on the aircraft in question, though by a strange twist of fate he was ordered to fly on the first Bombay with Tony Ancrum and the ground crew:

I was extremely lucky because we had two Bombays to take the ground crew and those pilots who weren't flying aircraft themselves to France. I wasn't one of those flying, as I hadn't been allotted an aircraft at the time, so I had to be on one of the Bombays. Some of the aircrew got into one of the aircraft so I went to get in as well, but one of the flight sergeants on the squadron who didn't like me for some reason - I can't remember why now - said 'no not you, come on Farnes you can get out and go in the other one', which I did. We took off first and landed at

Bétheniville in France, where I went over to dispersal to watch the other Bombay come in. As it approached it half stalled and went round again. But it stalled again and this time went straight in and crashed, so I was extremely lucky.

Another pilot who arrived with the rest of No. 501 Squadron in the Imperial Airways Ensign the following day was Peter Hairs, who recalled that it did not take long before they were in action:

The squadron flew out from Tangmere on 10 May and I joined them with others the next day. We flew out in an Imperial Airways Ensign. We experienced a very rapid transition from the relative peace and comfortable surroundings of a permanent RAF base in England, to temporary and less civilised accommodation in France. We operated mainly from flying fields, which were adequate and not always easy to spot from the air! Our living conditions were not quite on a par with those to which we had become accustomed. Furthermore we were immediately thrown into the battle. It was a new experience for all of us to fire at an enemy aircraft.

The morning after I arrived at Bétheniville I found myself flying early in the day as number two to Charles Griffiths, who was section leader. I cannot remember who was flying as number three on this occasion. We spotted a Dornier Do 17Z and were ordered by our leader to attack in vic formation. I was concentrating on keeping the target in my sights and in the nature of things my Hurricane was getting closer and closer to our section leader. In retrospect it seems surprising that I did not damage his starboard wing by my fire as I really was in tight formation by this time – my port wing cannot have been very far away from the leader's cockpit! It was experiences of this kind that caused changes in tactics.

As a result of this action the Dornier was in fact shot down by at least one, if not all, of the section. After they had landed back at their airfield, they went to their temporary mess for breakfast, a requisitioned estaminet, where they found one of the injured German crew, the rear gunner, lying on a couch drinking a cup of coffee and looking rather the worse for wear.

During this period two members of the RAF were awarded the Victoria Cross: Flying Officer Donald Garland of No. 12 Squadron and his navigator, Sergeant Thomas Gray. The incident leading to their awards took place on 12 May when five Fairy Battles of No. 12 Squadron, led by Garland, were ordered to destroy a vital bridge at Veldwezelt in Belgium that the Germans were using to cross the Albert Canal in force. On arriving over the target they were met by an inferno of anti-aircraft fire but pressed on to lead the assault and were consequently shot down and killed. Their citation for the decoration was published in *The London Gazette* on 11 June 1940, reading:

The King has been graciously pleased to confer the Victoria Cross on the undermentioned officer and non-commissioned officer in recognition of most conspicuous bravery: Flying Officer Donald Edward Garland (40105); 563627 Sergeant Thomas Gray

Flying Officer Garland was the pilot and Sergeant Gray was the observer of the leading aircraft of a formation of five aircraft that attacked a bridge over the Albert Canal which had not been destroyed and was allowing the enemy to advance into Belgium. All the aircrews of the squadron concerned volunteered for the operation, and, after five crews had been selected by drawing lots, the attack was delivered at low altitude against this vital target. Orders were issued that this bridge was to be destroyed at all costs. As had been expected, exceptionally intense machine-gun and anti-aircraft fire was encountered. Moreover, the bridge area was heavily protected by enemy fighters. In spite of this, the formation successfully delivered a dive-bombing attack from the lowest practicable altitude. British fighters in the vicinity reported that the target was obscured by the bombs bursting on it and near it. Only one of the five aircraft concerned returned from this mission. The pilot of this aircraft reports that besides being subjected to extremely heavy anti-aircraft fire, through which they dived to attack the objective, our aircraft were also attacked by a large number of enemy fighters after they had released their bombs on the target. Much of the success of this vital operation must be attributed to the formation leader, Flying Officer Garland, and to the coolness and resource of Sergeant Gray, who in most difficult conditions navigated Flying Officer Garland's aircraft in such a manner that the whole formation was able successfully to attack the target in spite of subsequent heavy losses. Flying Officer Garland and Sergeant Gray did not return.

On 13 May Billy Drake entered the cockpit of a Hurricane to go on patrol with a formation of four aircraft. When they got to 15,000 feet he realised that he was getting no oxygen, so he called his leader to report the situation, who told him to go back to base. While returning he observed a formation of Dorniers underneath him and decided that he would engage them. He got behind one of the Germans and fired his guns. On seeing that his bullets were hitting the target, he got behind another to do the same. By this time, a Messerschmitt Bf 109 had assumed position behind him without him noticing it and fired its cannons. He was hit and his Hurricane went up in flames. He found himself covered in petrol and glycol, and deciding 'enough was enough' went to get out. As he explained:

I undid everything and attempted to stand up and get out but I had forgotten to open the hood, which probably saved my life. Had I opened it, flying straight and level as I was, the flames would have come straight into the cockpit and being covered in petrol I would probably have been set on fire. Anyway, when I realised that I hadn't released the hood, I did so, turned the aeroplane upside down and fell out.

As I pulled the rip-cord to open my parachute, I really felt that I had been badly hit in my back and legs. I thought that one of my legs had been shot away. So as I got closer to the ground I wondered what was going to happen to me as I landed, would my legs collapse? But they didn't and as I sorted myself out on the ground, ten to thirteen French farmers with scythes, pitchforks and all sorts of things came at me in a rather menacing manner. I did my best, as I was able to speak French, to say 'don't do anything nasty I am an Englishman'. But because of the wounds on my back I was unable to undo my overalls and show them my RAF wings in a hurry. In the end I was able to show them and when they saw that I was one of their allies they couldn't have done more to help me.

The farmers took him to the nearest French military casualty station and handed him over to the orderlies there. They asked him if he could speak French and, after being told that he could, they explained that, with regret, there were no doctors with them anymore, only medics. They also explained that they had no anesthetics left but would have to treat his wounds as soon as possible regardless. They gave him some morphine, stripped the tattered clothing off his back and leg and then cleaned the wounds as best they could to remove all the clothing, debris and splinters. Billy described the following twenty minutes as 'very unpleasant', as he continues the story:

> They did what they had to do, cleaned me up and then took me by car to the local hospital. I was in the hospital for about two or three days. There was a lot of bombing going on, so eventually I was put onto a Red Cross train that took me all the way to the south of Paris to a French army hospital at a place called Chartres. While I was there I was able to ring up and get hold of my girlfriend Helen who lived in Paris and who was a member of the American Ambulance Corps. She said bear with me and I will come down as quickly as possible and take you back to Paris in my car, which she did about two days later in her uniform. Unfortunately I was in civilian clothes because my uniform had been destroyed. When we got to Versailles the French police stopped the car and asked my girlfriend, 'And who is this?' She said, 'He's a Royal Air Force officer, I'm taking him to Paris'. They were very doubting about the whole thing. They accepted that she was a bona fide person, but with so many Germans wandering around as blond as I was, they were very suspicious about me.
>
> Helen then said, 'Well hang on I will get on to the British Embassy if you take me to a telephone,' which they did only to

find that the British Embassy had already left Paris. Luckily she was very friendly with people at the US Embassy and I had met one or two of the Americans on my various leaves down into Paris myself. They were able to verify to the French police that I was indeed what my girlfriend was saying, and luckily I was not put up against a wall and shot.

Having finally arrived in Paris, Billy was taken to the American Embassy, where he was told to get out of the capital as soon as possible as the Germans would be there at any time. With that statement his girlfriend Helen, who came from a wealthy family, offered to fill up her car with petrol and let him borrow it in order for him to drive himself back to his squadron, which was now at Le Mans. He described this as a 'very distressful journey' because the road was lined with refugees all the way. Many of them were French troops without any weapons, simply fleeing from the Nazis. Eventually he made it back to the squadron just in the nick of time as only a rear party remained, who were busy destroying unserviceable aircraft and other equipment. He was offered a lift back to England with a Fairey Battle pilot via Jersey, after which he finally made his way to Tangmere to rejoin the main body of No. 1 Squadron. All in all, he had experienced a series of lucky escapes!

While all of this was going on in France, back in England RAF Fighter Command continued its job of protecting home shores while occasionally mounting patrols towards the French coast. By May 1940, No. 64 Squadron was based at Kenley in Surrey and equipped with Spitfire Mk Is. It was during this period that the squadron took part in its first operational sortie over the Channel. During this patrol James O'Meara was to damage a Junkers Ju 88. Over the ensuing months the *Luftwaffe* would suffer heavily through his marksmanship. He wrote a very eloquent and thought-provoking account of this first operational sortie:

On the morning of 21 May the squadron nearly went mad. Twelve aircraft of 64 Squadron were to patrol the French coast, that afternoon from Calais to the Belgian border. It was with a sick and empty feeling that I received this news. Yet, for the

Above: The Reichstag building in Berlin, which was built to house the parliament of the German empire and would be the scene of many of the important political events that led to the outbreak of the Second World War. (Photo copyright 'Nathan': reproduced under the terms of the Creative Commons License)

Below: The commanding Ehrenbreitstein Fortress near Koblenz, at the confluence of the rivers Rhine and Moselle, which after the First World War was used by the American occupation forces in Germany led by Major General Joseph Dickman as their headquarters. (Photo copyright Axel Magard: reproduced under the terms of the Creative Commons License)

Above: Fascist allies: Benito Mussolini who became prime minister of Italy in 1922 and Adolf Hitler who was appointed chancellor of Germany in 1933. (Photo copyright Marlon Doss: reproduced under the terms of the Creative Commons License)

Below: Nazi propaganda posters promoting the Hitler Youth, the future of the Führer's Aryan master race. (Photo copyright Will Manley: reproduced under the terms of the Creative Commons License)

Above: The remains of Ouvrage du Fermont, one of the formidable concrete forts along the Maginot Line on the French side of the borders with Switzerland, Germany and Luxembourg. (Photo copyright Morten Jensen: reproduced under the terms of the Creative Commons License)

Below: This picture shows the inside of a fort on the Maginot Line and gives a good idea of the scale of the fortifications, with a vast network of underground tunnels even supporting rail lines to move ammunition up to the guns. (Photo copyright Morten Jensen: reproduced under the terms of the Creative Commons License)

Left: Lieutenant General Erich von Manstein would be the unlikely architect of Germany's successful military campaign on the western front in 1940.

Below: British soldiers wait for the Germans to attack during the winter months of the Phoney War. (Reproduced with the permission of Michael Virtue, Virtue Books)

Right: Recruiting poster for the Waffen SS, which was the fourth service of the Wehrmacht. The term SS stood for 'schutzstaffel', which meant 'protective squadron', and its members were all fanatical Nazis.

Below: The French Char B1, armed with a 47 mm gun in the turret and a larger 75 mm howitzer in the hull, had better armour and firepower than any of the German tanks of the time but it was slow and did not have radios. (Photo copyright Nigel Brown: reproduced under the terms of the Creative Commons License)

Above: The Panzer I, the main German armoured fighting vehicle during the Battle of France, was only equipped with two 7.92 mm machine guns. However it was much faster than the French and British tanks and had radios as standard. This surviving example is pictured on display in the United States. (Photo copyright Vall Marston: reproduced under the terms of the Creative Commons License)

Below: The main British tanks during the build-up of forces in France were the Matilda I (A11), seen here, and the Matilda II (A12). It was apparently named 'Matilda' by General Hugh Elles, who was master general of the ordnance at the time, because of its diminutive size and duck-like shape. (Photo copyright Roland Turner: reproduced under the terms of the Creative Commons License)

Above: On 10 May 1940 the Luftwaffe used Junkers Ju 52 transport aircraft to land airborne forces during the Battle of The Hague. The operation went badly for the Germans, who would lose 182 aircraft, mainly Ju 52s. (Photo copyright D. Miller: reproduced under the terms of the Creative Commons License)

Below: Fort Eben-Emael, one of the largest and most modern forts of its type, was considered to be impregnable. It was positioned at the junction of the Albert Canal and the River Meuse, which allowed it to control the movement of anything trying to cross this part of the country. To proceed the Germans would have to capture it. (Photo copyright Anton Raath: reproduced under the terms of the Creative Commons License)

Above: A Luftwaffe crew from a fighter wing resting at an airfield during the Battle of France near a Messerschmitt Bf 109 with an open bonnet. In the background is a Junkers Ju 52. (Photo copyright Bundesarchiv)

Below: On 10 May, after the Germans began their attack in the Low Countries, the main body of British troops had accompanied the French 1st Army Group as it crossed the Belgian border and moved up to the KW-Line. Here we see a British gun just about the cross the frontier. (Reproduced with the permission of Michael Virtue, Virtue Books)

Right: Vice Admiral Sir Bertram Ramsay, commander of naval forces in Dover, who conducted naval operations at Boulogne, Calais and Dunkirk. This statue stands in the grounds of Dover Castle, where he had his headquarters. (Photo copyright Karen Roe: reproduced under the terms of the Creative Commons License)

Below: The PS *Medway Queen* made seven trips to the evacuation beaches of France and rescued 7,000 men, earning her the nickname 'The Heroine of Dunkirk'. (Photo copyright Tom Lee: reproduced under the terms of the Creative Commons License)

Left: General Erwin Rommel, commander of the 7th Panzer Division, who was tasked with the capture of Cherbourg. (Photo copyright Bundesarchiv)

Below: The MY *Sundowner* pictured in Ramsgate Harbour. She was owned by Charles Lightoller, former second officer of the RMS *Titanic*. Under his command she rescued 130 soldiers from Dunkirk, as well as a number of survivors from the motor cruiser *Westerly*, which had broken down in the Channel. (Photo copyright Lisa Larsson: reproduced under the terms of the Creative Commons License)

Right: General Rommel and his staff observe while the 7th Panzer Division cross a river in France. (Photo copyright Bundesarchiv)

Below: Erwin Rommel is pictured here with Major General Victor Morven Fortune, Commander of the 51st (Highland) Infantry Division, which had just surrendered at Saint-Valery-en-Caux. (Photo copyright Bundesarchiv)

Above: Captured British soldiers await their fate at Saint-Nazaire. (Photo copyright Bundesarchiv)

Below: British and French troops marching through a street in Dunkirk, littered with debris and surrounded by burning buildings, during a lull in the German air bombardment of the town. A burning lorry can be seen on the right.

Right: On 2 June, Mr Anthony Eden, the War Minister, stated that the magnificent defence of the Citadel of Calais by a small Allied garrison drew off powerful German forces which would otherwise have been available to attack the flank of the BEF.

Below: A double-barrelled machine gun on a destroyer pointing skywards as troops of the BEF, who fought in one of the greatest rearguard actions in history, make their way along the pier at Dunkirk to embark.

Above: British and French troops are seen here massed on the dunes at Dunkirk in readiness to be taken aboard ships assisting in the evacuation. In the background, troops are marching out towards the sea to the waiting vessels near the shore.

Below: Heading bravely for England here is a fussy little tug, with a motor-launch in tow, laden with heroes of Dunkirk, like the hundreds of other vessels that comprised this amazing armada which performed a 'miracle of deliverance'.

Gratitude to the Royal Navy for the great part they played in the famous withdrawal of Allied troops from Dunkirk has been expressed by thousands of men who were brought safely home. Destroyers are seen above packed with troops on their arrival at a British port.

Above: Fires raging in Dunkirk as seen from aboard a destroyer taking part in the epic evacuation. Despite heavy attacks by the enemy from land and air, four-fifths of the BEF were withdrawn from Flanders against tremendous odds.

Below: On 17 June the *Lancastria*, pleasure cruiser of peacetime, had taken her full complement of British troops and civilians aboard from the evacuation port of St Nazaire when three aeroplanes attacked and sank her.

last ten months, I had been hoping for a chance like this, now that the chance had come I would have given anything to get out of it. It was so sudden, so unexpected. But I could not say no. I had, if only for the sake of keeping my pride, to appear as pleased and enthusiastic as the rest of the boys. There seemed to be something rather set about their smiles, too; something forced about their keenness to go.

At half past two that afternoon, twelve Spitfires taxied out, and roared into the air. We were off. Circling Kenley once, Roo (the CO) climbed towards the coast, passing high over Manston, and headed towards Calais. Ahead lay the French coastline. Far inland I could see black bursts of anti-aircraft fire dotting the sky. I wondered if I should see England again. There was a horrible sensation in the pit of my stomach: I felt empty and tight inside. I could feel myself shaking all over. I was afraid: I could not stop my hands and knees from shivering. France was close now; I could see fields, and roads and villages spread out before me, stretching away into the blue haze of distance. I looked round me feverishly, trying to see behind. 'O Christ help me', I whispered, 'let me get back safely.'

A shout in my ears, I jumped. It was blue section leader: he had sighted something. I strained my eyes, searching, searching – looking to see what it was, where it was. My guts seemed to turn over, leaving me sick and stiff, leaning forward, my eyes wide, my head turning from side to side, looking, searching, praying, my lips moving: 'Where are they? Where …?' And then I saw them, five thousand feet below – nine grey bombers; squat, silent, evil shapes; the black crosses in relief on the blue-grey wings. Roo's aircraft turned and dived. The sections opened and followed.

'Line astern – Line astern – Go'! Blue section turned away, quickly taking up their positions. Green followed. The squadron was straggling now, as the speed of the dive increased. Below, against the silver, shining background of the sea, I could see the diving, speeding shapes of the German bombers. They were apart now, going for their objectives. Far down were toy ships, tiny pinpoints of flame lancing up at the attacking raiders. Beside one, a huge column of water leapt suddenly into the air, leaving on the surface a great wing of white, frothing, heaving foam. A bomb!

Immediately the Hun turned away, headed to the east. I steepened my dive to cut him off. Down, down, down; closer and closer. Fear was gone, forgotten. I was tense, leaning forward, my eyes glued on the enemy; tense, not with fear and not with excitement, I was cool now, and calm. Calm with a cold, intense determination.

Now I was almost in range; the black crosses on the wings and the swastikas on the tail were plain to see. Another second and I opened fire. Tracer leapt across the sky between us, and the Hun, seeing it, turned sharply to the right and dived to sea-level. Stabs of fire from amidships shot out to meet me. Instinctively, I ducked in the cockpit. Hardly breathing now, I concentrated on getting a correct sight. Again I shot, this time with effect. The bullets tore into the fuselage of the German. He was huge now, almost dead ahead, almost too close. With my thumb on the firing button still I broke violently away to port. As I did so, I could see, over my shoulder, the port engine of the Hun burst into a startling, yellow star of flame. That was the last I saw of him. When I circled again nothing was to be seen. There were no aircraft, no ships; nothing but the smooth, calm sea in every direction.

After trying a few calls over the R/T and getting no reply, I decided to go home. Now almost beside myself with excitement, I flew for some time and crossed the coast west of Folkestone. Everything had happened with such incredible swiftness. Ten minutes ago I had been with the squadron, sick with fear and apprehension, turning and twisting to watch for death: now I was back; I had been in action; I had won an air-fight. It seemed fantastic.

On 31 May James O'Meara would record his first definite kill when he brought down a Me 109 over the beaches of Dunkirk. Other fighter pilots would also make their name while serving in France, perhaps the most notable at the time being Edgar James (Cobber) Kain, a New Zealander flying Hurricanes with No. 73 Squadron.

He claimed his and the squadron's first victory during the Phoney War on 8 November 1939, shooting down a Dornier Do 17; a second Dornier followed days later. These were followed by three Messerschmitt Bf 109s, with the fifth in March making him a fighter ace (a pilot credited with five or more enemy aircraft destroyed in aerial combat). He was also the first recipient of the Distinguished Flying Cross (DFC) during the Second World War. Within seventeen days from the start of *Fall Gelb,* he had claimed a further twelve aerial victories. His success so early in the war made him a household name back in Britain. Sadly he would be killed in a flying accident on 7 June, the day he had been ordered home for a rest. At the time of his death he held the rank of flying officer and was credited with seventeen aerial victories.

The situation with the RAF in France would become unsustainable in view of the fact that Fighter Command, which was responsible for protecting Britain, was being steadily eroded in order to strengthen Air Marshal Barratt's forces. This would leave Britain increasingly vulnerable to air attacks, and, besides, on the Continent British aircraft were being lost needlessly against a numerically superior enemy.

After the Germans launched the offensive, Air Vice-Marshal Playfair ordered the Fairey Battle and Bristol Blenheim bomber squadrons of the Advanced Air Striking Force to attack German troops, particularly convoys of vehicles and key bridges. However they were easy prey to both the Messerschmitt Bf 109 fighter aircraft and the mobile anti-aircraft guns used to protect troop movements. Subsequently they quickly suffered heavy losses, and by the end of 12 May the number of serviceable bombers available to Playfair had been reduced from the 135 he had at the start of the offensive to just seventy-two. At a meeting of the War Cabinet in London that evening, the chief of the air staff, Air Chief Marshal Sir Cyril Newall, made the stark warning that 'bomber losses had been disproportionate to the results achieved'.

Lord Gort and Air Marshal Barratt both requested further reinforcements to be sent to France. After lengthy discussions between the chiefs of staff committee and the War Cabinet on the morning of 13 May, Churchill gave the go ahead to send a further two Hurricane squadrons, even though the committee had strongly advised against it. They had recommended that no further air support should be given to the British Air Forces in France, as this would seriously undermine Britain's home defence. The matter was raised again that evening at a War Cabinet meeting at which the secretary of state for air, Sir Archibald Sinclair, made it clear that in order to defend Britain the air staff had estimated Fighter Command would need a minimum of sixty fighter squadrons; they had already been reduced to only thirty-nine. Churchill was beginning to accept that in spite of his assurances to the French government, it was simply not possible to send further large numbers of fighters to France.

IO

BREAKOUT FROM
THE ARDENNES

While Army Group B continued to press down on the K-W Line, the situation further south was becoming steadily clearer although General Gamelin was still not overly concerned. He still believed that the conditions posed by the Ardennes coupled with the forces he had deployed to the area would be sufficient to stop the Germans breaking through there. To begin with it seems that he may have been right.

One of the biggest problems facing General Gerd von Rundstedt and his Army Group A was the vast numbers of vehicles he had to get through the forest using its network of poor roads: General Kleist's Panzer Group alone had over 41,000 vehicles. There were only four possible routes they could take and these were soon blocked and congested with queues stretching all the way back to the Rhine. This made Army Group A vulnerable to air attacks, but these did not materialise as although Gamelin was aware of the situation, the Allied bomber force was not dominant enough to challenge German air superiority so close to the border.

Instead the Allies relied on ground troops to try and defeat the German advance guard. These largely consisted of the Belgian 1st Chasseurs Ardennais and the French 5th Light Cavalry Division. From their name it is clear that the Belgian troops were designed to fight in this particular terrain: their regiment comprised a mixture of battalions of cyclists made up of riflemen and machine gunners, motorbike squadrons, and armoured squadrons equipped with British-built Vickers T-15 light tanks armed with 13.2 mm Hotchkiss machine guns, or Vickers T-13 tank destroyers armed with a 47 mm anti-tank weapon. The French 5th Light Cavalry Division, commanded by Lieutenant General Baron Subervie, consisted of the 6th Cavalry Brigade, 15th Light Mechanised Brigade, and the 78th Artillery Regiment. Unfortunately these forces simply did not have enough anti-tank weapons to make an effect on the vast numbers of German tanks they encountered. They were quickly forced to retreat and withdrew to positions on the west bank of the River Meuse, which formed a natural boundary through this part of Belgium and eastern France.

On 11 May, General Gamelin at last seemed to recognise that the Germans did indeed pose a threat in the Ardennes sector and ordered reserve troops to reinforce the positions along the River Meuse. These reinforcements largely came by train, but because the *Luftwaffe* had air superiority their movement was restricted to night-time only, which made the build-up painfully slow. The French units fortifying the sector were also extremely short of anti-aircraft and anti-tank guns, while their artillery was designed to withstand attack from infantry, not armoured divisions.

By the late afternoon of 12 May General Rundstedt's Army Group A had reached the east bank of the River Meuse. In order for his three armies to cross he needed to establish bridgeheads, and he focused his efforts on three places: Dinant (Belgium) in the north, Monthermé (France) in the centre and Sedan (France) in the south.

Even though General Guderian had identified the Sedan area as being vulnerable because it was twelve miles west of Ouvrage La Ferté, the final position on the Maginot Line, General Rundstedt was still not totally convinced that it would be easy to force a breakthrough here. The River Meuse at this point sat in a deep gorge which he was led to believe was guarded by 103 pillboxes manned by the 147th Fortress Infantry Regiment; these looked down across the valley from the high ground along the west bank. The area was also guarded by the 55th Infantry Division commanded by Brigadier General Henri-Jean Lafontaine. This was what was termed a grade B reserve division, and was certainly not a frontline unit. However on the morning of 13 May they had at least been reinforced by the arrival of the 71st Infantry Division, under Brigadier General Joseph Baudet.

In photographs taken by *Luftwaffe* reconnaissance aircraft the steep banks of the Meuse, dotted with this formidable barrier of bunkers and other defences, gave Rundstedt grave concerns about Guderian's choice of Sedan as the point where they should make their maximum effort. To identify just how strong these defences were, a team of photographic specialists evaluated the pictures and concluded that many of the bunkers were in fact half-built shells with no weaponry inside them. This intelligence swayed the Sedan attack plan in Guderian's favour and Rundstedt gave the order to proceed.

Prior to the attempted crossing, on 13 May the *Luftwaffe* concentrated most of their air power on smashing a hole in a narrow sector of the French line. They did this by both carpet-bombing and precision dive-bombing. Reichsmarschall Hermann Göring had promised Rundstedt that he would provide a continual eight-hour air attack beginning at 8:00 a.m. and finishing at dusk. He was true to his word, and the *Luftwaffe* executed the heaviest air bombardment the world had ever witnessed up until that point and probably the most intense period of bombing the *Luftwaffe* would carry out during the entire war. Nine complete *Kampfgeschwaders* (bomber wings) and two *Sturzkampfgeschwaders* (dive-bomber wings) took part in the assault. The bombers flew a total of 3,940 sorties, while the dive-bombers completed 300.

Screened by this fearsome onslaught, Guderian's XIX Corps, which was made up of the 1st Panzer Division, 2nd Panzer Division and the 10th Panzer Division, started to cross the river near Sedan in three places. They were reinforced by the elite *Großdeutschland* Panzer Grenadier Division. Where the French had previously destroyed bridges, German engineers quickly constructed pontoon replacements.

As a result of this terrifying bombardment many of the French defenders, particularly those soldiers stationed at artillery batteries or serving with the 55th Infantry, fled from their positions. By midnight, at a cost of just a few hundred casualties, the German infantry had penetrated the French defensive zone to a depth of about five miles, while in the rear German troops continued to cross the river throughout the night.

Rumours quickly began to spread through the French lines that the German tanks were already behind them. By 19:00 on 13 May, the 295th Regiment of the 55th Infantry Division, which was holding the last prepared defensive French position at the Bulson Ridge about six miles west of the river, panicked and fled, believing that the Panzers had already outflanked them. Effectively, this left the door to France wide open to the attackers.

General Gaston-Henri Billotte, the commander of the French 1st Army Group, whose right flank pivoted on Sedan, requested that the bridges across the Meuse be destroyed by air attack immediately to try and stop the flood of vehicles and men pouring over them. His request was granted and every available Allied light bomber was employed in an attempt to destroy the three crossings. However they failed to hit any of them and suffered heavy losses in the process. The Advanced Air Striking Force of the BEF committed its last seventy-one aircraft. Forty of these failed to return. On hearing the news, Air Marshal Barratt was said to have wept.

From the start General Guderian wanted to press on immediately towards the English Channel by enlarging the German bridgehead to at least twelve miles. This caused a conflict with his superior General Kleist, who basically wanted to consolidate his positions first by digging in and waiting for the whole army to cross the river and move together. However Guderian did manage to get permission from Kleist to reconnoitre ahead in force, which effectively was the same thing as pushing on.

Manstein's original plan had included secondary attacks that would be carried out from the Sedan bridgehead to the rear of the Maginot Line to act as another diversion. This element of the plan had quite possibly been Guderian's own idea in the first place, but Franz Halder, the chief of the general staff, had removed it. Guderian now took it upon himself to reinstate the idea and consequently sent the 10th Panzer Division and the *Großdeutschland* Panzer Grenadiers south to execute precisely such a feint attack. They would use the only available route south towards the village of Stonne.

As a coincidence General Charles Huntziger, the commander of the French 2nd Army, had intended to launch a counter-attack from the high ground around Stonne aimed at destroying the bridgehead. This resulted in a tank battle between the 10th Panzer Division and elements of the 2nd Army, which took place between 15 and 17 May.

On the morning of 16 May the French made a counter-attack led by the 3rd company of the 41st Tank Battalion, equipped with Char B1 tanks. During this engagement a single B1, commanded by Captain Pierre Billotte, the son of General Billotte, entered the occupied village and found itself in the middle of the German defences. Before withdrawing it single-handedly proceeded to destroy two Panzer IV tanks, eleven Panzer IIIs and two PaK 36 anti-tank guns of the 8th Panzer Regiment.

After 16 May, the 10th Panzer Division withdrew to be replaced by the 16th and 24th Infantry divisions. The *Großdeutschland* Panzer Grenadiers had lost 570 men at Stonne – in fact the majority of the casualties they suffered during the entire 1940 campaign were lost during this one battle.

The village itself would change hands between the Germans and the French on several occasions. Huntziger knew that if he could hold Stonne and recapture Bulson, it would mean that the French would have the advantage of occupying the high ground overlooking Sedan. However, after heavy and determined fighting, Stonne would finally fall to the Germans for the last time on the evening of 17 May.

While all of this was taking place the 1st and 2nd Panzer Divisions were quickly moving west along the Somme valley towards the English Channel. French forces everywhere were in flight or capitulating, with the Ninth Army surrendering in its entirety. The 7th Panzer Division, commanded by Major General Erwin Rommel, had crossed the River Meuse at Dinant in Belgium and was given the task of breaking through what was termed the extended Maginot Line. This was a barrier of hurriedly built minor fortifications and anti-tank ditches along the border between France and Belgium. Erwin Rommel, who would later gain fame for his exploits in North Africa as the 'Desert Fox', kept a journal of his experiences. In the following excerpt, he describes the moment they breached the daunting line. Although this section was nothing like the real Maginot Line further east, from his writing you can still sense his obvious pride in this achievement:

The tanks now rolled in a long column through the line of fortifications and on towards the first houses, which had been set alight by our fire. In the moonlight we could see the men Of 7th Motorcycle Battalion moving forward on foot beside us. Occasionally an enemy machine gun or anti-tank gun fired, but none of their shots came anywhere near us. Our artillery was dropping heavy harassing fire on villages and the road far ahead of the regiment. Gradually the speed increased. Before long we were 500 -1,000 - 2,000 - 3,000 yards into the fortified zone. Engines roared, tank tracks clanked and clattered. Whether or not the enemy was firing was impossible to tell in the ear-splitting noise. We crossed the railway line a mile or so southwest of Solre-le-Château, and then swung north to the main road which was soon reached. Then off along the road and past the first houses.

The people in the houses were rudely awoken by the din of our tanks, the clatter and roar of tracks and engines. Troops lay bivouacked beside the road, military vehicles stood parked in farmyards and in some places on the road itself. Civilians and French troops, their faces distorted with terror, lay huddled in the ditches, alongside hedges and in every hollow beside the road. We passed refugee columns, the carts abandoned by their owners, who had fled in panic into the fields. On we went, at a steady speed, towards our objective. Every so often a quick glance at the map by a shaded light and a short wireless message to Divisional HQ to report the position and thus the success of 25th Panzer Regiment. Every so often a look out of the hatch to assure myself that there was still no resistance and that contact was being maintained to the rear. The flat countryside lay spread out around us under the cold light of the moon. We were through the Maginot Line! It was hardly conceivable. Twenty-two years before we had stood for four and a half long years before this self-same enemy and had won victory after victory and yet finally lost the war. And now we had broken through the renowned Maginot Line and were driving deep into enemy territory. It was not just a beautiful dream. It was reality.

At this point in the battle Rommel was marginally ahead of General Guderian's 1st Panzer Division, under Major General Kirchner, and 2nd Panzer Division, led by Major General Veiel, which had crossed the Meuse to the south at Sedan. Not far behind him in his own sector was the 5th Panzer Division, commanded by Major General Max von Hartlieb-Walsporn. Rommel urged his troops onwards with little rest, willing them to be first to the coast. His immediate superior General Hermann Hoth, commander of the XV Corps, ordered him to wait for support troops to catch up. However, by a strange twist of fate their lines of communications were severed, which provided Rommel with the opportunity to disobey his orders and press on.

Rommel continued to advance north-west towards Avesnes-sur-Helpe, where he found the troops of the French 5th Motorised Infantry Division camped for the night with their vehicles neatly lined up along the sides of the road. Together with the 5th Panzer Division Rommel's tanks drove in amongst them, destroying the French tanks at close quarters. Some of the French did manage to mount their vehicles and begin to fight back. Those that did were successful in causing damage to the attackers, but due to the slow speed of their vehicles and their lack of radio communication they could not deal with the speed of the German attack.

By 17 May, Rommel claimed to have taken around 10,000 prisoners. Guderian was enthralled by the speed of the advance and pressed his own Panzer commanders to keep pushing towards the Channel, only stopping if and when they ran out of fuel. However, the success of his troops in the field began to concern Hitler, who thought that they were perhaps moving too quickly and would open themselves up to effective Allied counter-attacks due to lack of support and supply lines. Franz Halder recorded in his diary on 17 May that the 'Führer is terribly nervous. Frightened by his own success, he is afraid to take any chance and so would pull the reins on us ... he keeps worrying about the south flank. He rages and screams that we are on the way to ruin the whole campaign.'

Through making different interpretations of their orders, Guderian, Rommel and other commanders in the field were yet able to largely ignore Hitler's concerns and maintain their momentum. Rommel in particular was moving so fast that the 7th Panzer Division earned the nickname of 'the ghost division' because it seemingly appeared out of nowhere and in places least expected. Even his own superiors were not sure of where Rommel was all the time, much to the chagrin of his superiors who looked upon the general as something of an out of control maverick.

How did all of this affect the British Expeditionary Force? The force had, on 10 May, complied with the Dyle Plan and crossed the Belgian border to face the enemy who were bearing down from the north. By breaking through the Ardennes, Army Group A had come in behind the British to the south, which meant that they were now trapped in a pocket with the enemy on three sides. If they had to withdraw, they now had only one escape route, west towards a narrow strip of coastline and the port of Dunkirk.

We can get some idea of the confusion facing the British and how little prepared some of them were from the memoirs of John Peyton. In the summer of 1939 he applied for and received a commission in the supplementary reserve of the 15th/19th The King's Royal Hussars. Peyton joined the regiment for a two months' attachment in York, where they had already been equipped with Mark VIB light tanks and carriers; the regiment had still employed horses up until a year before. However, his two months' attachment suddenly became full time as war was declared.

In due course he was sent to join the 54th Armoured Training Regiment at Perham Down, near Tidworth. At the start there was very little in the way of organised training: there were no tanks to train with anyway. Eventually he attended a driving and maintenance course at Bovington, a gunnery course at Lulworth, and an intelligence course at Aldershot. In March 1940 he was considered fit to join his regiment in France. After a week or so in tents at Pacy-sur-Eure, he rejoined the regiment near Lille.

On 10 May the Germans began their attack and the regiment entered Belgium, where they were met at the border by cheering crowds who draped their vehicles with lilac. However, as they moved forward to face the enemy, there was a sense of bewilderment among the troops: there had been no time to prepare for such an operation, and they had no idea of what they were expected to achieve or how they would go about achieving it.

As the Germans continued their advance and the British began to pull back, the regiment was transferred to the 4th Division to provide cover. Eventually, with the bridge over the River Dendre in German hands, they found themselves cut off. John Peyton was sent by his commanding officer to inform the regiment's C squadron of the situation and to see if they could cross the river at Liedekerke. From there he went to look at the bridges in the area to see if any of them were not yet in enemy hands. On the way he met a troop leader in his regiment and took a ride on the back of his carrier. Suddenly, as they entered a small town, they came under fire and the officer was killed instantly. John Peyton returned to C squadron in haste, but found confusion all around him. Joining others he took shelter in a cornfield and then a pig-sty. Before long swarms of Germans appeared, and they were taken prisoner. So ended his short inauspicious war: a similar fate would befall many other soldiers of the British Expeditionary Force.

11

ADVANCE TO THE COAST

On the morning of 15 May, Winston Churchill, who had then only been prime minister for five days, received a desperate telephone call from the distraught prime minister of France, Paul Reynaud. He stated: 'We have been defeated; we are beaten; we have lost the battle.' Churchill did his utmost to try and console Reynaud by reminding him that during the First World War the Germans had broken through the Allied lines on a number of occasions only to be repulsed again later. However, Reynaud seemed to be inconsolable. Churchill vowed to fly out to Paris the following day.

It was never going to be an easy meeting, as Churchill knew full well that what the French needed and were certain to ask for was more fighter aircraft. On 14 May, the French government had requested yet another ten fighter squadrons. This was discussed by both the committee of the chiefs of staff and the War Cabinet, and both decided that it would be unwise to take any immediate action on the question. At a further meeting of the chiefs of staff, on 15 May, the issue was raised again and Air Chief Marshal Sir Hugh Dowding, the commander-in-chief of Fighter Command, made it absolutely clear that if any more aircraft were sent to France it would leave his forces too weak to defend Great Britain. Besides, he furthered to suggest, if they did send more fighter aircraft to aid the French, it would not achieve any decisive results. The committee therefore decided against sending reinforcements at that time.

The following day, 16 May, General Gamelin made a personal plea begging for ten fighter squadrons, stressing that without them the battle would be lost. Due to this added pressure the committee reconsidered the matter and offered to send eight flights of aircraft (basically half–squadrons). This was later discussed by the War Cabinet and sanctioned, even though Churchill himself was still set on sending more. Archibald Sinclair, the Secretary of State for Air, still had grave reservations and insisted that four squadrons should be the absolute maximum; and even that would be taking a very serious gamble with Britain's security, and would go against the advice of Sir Hugh Dowding, who was very much the architect of Britain's air defence and had been through much of the 1930s. The chiefs of staff feared that to go against Dowding's advice could be catastrophic.

Churchill flew to Paris on 16 May, where he could immediately see for himself the gravity of the situation. The French government was already burning its archives and preparing to evacuate the city. In a grim meeting with the French commanders, he asked General Gamelin where was the strategic reserve that had saved Paris in the First World War? 'There is none,' Gamelin replied, although after the war he claimed his response was 'there is no longer any' – not that this misinterpretation of his words would have made any difference to the situation at the time. Churchill later described hearing this news as the single most shocking moment in his life. He then asked Gamelin where and when he proposed to launch a counter-attack. Gamelin did not have an answer other than to make excuses suggesting that the Germans had the upper hand because the Allies were inferior in numbers, equipment and strategy.

At the meeting the French continued to press for the RAF to send ten full fighter squadrons. Churchill tried to explain the fact that if they did, it would leave Britain unable to defend its own airspace. He also doubted that sending these aircraft would make any difference whatsoever, as the Germans had total air superiority in the theatre: the fighters would simply be lost. Over Britain it would be a different matter as Dowding and Fighter Command had an air defence system in place where they would have air supremacy. Édouard Daladier disagreed with Churchill. Although he was no longer prime minster of France, he still had the ear of its Cabinet and he asserted that the extra air cover that these aircraft would provide would give the French infantry the confidence they needed to fight Hitler's tanks. Reynaud also insisted that with the help of these aircraft, the French still had a good chance of stopping the Germans advancing on Paris. In light of this, Churchill sent a telegraph to his War Cabinet in London explaining that the situation was 'grave in the last degree' and giving his final decision on the matter:

> I personally feel that we should send squadrons of fighters demanded and ... dominate the air above the bulge for the next two or three days, not for any local purpose, but to give the last chance to the French Army to rally its bravery and strength. It would not be good historically if their requests were denied, and their ruin resulted ...

After receiving Churchill's message the War Cabinet was left with no alternative except to agree to France's demands. However the chief of the air staff, Sir Cyril Newall, did have the choice of how to deploy these squadrons. He therefore decided that the Hurricane fighters in question would fly to forward airstrips in the north of France on a daily basis but remain based at home. Three squadrons would go each morning and three in the afternoon. This would effectively bring the number of fighter squadrons available to the Air Component up to thirteen. In this way the fighters would not be on the ground for lengthy periods and vulnerable to air attack.

Even so the situation in France had become clouded as the Germans, continuing their push towards the coast from the Sedan bridgehead, had begun to drive a wedge between the Allied forces. The airfields being operated by the Air Component were based to the north of the German line of advance, whereas those of the Advanced Air Striking Force, as well as Air Marshal Barratt's British Air Forces in France's (BAFF) headquarters, were to their south. By 17 May the Germans had severed all landline connections between BAFF and the Air Component. This meant that they were no longer able to take orders from Air Marshal Barratt and instead operated as directed by Lord Gort and the Air Ministry in London.

As the Germans continued their advance, one by one they overran the Air Component's airfields forcing Air Vice-Marshal Blount to re-base all his units in the south of England and continue the fight from there. Of the 261 fighters that had operated with the Air Component from within France, only sixty-six made it home to fight another day.

A major problem with the Dyle Plan was the fact that in executing it Gamelin had sent most of the elite Allied forces, including the BEF, north through the Low Countries in order to keep the fighting on foreign soil. By breaking through at Sedan the Germans had brought the war directly to France, where the troops were largely second rate. Had some of the better quality units been kept in reserve in France, they might have been able to mount a credible counter-offensive, but these were now trapped in the northern pocket and isolated from their supplies, communications and reinforcements.

So far the campaign had also gone completely against French planning. They had anticipated a long, drawn out slog where armies checked one another at heavily defended front lines while the politicians negotiated. The Germans had, of course, used their fighting vehicles in large operational formations and moved quickly across the various terrains for maximum impact. The world had never experienced warfare like this before and the Allies were not equipped to cope with it. Although numerically superior, the French had used the bulk of their armour in small, scattered formations all along the front. A big problem for the French tanks trapped in the northern pocket was that the Germans had isolated them from their supply routes, most particularly fuel. When the petrol ran out the tanks simply stopped working.

The French had four armoured divisions in the field, known as DCR's (*Divisions Cuirassées Rapide*). These were the troops that could in theory combat the German tanks. However the 1st DCR had gone to Belgium, where it had been completely eliminated after running out of fuel; the 3rd DCR could have mounted a counter-attack at Sedan, but because it was taken by surprise and lacked radio systems it was unable to coordinate itself, and any threat it posed fizzled out.

On 16 May the 2nd DCR was ordered to defend the bridges across the River Oise to the west of Saint-Quentin with a view to mounting a counter-offensive from that position, but its commander could not locate half of his companies who were thinly stretched over a forty-nine-mile front. While he was in the process of doing this they were overrun and almost completely destroyed by Kleist's Panzer Group, between 17 and 19 May, particularly the 8th Panzer Division under Colonel Erich Brandenberger. The 2nd DCR did manage to regroup and would fight again at Abbeville.

Finally there was the 4th DCR, which had been hurriedly formed under the command of Colonel Charles de Gaulle. On 17 May he launched an attack on Montcornet, the village where General Guderian had set up his temporary headquarters as he had been ordered to slow the advance and allow the forces behind to catch up and secure the corridor they had established. The 1st Panzer Division also had its service area here, where its tanks could be prepared for further action. It was also strategically important as it cut the roads to Reims, Laon and Saint-Quentin. De Gaulle's Char B1 tanks came under heavy fire from both Panzers and 3.7-cm Pak 36 anti-tank guns. Consequently several were lost to enemy fire while others had to be abandoned when they ran out of petrol or got stuck in the surrounding swamps.

At around 16:00 de Gaulle ordered a second attack on Montcornet, but the tank crews did not have adequate maps of the sector and, after coming under fire from 88-mm flak guns, the assault floundered. Guderian rushed up the 10th Panzer Division to threaten de Gaulle's flank, which together with the aircraft of General Richthofen's VIII Fliegerkorps broke up the attack. At around 18:00 the 4th DCR retreated to its original positions having lost thirty-two tanks and armoured vehicles.

On 19 May, after receiving reinforcements de Gaulle rallied his troops to attempt one final attack. However this effort was also repulsed, with the loss of eighty of his remaining 155 tanks, mostly at the hands of VIII Fliegerkorps.

Up until this point the main British effort had been focused well to the north, where seven of Lord Gort's divisions were engaged against

Fedor von Bock's Army Group B along the Scheldt River. The chief of the British imperial general staff, General Edmund Ironside, visited Gort at his headquarters near Lens in the Pas-de-Calais on 19 May, to try and find out what was happening and how, in view of the deteriorating state of France's competence to wage war, the BEF could be saved, which might involve making an attack towards Amiens. Gort explained that the BEF was technically under the control of the French 1st Army, and as such he took his orders from General Billotte. Having said that, Billotte had not actually issued any orders for eight days, so the BEF was, in effect, working independently.

Ironside subsequently confronted General Billotte at his own headquarters in Douai and was disturbed to find that the general seemed incapable of making decisions. He returned to Britain and reported that, in his opinion, the BEF was 'already doomed' and that measures should be taken to extricate them from the situation; more importantly, he recommended they begin anti-invasion plans, as it was only a question of time before France collapsed and the Germans reached the coast.

While the French were in disarray, General Guderian demanded that his troops should be allowed to keep moving forward to prevent the Allies reorganising themselves and forcing a counter-attack. Ideally, he ventured, they would also like to capture as much of the BEF as possible to deny Britain these troops during its proposed occupation.

On 19 May Rundstedt allowed Guderian to push on. His first adversaries were the 12th (Eastern) Infantry Division, commanded by Major General Petre, and the 23rd (Northumbrian) Infantry Division, under Major General Herbert, both of which were territorials located on the River Somme near Amiens. Many of the soldiers in these units were barely trained, with some receiving little more than a week's instruction. Many had apparently not even fired a rifle before they were deployed. They were also under-equipped and did not have signals, artillery or administrative backup. Consequently the Germans smashed through them with ease inflicting heavy casualties and opening the way to occupy Amiens and secure the westernmost bridge over the Somme at Abbeville.

On 20 May, a reconnaissance unit from the 2nd Panzer Division arrived at Noyelles-sur-Mer near the mouth of the River Somme. These were therefore the first German troops to be within sight of the English Channel. By now the Germans had trapped a vast army of Allied soldiers in a pocket between Army Group B in the north and Army Group A in the south. There were French, Belgian and British troops all squeezing towards the coast, descending on the area around Dunkirk.

On the previous evening the French prime minister, Paul Reynaud, had decided that it was at last time for a change at the top. He summoned and dismissed General Gamelin as supreme commander of the French armed forces for his ineptitude in making the correct decisions and inability to contain the German offensive. In his place he appointed General Maxime Weygand, who had been recalled from Syria where he had been commander-in-chief of the Orient's theatre of operation. However it seems that Weygand was not much of an improvement to his predecessor. On appointment he asserted that his first mission as commander-in-chief would be to get a good night's sleep. He then wasted several days making courtesy visits to dignitaries in Paris while the Germans continued to wreak havoc in the countryside.

After finally giving consideration to the job in hand, he offered up a similar plan to the one Gamelin had proposed himself at the time of his dismissal. The idea was to make a counter-offensive against the narrow German corridor that now stretched from Sedan to the coast. The Allied troops trapped in the pocket above the German corridor would attack in strength to the south; simultaneously, the newly formed French 3rd Army Group, led by General Antoine-Marie-Benoît Besson, whose troops were situated to the south of the corridor, would strike north. They would catch the Germans in the middle and annihilate them. In many ways it was the same plan that the Germans had used against them in the Low Countries.

Weygand planned to launch the attack on 21 May utilising the BEF in the north, the Belgian army and the French light mechanised divisions, known as DLMs (*Divisions Légères Mécanique*), which were equipped with a variety of light Hotchkiss and SOMUA medium tanks; to the south of the German corridor was the newly raised

French 3rd Army Group and what remained of Colonel de Gaulle's 4th DCR.

When General Gamelin had first put the plan forward it seemed feasible assuming that the necessary troops were available, but unfortunately the French forces in question were much more depleted than Weygand had imagined. Also during the preceding few days as had he dragged his heels, the *Wehrmacht* had meanwhile strengthened the corridor with infantry divisions, while Rundstedt's troops had begun to push further along the coast. By the time Weygand met with General Billotte and King Leopold, the commander-in-chief of the Belgian army at Ypres to outline the plan, the opportunity had already realistically been missed.

King Leopold made it quite clear to Weygand that his army could not possibly be used for offensive operations as they lacked armour and aircraft and were only trained for defence. They would therefore not be able to participate in his scheme. Furthermore, Leopold urged Lord Gort not to allow British troops to be used in a plan that could only end in failure. He suggested that the best course of action was to establish a beachhead covering Dunkirk and the Belgian channel ports, from where the Allies could reinforce and, in time, mount an offensive.

On 21 May Weygand ordered Billotte to launch an attack towards the south in the direction of the town of Bapaume, in the Pas-de-Calais, with whatever forces he could muster. At the same time General Besson, commander of the French 3rd Army Group, was ordered to attack from the Somme. Billotte's resources included only the remnants of the DLMs, while the 3rd Army was still in the process of building up and was not ready for offensive action. Neither of these attacks transpired and consequently Weygand rescheduled his offensive for 26 May, to give his forces time to strengthen.

In the meantime various actions still took place, including the Battle of Arras involving the BEF. By 21 May, Rommel's 7th Panzer Division had captured the town of Cambrai and pushed on to the area south of Arras. General Hoth, Rommel's superior, ordered the 7th and 5th Panzer Divisions to bypass the town flanked by the SS *Totenkopf* Division. The 7th were to capture the bridges over the River Scarpe at Acq. This was a risky manoeuvre as it left the division vulnerable to a counter-attack from the British forces in and around Arras, which were substantial, led by Major General Harold Franklyn. These troops included his own 5th Infantry Division; the 50th (Northumbrian) Infantry Division, under Major General Giffard Le Quesne Martel, and the 1st Army Tank Brigade, led by Brigadier D. H. Pratt, with seventy-four varied Matilda tanks and fourteen Vickers Mark IV light tanks.

Franklyn's original orders were to plan a limited assault south of Arras, relieve the garrison and cut German communications. Ironically his own communications had been lost and he was not aware that the French were planning an attack at Cambrai. They were likewise unaware of his plans at Arras. In view of the changing situation, General Ironside, who was now getting more involved with Allied planning, considered a more ambitious move in conjunction with the French, but his instructions did not reach Franklyn and consequently he was unaware of the importance of the operation.

Adhering to his original orders Franklyn attacked with only two infantry battalions and two tank battalions. He also had the French 3rd DLM available for use but they were only given the role of protecting his flanks with their SOMUA S35 tanks. Had Franklyn been aware of Ironside's new instructions, he would undoubtedly have used a much stronger force, and although he achieved surprise and some initial success against Rommel's forces, ultimately the assault was destined to fail. Radio communication between the tanks and infantry was poor and although both French and British aircraft had been requested to aid the attack, communications could not be raised with these either. On the German side, a combination of 88 mm flak guns, 105 mm field guns, and the Junkers Ju 87 dive-bombers of the *Luftwaffe* broke up the Allied formations and destroyed sixty-eight of the British tanks. The French attack on Cambrai also failed.

Although these two attacks had been unsuccessful they sent a shockwave through German high command, who saw them as evidence that the Allies were massing with hundreds of armoured vehicles ready to engage the troops in the corridor. The panic was, of course, unjustified and the psychological effect of these attacks was out of proportion to their military achievement. Once the Germans realised this, their confidence was restored.

Also, on 21 May, further north in Belgium, troops of the BEF were holding back the German advance along the Scheldt River, sometimes referred to in French as the Escaut River, where two Victoria Crosses were won for outstanding bravery. Their citations give us some idea of the chaotic nature of the fighting there. The first was awarded to George Gristock, who was born in Pretoria, South Africa. At the time he was thirty-five years old and a company sergeant major in the 2nd Battalion of the Royal Norfolk Regiment. The following citation was published in *The London Gazette* on 23 August 1940:

> For most conspicuous gallantry on 21 May 1940, when his company was holding a position on the line of the River Escaut, south of Tournai. After a prolonged attack, the enemy succeeded in breaking through beyond the company's right flank which was consequently threatened. Company Sergeant Major Gristock having organised a party of eight riflemen from company headquarters, went forward to cover the right flank.
>
> Realising that an enemy machine gun had moved forward to a position from which it was inflicting heavy casualties on his company, Company Sergeant Major Gristock went on, with one man as connecting file, to try to put it out of action. Whilst advancing, he came under heavy machine-gun fire from the opposite bank and was severely wounded in both legs, his right knee being badly smashed. He nevertheless gained his fire position, some twenty yards from the enemy machine-gun post, undetected, and by well aimed rapid fire killed the machine-gun crew of four and put their gun out of action. He then dragged himself back to the right flank position from which he refused to be evacuated until contact with the battalion on the right had been established and the line once more made good.
>
> By his gallant action, the position of the company was secured, and many casualties prevented. Company Sergeant Major Gristock has since died of his wounds.

The second of these awards went to Harry Nicholls, who was twenty-five and serving as a lance corporal in the 3rd Battalion, Grenadier Guards. His citation appeared in *The London Gazette* on 31 July 1940:

> On 21 May 1940, Lance Corporal Nicholls was commanding a section in the right-forward platoon of his company when the company was ordered to counter-attack. At the very start of the advance he was wounded in the arm by shrapnel, but continued to lead his section forward; as the company came over a small ridge, the enemy opened heavy machine-gun fire at close range.
>
> Lance Corporal Nicholls, realising the danger to the company, immediately seized a Bren gun and dashed forward towards the machine guns, firing from the hip. He succeeded in silencing first one machine gun and then two other machine guns, in spite of being again severely wounded.
>
> Lance Corporal Nicholls then went on up to a higher piece of ground and engaged the German infantry massed behind, causing many casualties, and continuing to fire until he had no more ammunition left.
>
> He was wounded at least four times in all, but absolutely refused to give in. There is no doubt that his gallant action was instrumental in enabling his company to reach its objective, and in causing the enemy to fall back across the River Scheldt.
>
> Lance Corporal Nicholls has since been reported to have been killed in action.

Contrary to his citation, Nicholls was actually taken a prisoner-of-war and was later presented with his VC ribbon by a German commandant while in captivity in Poland.

Having secured the bridgehead over the River Somme, on 22 May General Guderian's XIX Panzer Corps ploughed on towards the channel ports. The 1st Panzer Division was sent to capture Dunkirk; the 2nd Panzer Division was dispatched towards Boulogne (Boulogne-sur-Mer); and the 10th Panzer Division was ordered to take Calais. The Germans knew that these ports were a crucial lifeline for the Allies as they could be resupplied through them. Possibly they also by now realised that it was from this area that the British might also attempt an evacuation.

At this point Weygand's plan had still not been executed. To complicate matters further, on 23 May General Billotte died in a road traffic accident, which left the French 1st Army Group without a commander for three days until the appointment of General Blanchard to succeed him. Billotte was the only person who knew the full details of General Weygand's plan and with his death it was virtually abandoned. Although the British and French would still make one last attempt to cut through the German corridor, at Abbeville, and relieve the Allied forces trapped in the northern pocket, the decision had already been reached to evacuate the BEF from Dunkirk.

12

BATTLE FOR THE CHANNEL PORTS

In the early hours of 23 May Lord Gort ordered his troops to retreat towards the Allied pocket along the coast of northern France and Belgium. By now he had lost all confidence in General Weygand and his new plan to establish a fortified redoubt around Dunkirk and its neighbouring ports, which he termed a '*Réduit de Flandres*'. This was basically the same idea proposed earlier by King Leopold of Belgium: to establish a beachhead where the Allies could regroup and implement the long-awaited counter-offensive. As the ports in question were already being targeted by the *Wehrmacht*, Gort knew that the suggested counter-offensive would never actually happen and that the best they could hope for was to save as many Allied soldiers as possible and ferry them to safety in England; but it was a decision that would still have to be made by higher authorities.

One of the ports from which the Allies could evacuate some of their forces was Boulogne, which had been used by the BEF as a communications base and an area for the movement of troops back and forth from the UK, but unfortunately on the same day as Lord Gort ordered the retreat, the 2nd Panzer Division arrived outside the city to begin its assault.

Two days previously the 20th Guards Brigade, under Brigadier William Fox-Pitt, consisting of the 2nd Battalion, Welsh Guards and the 2nd Battalion, Irish Guards, were undergoing training at

Camberley in Surrey. Orders arrived for them to embark for Boulogne immediately to hold the perimeter of the city while troops already gathered in the port were evacuated, notably about 1,500 men of the Auxiliary Military Pioneer Corps (AMPC).

On the morning of 22 May the brigade set sail aboard three merchant ships and the destroyer HMS *Vimy*. At the same time the French 21st Infantry Division, commanded by General Pierre Louis Félix Lanquetot, was ordered to hold the line against the advancing Germans between Samer and Desvres, some ten miles to the south east.

On arrival Fox-Pitt got straight to work deploying his troops on the high ground outside the city. The Irish Guards were sent south to Saint-Léonard on the River Liane to hold the right flank between there and the sea. The Welsh Guards would hold the left flank, mainly covering the west slopes of Mont Lambert to the east of the city. A few road blocks were already in place, manned by the 7th Battalion, The Royal West Kent Regiment, who were already in the vicinity. This formed a defensive perimeter of some six miles.

On arrival outside the city Major General Veiel divided the 2nd Panzer Division in two. One half was to circle the city and attack from the north while the other moved up from the south. In the early afternoon of 22 May this second column encountered elements of the French 21st Division who were in the process of moving south to their designated positions. What the Germans encountered was in fact the headquarters company of the 48th Infantry Regiment. The French had obviously not expected the enemy to be there quite so quickly and were caught completely unprepared. Although they managed to hold up the Germans for around two hours with two 75 mm field guns and two 25 mm Hotchkiss anti-tank guns, they were soon outflanked, and by evening as the new arrivals from Britain were still settling in, Veiel's tanks had arrived at the outskirts of Boulogne and immediately began shelling the positions held by the Irish Guards to the south of the city.

In the early hours of 23 May the column of panzers that had moved to the north of the city began to attack the positions held by the Welsh Guards, while in the south Veiel's tanks continued to press the Irish Guards, who by 10:00 a.m. had been forced back within the suburbs of the city.

At midday, HMS *Vimy* arrived in the harbour again, this time transporting a demolition party led by Lieutenant Commander A. Welman and a unit known as Force Buttercup, which consisted of four platoons of seamen, two platoons of Royal Marines, a section of machine gunners and a medical party, all commanded by Major C. Holford. Their job was to secure and control the docks during the evacuation and give cover to the demolition party. The ship's crew began to embark the wounded and troops of the AMPC immediately. They were also carrying orders for Brigadier Fox-Pitt as all radio contact had been lost with England. The Guards Brigade was told to hold Boulogne at all costs. This was not going to be easy, as Fox-Pitt also learned that the French 21st Division had abandoned all their blocking positions to the south-east.

During the afternoon the tanks temporarily halted and there was a lull in the ground fighting. However this was only in order for the *Luftwaffe* to dive-bomb Allied positions and ships in the harbour with their Ju 87 'Stukas'. HMS *Vimy* was hit and her captain, Lieutenant Commander Colin Donald, was killed by bomb splinters. Shortly before the air raid, the destroyer HMS *Keith* had arrived in the harbour and began embarking AMPC troops. As a coincidence, her captain David Simson was among those who also perished in the attack. Two French destroyers were also hit by dive-bombers, the *Frondeur*, which was disabled, and the *Orage*, which had to be scuttled. The air raid was eventually broken up by Supermarine Spitfires of No. 92 Squadron flying from RAF Tangmere.

One of the pilots who took part in this action was Squadron Leader Roger Bushell, who was credited with shooting down two Messerschmitt Bf 110s over Boulogne before he was shot down himself by Oberleutnant Günther Specht in a Bf 109 and subsequently taken prisoner. He would later gain notoriety among the Germans as the organiser of the famous 'Great Escape', when seventy-six prisoners broke out of Stalag Luft III at Żagań in Poland. At the time he was head of the camp's escape committee and known as 'Big X', as portrayed by Richard Attenborough in the Hollywood adaptation of the breakout, although in the movie his name had been changed to Bartlett. Seventy-three of the escapees were recaptured and fifty, including Bushell, were shot by the Gestapo on the personal orders of the Führer.

Around 18:00 on 23 May HMS *Keith* received orders from Vice-Admiral Bertram Ramsay, the officer in charge of the Royal Navy's Dover Command, to begin a full evacuation of the British forces in Boulogne, including the Guards Brigade; Ramsay would be in charge of all evacuations from the Channel ports at this time. HMS *Keith* would be supported by at least seven more destroyers: HMS *Vimiera*, HMS *Whitshed*, HMS *Venomous*, HMS *Wild Swan*, HMS *Venetia*, HMS *Windsor* and, of course, HMS *Vimy*.

Having boarded most of the AMPC soldiers from the jetty, HMS *Keith* and HMS *Vimy* were replaced in the harbour by HMS *Vimiera*, HMS *Venetia* and HMS *Whitshed,* who began to evacuate the Royal Marines and much of the Guards Brigade after Fox-Pitt had conducted a fighting withdrawal from their positions around the city. They were followed by HMS *Venomous* and HMS *Wild Swan*, who began to take off the rest of Force Buttercup and the last of the Irish Guards that had been fighting around the harbour perimeter to cover the evacuation.

As the Irish Guards withdrew from their positions, the Germans occupied them and began to fire on both the withdrawing soldiers and the ships in the harbour. Before long German tanks were rolling towards the quayside, but they were kept at bay by the 4.7 inch guns of HMS *Venomous*. Next, as the ships attempted to leave the narrow channel out of Boulogne harbour they came under increasing fire from German field guns. HMS *Venetia* was hit several times and set on fire but she still managed to manoeuvre out of the channel followed by *Venomous* and *Wild Swan*.

Shortly after dark, HMS *Windsor* arrived in Boulogne to complete the evacuation but on clearing the harbour she signaled to the other vessels to say that there were still some British soldiers waiting to be lifted. HMS *Vimiera* consequently returned to the harbour at around 1:30 a.m. The quayside was dark and deserted, but *Vimiera's* captain, Lieutenant Commander Roger Bertram Nettleton Hicks, called out on a loudspeaker to see if anybody was there, at which quite a considerable number of soldiers emerged from the shadows of the surrounding buildings and were packed onto the ship in every remaining available space. When the ship arrived in Dover at 4:00 a.m., quite seriously damaged by enemy fire, some 1,400 men were disembarked but unfortunately a party of around 300 men of the Welsh Guards and various other Allied troops had been left behind at the quay.

Due to a complete collapse in communication, General Lanquetot, who had established his headquarters at the Citadel, a medieval moated fortress in the old part of the city, did not know that his division, the 21st, had collapsed, or that the British had evacuated the city. Brigadier Fox-Pitt had no means of informing Lanquetot of the situation. At around 18:00 on the evening of 24 May the Germans attacked the Citadel but were initially repulsed; the French naval destroyers *Fougueux* and *Chacal* supported their besieged comrades by firing on the Germans from off-shore. However their efforts were thwarted when they were attacked and damaged by the *Luftwaffe*, with the *Chacal* later sinking. At dawn on 25 May the Germans assaulted the walls again, this time using ladders, grenades and flamethrowers. At 8:30 a.m. Lanquetot finally surrendered.

Back at the quayside and on realising that the evacuation had now finished, Major J. C. Windsor Lewis, the officer commanding 4 Company, 2nd Battalion, Welsh Guards, took charge of all the stragglers who had not been rescued. As well as guardsmen there were 120 French infantry soldiers, 200 unarmed members of the AMPC, 120 Royal Engineers and 150 civilian refugees. When the sheds in which they were sheltering came under German fire, the group occupied the harbour railway station and made improvised barricades with sandbags and anything else to hand. On the evening of 24 May, they came under fire from tanks, machine guns and a German assault party that approached the quay in a boat. They fought all of these off until eventually, short of food and running low on ammunition, and realising that there would be no further evacuation, the force surrendered at 13:00 on 25 May. In total the Germans captured 5,000 Allied troops in Boulogne, the majority of which were French; some 4,360 had been successfully rescued.

At the same time as the 2nd Panzer Division was attacking Boulogne, the 10th Panzer Division, led by Major General Ferdinand Schaal, had begun its siege of Calais, which had been used extensively throughout the Phoney War as a transit camp for men on compassionate leave. On 20 May, Colonel Rupert Holland, the base commandant, was ordered to arrange the evacuation of all unnecessary personnel and began the process of evacuating non-combatants on steamers from the Gare Maritime, a railway sidings and quay in the harbour.

The town and port would be defended by a group codenamed Calais Force, commanded by Brigadier Claude Nicholson, who relieved Colonel Holland. They were largely drawn from the 30th Motor Brigade, which was made up of the 1st Battalion, Rifle Brigade (Prince Consort's Own); the 2nd Battalion, King's Royal Rifle Corps (60th Rifles); and the 7th Battalion, King's Royal Rifle Corps (Queen Victoria's Rifles). Its main firepower was provided by the 229th Anti-Tank Battery, Royal Artillery and the 3rd Battalion, Royal Tank Regiment, equipped with twenty-one Vickers Mark IV light tanks and twenty-seven Cruiser tanks newly arrived from England. At the same time, the anti-aircraft defences around the town were enhanced when the 6th Heavy Anti-Aircraft Battery, Royal Artillery, the 172nd Light Anti-Aircraft Battery, Royal Artillery, and the 1st and 2nd Searchlight Batteries were moved up from Arras and deployed around the port.

Eight hundred French soldiers were also posted in Calais, commanded by Major Raymond Le Tellier, based at the Citadel, another moated medieval fortification similar to the one in Boulogne. In total there were around 4,000 men guarding Calais, while at full strength the 10th Panzer Division would have had approximately 15,000 men and at least 300 tanks. This meant that the defenders would be outnumbered by around three to one, although on 23 May General Kleist reported that half of his tanks were by then out of action.

On reviewing the situation at Calais Brigadier Nicholson realised that his available forces would not be able to defend the outer perimeter of the town for long, so instead he set up his headquarters in a clinic in the Boulevard Léon Gambetta and concentrated his main defences around an inner perimeter covering the north of the town, including the old town, the docks and the Citadel. Much of this area was naturally surrounded by water obstacles such as a series of canals.

The first elements of Calais Force, the Queen Victoria's Rifles and the 3rd Royal Tank Regiment, arrived in the port from Southampton on 22 May and began to prepare for action. At this point Nicholson was also given the task of creating a link up with the forces at Dunkirk further along the coast to the north-east. This would establish a new supply line for the BEF.

On the morning of 23 May elements of Major General Friedrich Kirchner's 1st Panzer Division began to approach Calais on their way to assault Dunkirk with orders to make an attempt to capture the town as they passed, if it seemed achievable. Presumably General Kleist was still unaware that the garrison in Calais had been strengthened. At the same time Brigadier Nicholson dispatched three squadrons of British tanks, under Lieutenant Colonel Reginald Keller, to patrol the area around Saint-Omer some twenty miles to the south-east. By the time they reached Guines, only five miles away, they stumbled across the advance units of the 1st Panzer Division, who were advancing north-east from Marquise. After a short fight the British retreated to Coquelles to the south-west of Calais; General Kirchner decided to spend no more time on the port and carried on towards Dunkirk, leaving Calais for General Schaal to deal with.

In the early hours of 24 May Nicholson began his attempt to open the link to Dunkirk. At 2:00 a.m. he led a squadron of tanks supported by a company from the Rifle Brigade up the road towards the more north-easterly port, but they soon came across strong enemy opposition and Nicholson realised that the task would be impossible. He therefore abandoned the attempt and withdrew his forces back to Calais, ordering his troops to stand-to and prepare to defend the outer perimeter of the town.

By 18:00 that evening the 10th Panzer Division had begun to probe the British defences around the perimeter, breaking through in several places and forcing Nicholson to relocate his headquarters to the Gare Maritime in the harbour area and pull his forces back to the inner perimeter. From the start he was short on artillery, but some fire support was provided by Royal Navy destroyers and the Polish warship ORP *Burza*, which fired on the enemy positions from offshore. These vessels made a great contribution to the battle, though at a heavy price: HMS *Wessex* was sunk by Stukas and HMS *Vimiera* and the *Burza* both sustained damage. Later in the evening HMS *Wolfhound* and HMS *Verity* arrived in the harbour with ammunition supplies.

Also aboard the *Verity* was Vice-Admiral James Somerville, a subordinate of Vice-Admiral Ramsay, who met personally with Brigadier Nicholson to make an appraisal of the situation and to inform him of Churchill's decision that there would be no evacuation of troops from Calais: they were to hold out to the very last man. Nicholson was reportedly quite unperturbed by this message and seemed to have resigned himself to such a fate. He explained to Somerville that his men were short of ammunition and he only had two anti-tank guns and two light anti-aircraft guns remaining. Somerville left Calais on the *Wolfhound* at 3:00 a.m. on 25 May, arriving in Dover at 4:30 a.m. On his return he made a broadcast to the nation describing his meeting with the heroic Nicholson.

The Royal Navy immediately started preparations to evacuate the troops at Calais in the event that Churchill's orders were reversed, but their plans were scuppered by the prime minister, who would not give his approval to them. He had come to the decision that Calais Force would have to fight for as long as possible in order to win precious time for the BEF to reach Dunkirk. It was an incredibly difficult order to issue, but Nicholson and his men would be sacrificed to try and save as many other Allied soldiers as possible. A final decision would be made later that day; there remained a glimmer of hope.

Throughout 25 May the Germans made concerted attacks against the British positions within the inner perimeter, which were successively repelled by the men of the rifle regiments. However with each renewed assault Nicholson's force grew weaker with its continued loss of men and expenditure of ammunition. In the afternoon he decided to move his headquarters for the last time, joining the French commanders in the Citadel.

That evening at 21:00 Churchill consulted with Anthony Eden, the Secretary of State for War, and General Ironside. After much deliberation, they finally confirmed that there would be no evacuation of the troops in Calais, a decision which Churchill later admitted made him feel physically sick. That night the following orders were sent to Nicholson, although it is not known whether or not he ever actually received them:

> Every hour you continue to exist is of the greatest help to the BEF. Government has therefore decided you must continue to fight. Have greatest possible admiration for your splendid stand. Evacuation will not (repeat not) take place, and craft required for above purposes are to return to Dover.

Consequently both HMS *Verity* and HMS *Windsor,* which had been poised in the harbour, returned to home waters. Vice-Admiral Ramsay did however make a flotilla of ships available just in case circumstances changed again. That night he also arranged for a small group of ships to sail across to Calais and rescue the wounded and any survivors from the force of Royal Marines who had been sent to protect the naval demolition crews.

The following day, 26 May, the 10th Panzer Division resumed their assault. Once again the riflemen held them off until their ammunition was almost exhausted and German medium tanks were pitted against them. At one point in the day Guderian was so frustrated by Schaal's inability to break the Allies down that he threatened to withdraw the 10th Panzer Division and ask the *Luftwaffe* to destroy the town. However by 16:00 the area surrounding the harbour had fallen, followed by a successful assault on the Citadel at 17:00 that saw Nicholson and his headquarters finally captured along with the surrender of the French contingent.

Yet this did not spell the end of the fighting as several groups refused to submit and fell back to Le Courgain, the maritime and fishing quarter of the port, from where they continued to resist until darkness fell. At this point they decided to break up and attempt to escape from the town. However by now every street was teeming with German soldiers and most were taken prisoner. As for Nicholson himself, he died on 26 June 1943 while in captivity and lies buried in the civil cemetery in Rotenburg, Germany.

In spite of the fact that the port had fallen there was still one heroic rescue to be made, when HM Yacht *Gulzar* entered the harbour just after midnight on 26 May, remaining until 1:00 a.m. after taking on board a party of fifty men who were waiting at the end of the breakwater. She then quietly made her way back to England.

The determination with which 30th Motor Brigade held the town of Calais, entrenched for four days against overwhelming odds, undoubtedly won time for the BEF to fall back on Dunkirk and the neighbouring beaches. How significant their glorious stand was remains a matter of debate. However on 4 June Churchill made the following statement in Parliament:

> The Rifle Brigade, the 60th Rifles and the Queen Victoria's Rifles, with a battalion of British tanks and one thousand Frenchmen – in all about four thousand strong – defended Calais to the last. The British Brigadier was given an hour to surrender. He spurned the offer, and four days of intense street fighting passed before silence reigned over Calais, which marked the end of a memorable resistance. Only thirty unwounded survivors were brought off by the Royal Navy, and we do not know the fate of their comrades. Their sacrifice was not however in vain. At least two armoured divisions, which otherwise would have been turned against the British Expeditionary Force, had to be sent to overcome them. They have added another page to the glories of the Light Division and the time gained enabled the Gravelines Walnlieu to be flooded and to be held by French troops; and thus it was that the port of Dunkirk was kept open.

The Gravelines of which Churchill spoke was a moated town at the mouth of the River Aa, some fifteen miles south-west of Dunkirk. It was established in the twelfth century when it was the western border of Spanish-held territory in Flanders and as such was heavily fortified. It was also the start of a canal and river system that the Allies could use as a flooded stop line. It was also here that German high command with Hitler's approval ordered the 1st Panzer Division to wait on 24 May during a general halt of Army Group A's forces moving on Dunkirk, which elsewhere had commenced two days earlier. They forbade Rundstedt's tanks from crossing a line running south from Gravelines because they feared, wrongly, that the Allies were about to launch a major counter-offensive that would trap their own forces.

This halt order remained in place until 26 May. It gave the trapped Allied forces time to construct defensive works around Dunkirk, establish a flooded stop line to the south, and pull back large numbers of troops. Also, between 28 and 31 May elements of the once-formidable French 1st Army fought a delaying action against seven German divisions, including three armoured divisions in the Siege of Lille. All of these including the defence of Calais were factors in the successful evacuation of the BEF.

13

OPERATION DYNAMO

Operation Dynamo was the codename for the mass evacuation of Allied soldiers from the beaches, breakwaters and harbour of Dunkirk between 26 May and 4 June 1940. Lord Gort, the commander-in-chief of the British Expeditionary Force, chose the French town as a focus point when he ordered the BEF to retreat towards the English Channel because it was the closest available location to England offering adequate port facilities. The British had started planning the evacuation on 20 May, initially without consulting with General Weygand who had only been appointed as supreme commander the day before but Lord Gort had already lost faith in following France's leadership and Weygand proved no better than his predecessor General Gamelin. It was clear to the British by this point that France was lost and in order to save Great Britain from invasion every soldier that could be saved to defend the home islands would be a blessing.

The operation was named after the dynamo room in Dover Castle, where Vice-Admiral Bertram Ramsay had his naval headquarters. It was here that he planned the operation and briefed Winston Churchill constantly while it was under way. The dynamo room provided the electricity for a complex web of secret underground rooms and tunnels dug out of the rock beneath the fortress that had guarded the shortest route across the English Channel since the time of the Norman Conquest. In fact protruding from his headquarters on to the cliff was a balcony from where Ramsay could clearly see his ships plying their way to and fro.

As soon as the evacuation had been decided upon Lord Gort sent one of his staff officers, Brigadier Gerald Whitfield, to Dunkirk to start the process of sending all unnecessary personnel back to Britain. He was astonished by the scale of the problem facing him, with thousands of soldiers descending on the port all attempting to get away. He was equally surprised to find that many of the officers he commandeered to help him process these troops also vanished onto the boats without a word.

On 22 May, Churchill ordered what remained of the BEF to fight its way southwards alongside the French 1st Army, at that time still under the command of General Georges Blanchard. At this point they were still seemingly complying with the Weygand Plan even though Gort was planning the evacuation in the background. However, on 25 May Gort acted on his own initiative and withdrew his men to behind the Ypres–Comines Canal, part of a canal system that eventually reached the sea at Gravelines, where sluice gates had been opened to flood the system and create a barrier called the Canal Line.

It was here that Lord Gort decided to make a stand with part of his force while others were allowed to continue the retreat. This stand became known as the Battle of the Ypres–Comines Canal, or just simply the Battle of the Canal for short. It started in the afternoon of 26 May and reached its maximum intensity on 27 and 28 May.

Although at this point Gerd von Rundstedt had ordered Army Group A to halt, Army Group B was still advancing along the eastern front. On 24 May General Fedor von Bock launched an attack on the Belgian forces stationed along the River Lys to the east of Menen. By 25 May the Belgian armies were retreating in a northerly direction and a gap between them and the British was opening up. It was after being informed of the Belgian collapse that Gort abandoned his participation in the French-led attack southwards and ordered Major General Harold Franklyn's 5th Infantry Division, which had already fought bravely at Arras, to go north instead in order to defend the section of the Ypres–Comines Canal running between those two towns and effectively plugging the gap. The division comprised the 13th Infantry Brigade under Brigadier Miles Christopher Dempsey and the 17th Infantry Brigade, commanded by Brigadier Montagu George North Stopford, augmented by the 143rd Infantry Brigade, led by Brigadier James Muirhead, part of the 48th (South Midland) Infantry Division. At the same time the 50th (Northumbrian) Motor Infantry Division, under Major General Giffard Le Quesne Martel, was sent to Ypres itself, arriving during the night of 26/27 May.

The German attack force came from General Walther von Reichenau's 6th Army, led by its IV Corps commander General Viktor von Schwedler and consisted of three infantry divisions. They began to probe the British positions on the afternoon of the 26th and launched a full-scale attack on the morning of 27 May. Soon the British line had been forced to retreat but from late afternoon onwards they launched a series of counter-attacks. Throughout the various stages of the battle the Royal Artillery, positioned on the Messines–Wytschaete Ridge, constantly broke up the German attacks. Here they had the equivalent of six field artillery regiments and five medium and heavy regiments, and there is little doubt that the successful British defence would not have been possible without this artillery support.

Both the 5th and the 50th divisions finally pulled out on the night of 28/29 May in order to continue their own withdrawal, but their stand, in particular that of the 5th Division, was critical in allowing a substantial part of the fighting strength of the BEF to reach Dunkirk.

While this battle had been taking place most of the French 1st Army was defending the area around Lille, again giving the BEF time to pull back towards the coast but ultimately sacrificing its own opportunity to escape. During the next few days its 50,000 men would put up a heroic defence against seven German divisions.

The fact that Army Group A had halted before they got to Gravelines, convinced that the sudden mass movement of Allied troops was the start of a counter-attack, also gave the retreating armies the opportunity to establish a defence cordon around Dunkirk, largely along the Canal Line. After capturing the port of Boulogne, General Veiel had sent the engineers of the 2nd Panzer Division to build five pontoon bridges across the Canal Line where at that time only one battalion of British infantry barred their way. However, having established these bridgeheads, the Germans failed to capitalise on the situation as General Rundstedt had of course ordered all Army Group A units to cease their advance. There were several reasons for this halt order other than just the consideration that the Allies might be planning an attack. Firstly, German high command, in accordance with Hitler, was concerned about the vulnerability of Army Group A's flanks as they had ploughed through a moderately narrow land corridor. If the Allies did attack they could potentially cut off supplies from reaching the forward troops. As a more practical consideration Rundstedt himself was also worried that the marshy ground around Dunkirk would prove unsuitable for the tanks of the 1st Panzer Division tasked with attacking the town; he needed to make sure that conditions were conducive before committing them.

With Army Group A effectively at a temporary standstill, Reichsmarschall Hermann Göring insisted that, with the help of General Fedor von Bock and his Army Group B pressing down on Dunkirk from the north and east, the *Luftwaffe* would be able to finish the BEF off once and for all. Franz Halder, the chief of the general staff, was not convinced, arguing that the *Luftwaffe*'s aircrews were exhausted after two weeks of relentless action. He also pointed out that aircraft, unlike tanks, were totally dependent on favourable weather conditions. Despite this, Göring evidently won the argument, as on 24 May Hitler issued directive number thirteen, which called for the *Luftwaffe* to defeat the Allies and prevent their escape. It included the following:

> The next object of our operations is to annihilate the French, English, and Belgian forces which are surrounded in Artois and Flanders, by a concentric attack by our northern flank and by the swift seizure of the Channel coast in this area.
>
> The task of the Air Force will be to break all enemy resistance on the part of the surrounded forces, to prevent the escape of the English forces across the Channel, and to protect the southern flank of Army Group A.

At 15:30 on 26 May, Hitler finally lifted the halt order and authorised all German divisions to continue their advance. Unfortunately for them the momentum had been lost, and the Allies had been able to fortify Dunkirk and implement preparations for the evacuation of the BEF. In hindsight, General Guderian considered the failure to execute an early assault on Dunkirk to be one of the worst German errors of the campaign on the western front in 1940, while Erich von Manstein later described it as 'one of Hitler's most critical mistakes'. Hitler himself would later claim that he permitted the BEF to escape as a sporting gesture, hoping it would encourage peace negotiations with Churchill. However his instructions to the *Luftwaffe* in directive number thirteen demanding the 'annihilation of French, British and Belgian forces in the Dunkirk pocket' and to 'prevent the escape of the English forces across the Channel' give this no credence whatsoever.

Under constant attack from the *Luftwaffe,* British units steadily made their way towards Dunkirk, while in the opposite direction French civilians flooded out of the town towards the sanctuary of the surrounding countryside to escape the bombs. Abandoned vehicles and the burned-out shells of Allied tanks that had fallen victim to Stuka attacks blocked every road.

Although the disaster unfolding in Dunkirk was kept secret from the general public back in Britain, King George VI called for a national day of prayer to be held on 26 May. In a national broadcast he asked the people of the UK to turn to God in a spirit of repentance and plead for divine help. Millions of people across the British Isles responded and filled churches around the country, praying for deliverance; the king himself attended a special service at Westminster Abbey. The Archbishop of Canterbury, Cosmo Gordon Lang, led prayers 'for our soldiers in dire peril in France'. Similar prayers were offered in churches and synagogues throughout the UK that day, all of which perhaps intimated to the public the desperate plight their troops were facing. Fortuitously it appears that God may have answered the nation's prayers – a calm descended on the English Channel, which provided perfect conditions for the subsequent operation.

Even before Operation Dynamo had officially begun, around 28,000 British soldiers had already been rescued from Dunkirk. The original plan anticipated that potentially 45,000 men could be rescued during a two day period, after which it was believed that the

Wehrmacht would be in a position to prevent further movement in and out of the port. Just before 19:00 on 26 May, Winston Churchill gave the order for the operation to commence and, largely due to the fact that the Germans were slow to seize the port, the totals saved would far exceed the estimates.

During the evacuation Vice-Admiral Ramsay made available the light cruiser HMS *Calcutta,* thirty-nine Royal Navy destroyers and numerous other smaller naval vessels, but from the start the Admiralty was well aware that they would need more boats. The BEF had sailed to France in stages over a lengthy period of time, so to rescue its troops all at once would entail a massive deployment of naval resources; they would need help from elsewhere.

The Merchant Navy volunteered passenger ferries, hospital ships and other craft. France, Belgium and Holland also provided what they could. The Admiralty also decided to try and enlist the services of any suitable craft that were available in local boatyards and harbours that had the potential to ferry personnel. Consequently naval officers scoured likely locations looking for possibilities. They were searching in particular for small craft that would be able to pick up men from the beaches and transport them to the larger ships waiting in the harbour or offshore. This was because the shallow water along the coast at Dunkirk meant that British destroyers were unable to approach the evacuation beaches; soldiers would have to wade out to them or ideally be lifted by flat-bottomed craft that could get as close to the shore as possible.

On 27 May the Ministry of Shipping telephoned boatbuilders around the coast, asking them to gather together all craft with shallow draft. Some of these would be taken with the permission of the owners, while others were requisitioned by the government with no time for the owners to be contacted. They also put out an emergency call for additional help to man these craft, and over the next few days nearly 700 private vessels were voluntarily employed in the evacuation, the famous 'little ships of Dunkirk', a ramshackle armada of fishing boats, lifeboats, speedboats, car ferries, Thames vessels and pleasure craft. All of these boats were checked over to make certain they were seaworthy, and then fuelled and taken to Ramsgate from where they would embark for France. They were manned by naval officers, ratings and experienced volunteers. Contrary to common myth, very few owners manned their own vessels with the exception of fishermen and one or two others.

Interestingly, an original appeal for little boats had been broadcast following the BBC's 9 O'Clock News on 14 May, so there must have already been some contingency planning towards evacuating the BEF as early as then. This appeal ran as follows:

> The Admiralty have made an order requiring all owners of self-propelled pleasure craft between thirty and 100 feet in length to send any further particulars of them to the Admiralty within fourteen days from today, if they have not already been offered or requisitioned.

The emergency appeal for extra volunteers with the necessary experience to help man these craft was broadcast during the BBC's 9 O'Clock News on 29 May and went as follows:

> The Admiralty wants men experienced in marine internal combustion engines for service as enginemen in yachts or motorboats: others who have had charge of motorboats and have a good knowledge of coastal navigation are needed as uncertified second-hands. Application should be made to the nearest registrar, Royal Naval Reserve, or to the fishery officer.

Vice Admiral Ramsay circulated a thousand copies of the necessary charts and arranged for a system of buoys to be laid from Goodwin Sands all the way to Dunkirk. He also methodically organised the flow of shipping to make sure that this huge number of craft could cross the straits without hindering each other. It was estimated that once completely loaded, the largest of the destroyers would be able to carry about 900 men per trip, most of which would travel on the upper decks as a precaution against being trapped below decks if the ships were attacked and sunk.

Each of the vessels was allocated to one of three cross-channel routes coded X, Y and Z. The shortest of these, Route Z, was also unfortunately the most precarious. It was a distance of thirty-nine nautical miles, which included a section that hugged the French coast. This consequently made the ships easy prey to gun batteries on shore, particularly during daylight hours.

Route X was around fifty-five nautical miles, and although it largely avoided the shore batteries, the ships on it had to pass through a heavily mined section of water. Returning from Dunkirk, this route would take the vessels north around the Ruytingen Bank from where they would steer towards the North Goodwin Lightship before heading south around Goodwin Sands to Dover. Unfortunately, although this route was the least likely to attract enemy fire, because of the minefields and sandbanks it could not be negotiated at night.

The longest route, at eighty-seven nautical miles, was Route Y, which followed the French coast as far as Bray-Dunes, then turned north-east until reaching the Kwinte Buoy. Here, after making an almost 270 degree turn, the ships sailed west to the North Goodwin Lightship and headed south around Goodwin Sands to Dover. Ships on Route Y were the most likely to be attacked by German surface vessels, submarines, or the *Luftwaffe*. Unfortunately because of the vast quantity of vessels taking part in the venture, not all of them could use the same channels; with all factors considered, the pros and cons of each were marginal and all were extremely dangerous.

In spite of the enemy shore batteries, submarines and surface vessels, the biggest problem facing the evacuation from the start was the unwelcome attention of the *Luftwaffe*, which began a heavy bombardment of Dunkirk on 27 May. Unfortunately many of the bombs missed the harbour and docks and landed in the town, killing an estimated 1,000 civilians, roughly one-third of the population that had not already fled from their homes. To compound matters, the bombing knocked out water supplies to the town so it was impossible to extinguish the widespread fires.

Sixteen RAF fighter squadrons were ordered to fly over Dunkirk to engage the German bombers during the evacuation. On 27 May, these squadrons shot down thirty-eight enemy aircraft for the loss of fourteen of their own. The British fighters would take part in 3,500 sorties throughout the whole of Operation Dynamo, but the soldiers awaiting evacuation on the beaches were largely unaware of the battles taking place high above their heads and bitterly accused the RAF of doing nothing to help them. In reality the RAF had already given all they could. Since the launch of *Fall Gelb* on 10 May and up until the start of Operation Dynamo, more than 900 aircraft had been lost, as well as 915 aircrew including 435 pilots; during the operation itself they would lose a further 145 aircraft and sixty pilots. In comparison, the *Luftwaffe* flew 1,882 bombing sorties and 1,997 fighter sorties and lost an estimated 156 aircraft; 1,279 were lost during the whole campaign.

By May 27, King Leopold of Belgium had come to the conclusion that his depleted army could no longer fight or retreat. He sent an emissary through the German lines to request an armistice, which the Germans rejected: Hitler demanded their unconditional surrender. With no army left to sustain the fight, and against the wishes of the exiled Belgian government in Paris, the king was given no choice but to accept Germany's terms. The Belgian prime minister, Hubert Pierlot, insisted that capitulation was the decision of the Belgian government, not one the king could make alone. However, as commander-in-chief of the army Leopold refused to abandon his men and was consequently taken prisoner. Throughout the period of the Nazi occupation of his country he would be confined mostly to the royal palace of Laeken in Brussels. In the House of Commons, Winston Churchill defended Leopold's decision, even though it made the British position more precarious.

At Lille elements of the French 1st Army would continue to hold out until midnight on 3 June, when they ran out of food and ammunition. The defence here had been led by General Jean-Baptiste Molinié in charge of a force mainly consisting of French North African troops. After their final and honourable surrender the Germans permitted 35,000 men to march proudly out of the town to await captivity. Their heroic stand was yet another factor that helped the BEF and the remainder of the 1st French Army to reach Dunkirk.

By 30 May all British troops had finally reached the Dunkirk defensive perimeter along with half of the French 1st Army; those not initially earmarked for evacuation would hold the Germans back at the Canal Line and elsewhere. The countryside around Dunkirk was marshy and, just as General Rundstedt had feared, totally unsuitable for his tanks to operate in. The German offensive therefore continued to largely depend on the *Luftwaffe* and infantry.

In Dunkirk itself men were waiting everywhere to be lifted amidst chaotic scenes, badly in need of some sort of organisation. Vice-Admiral Ramsay dispatched Captain William Tennant to Dunkirk on board the destroyer HMS *Wolfhound* to take charge of organising the troops and getting them safely on board the ships waiting to take them away.

On arrival Tenant discovered that the *Luftwaffe* had virtually destroyed both the harbour and the docks so any further evacuation from here would be severely restricted. He therefore needed alternatives and initially ordered the men to be evacuated from the town's beaches. Then, in an attempt to speed up the process as many of the boats were unable to get close to shore, he directed evacuees to queue up at two breakwaters, known as the East and West Moles. These structures were lengthy piers or jetties made of stone and concrete that stretched out to sea. Over the next few days some 200,000 troops embarked on ships from the East Mole alone, which stretched nearly a mile out to sea, making it the crucial hub of the evacuation. Many of the evacuees stood shoulder-deep in water for several hours while the *Luftwaffe* continued to execute Hitler's orders to stop the British from escaping across the Channel.

14

THE LITTLE SHIPS
OF DUNKIRK

The so-called 'little ships of Dunkirk' were 700 private vessels that mainly sailed from either Ramsgate or Dover in England to Dunkirk in France between 26 May and 4 June 1940 as part of Operation Dynamo, helping to rescue the men of the British Expeditionary Force as well as large numbers of Allied soldiers. They were there to supplement the efforts of roughly 220 vessels from the Royal Navy, commanded by Rear Admiral Frederic Wake-Walker, who in point of fact had been sent to Dunkirk by Vice-Admiral Ramsay to coordinate the participation of all Allied vessels off the Franco-Belgian coast.

This was a remarkable and typically British response to a disaster that very few other nations would even have contemplated. Some of the owners of these little boats and the volunteers who sailed them had responded to the Admiralty's pleas broadcast by the BBC. Many of the craft were flat-bottomed river boats that had never even been to sea before and were certainly not designed for open waters. Yet for several days these fishing boats, yachts, barges and other little vessels faced constant attacks from the aircraft of the *Luftwaffe* or the E-boats of the *Kriegsmarine* to rescue the remnants of an entire army, with some making three or more journeys.

The skippers of these craft could use plumes of billowing smoke as beacons to navigate by, the result of oil tanks set on fire at various locations along the French coast by German bombing. Thick clouds of this smoke covered most of Dunkirk and its nearby beaches, and many waves of bombers had to return to their bases with their bomb loads unused as they were unable to see any targets through the obscurity. On the beaches themselves as well as the existing breakwaters, units of Royal Engineers built makeshift jetties out of abandoned trucks and anything else they could get their hands on so that troops could clamber out to the boats as they arrived. Every time a flotilla was sighted, long lines of desperate men formed up hoping it was their turn to be rescued.

It would be impractical and impossible to tell the stories of all 700 ships. Here I have selected a few examples that will hopefully give a good representation of what happened during those momentous days. They range from large passenger ferries requisitioned for military use to small private yachts and fishing boats. The larger craft were used to shepherd men from coast to coast while the smaller craft generally took them from the beaches out to the bigger boats for onward transportation.

The MV *Royal Daffodil*, for example, probably rescued more soldiers than any other little ship. It was a ferry boat, launched in 1939, and in her inaugural season was used for Continental trips from Tower Pier in London to Ostend in Belgium. She was requisitioned for war service at the onset of hostilities, and from 15 September 1939 she was used to carry troops of the BEF to France, continuing this duty until October that year. On 23 May 1940, along with the passenger steamer SS *Archangel* she carried some of Brigadier Claude Nicholson's 30th Motor Brigade to Calais. At Dunkirk she is credited with evacuating around 9,500 men during seven trips – the largest number evacuated by a single passenger vessel in the operation.

On 2 June a bomb passed completely through her decks exploding beneath her. The explosion caused a gaping hole in her starboard side which began to let in water, so her master, Captain G. Johnson, ordered everyone on board to move to port side and in so doing the ship tilted, raising the hole above the water line. This enabled the crew to patch her up temporarily with mattresses and wood, repairs sufficient for her to make it back to Ramsgate and disembark her evacuees. Later she was sailed to Deptford under her own power and repaired. As well as the bomb, she had survived both machine gun and torpedo attacks.

The PS *Medway Queen* was built in Troon, Scotland in 1924 for service in the River Medway and Thames Estuary. She was requisitioned by the Royal Navy in 1939 and became HMS *Medway Queen,* employed as a minesweeper helping to protect the English Channel. Prior to Dunkirk she had been fitted with a 12-pounder gun and two machine guns. She left Dover in a flotilla that was also made up of PS *Sandown,* PS *Thames Queen,* PS *Gracie Fields,* PS *Queen of Thanet,* PS *Princess Elizabeth,* PS *Laguna Belle* and PS *Brighton Belle.* She was to make seven crossings, and on her first trip soldiers were taken off the beaches in lifeboats and ferried out to her. She arrived back at Dover during an air raid and proceeded to shoot down one of the enemy aircraft just outside the harbour: the first of three she would destroy during the operation. Also on this trip the *Brighton Belle* ran over sunken wreckage and began to sink. All of her passengers and crew were rescued by the *Medway Queen* without loss and she finally reached the harbour heavily overloaded but safe.

On her second trip she took soldiers directly off the beach itself, which was obviously quicker but needed a steady hand in the shallows. On later trips she rescued men from the concrete jetties and took them to Ramsgate where she could be refuelled and take on provisions. On Monday 3 June Vice-Admiral Ramsay gave the order that all ships were to leave Dunkirk by 2.30 a.m. the following morning. At the time the *Medway Queen* was on her seventh trip and docked at one of the Moles when a destroyer moored astern of her was driven forwards by an explosion and smashed her starboard paddle box, causing her considerable damage. Undaunted, she managed to limp back to England carrying 400 French soldiers, by which time she had rescued 7,000 men. She subsequently became known as *The Heroine of Dunkirk.*

The motor yacht MY *Sundowner* was originally built in 1912 and was later owned and relaunched by Charles Lightoller, former second officer of the RMS *Titanic.* In 1939, with the threat of war looming, Lightoller was tasked to secretly survey the European coast for the Admiralty from aboard his yacht. On 31 May *Sundowner* was requisitioned and ordered to sail to Dunkirk. Lightoller, who was then sixty-six years old and retired, volunteered to take her himself, along with his eldest son Roger and eighteen-year-old sea scout Gerald Ashcroft.

Leaving Ramsgate at 10:00 a.m. on 1 June, the yacht crossed the Channel in the company of five other ships. On their way they rescued the crew of the motor cruiser *Westerly*, which had broken down and was on fire. On arrival at Dunkirk, Lightoller found that the piers were too high for the craft, so he drew her alongside the destroyer HMS *Worcester* and took on board 130 of her evacuees. *Sundowner* then returned to Ramsgate and managed to avoid the German dive-bombers. Being slow the greatest danger she faced was having her decks swamped by the wash caused by destroyers as they sped by. After disembarking the troops, she was preparing to return when Lightoller was informed that in future only ships capable of doing twenty knots would be allowed to continue.

The motor launch ML *Advance* was another of the very few ships to be skippered by her owner, Colin Dick. He and his crew had left Dover for Dunkirk with a small flotilla at 6:45 a.m. on 29 May. When they approached the shore, they were attacked by two aircraft and her signal mast was torn off after being struck by the undercarriage of the second of these. At 13:00 they started rescuing troops, ferrying them to various vessels offshore. At 20:45 *Advance* and MY *Elizabeth Green*, another of the ships in the group, returned to Ramsgate having both suffered damage; *Advance* had to be beached on arrival at 5:30 a.m. to prevent her sinking.

Colin Dick and his crew member Eric Piercy were each given an official letter recording their brave participation in this operation, but forty-eight hours later the story took a strange twist as both were detained by the police under defence regulation 18B, which allowed the internment of British citizens without charge or trial if they were seen as a danger to the country. Their offence was that they had both been known members of Oswald Mosley's Blackshirt party, but they were released ninety days later. Meanwhile *Advance* had made one further trip to Dunkirk with Sub-Lieutenant P. Snow as skipper on 2 June.

The motor yacht MY *Bluebird* had belonged to Malcolm Campbell, who had broken the world land-speed record nine times between 1924 and 1935 and the world water-speed record four times, the last in

1939. He adopted the name *Bluebird* from Maurice Maeterlinck's play *L'Oiseau bleu* and gave it to all his record-breaking cars and boats, as well as three successive yachts. The *Bluebird* at Dunkirk, which was later renamed *Bluebird of Chelsea*, was Malcolm Campbell's second yacht, which he sold after only three years. After two false starts, she finally arrived off France commanded by a yachtsman, Lieutenant Colonel Harold Barnard, with a crew of naval ratings. However her draft was too great to let her work comfortably near the beaches so she ferried troops from the harbour to the ships. She suffered no major damage but her twin screws were fouled by debris, causing her engines to stop, and she had to be towed back to England.

As a coincidence, another of Malcolm Campbell's ex-yachts, also called *Bluebird* but later renamed the MY *Chico*, participated in the evacuation. Under the command of Sub-Lieutenant Jack Mason, she embarked 217 troops on one trip and nearly 1,000 on a second, which she then ferried to waiting ships; back in Dover she would disembark a further estimated 100 troops that she had carried herself.

On 29 May the MY *Cordelia* left for Dunkirk, commanded by Sub-Lieutenant C. A. Thompson, together with a whaler and three former Belgian fishing trawlers, all of which were towed to France by a drifter. By 5:30 a.m. on 30 May they arrived off the beach to the west of La Panne and during the next five hours ferried 300 troops from the beach to off-lying ships. The *Cordelia*'s port engine then seized up and the starboard propeller was fouled by flotsam, so she was towed back to Dover, arriving at 20:30 that same evening.

Another interesting story belongs to the fifty-foot barge *Count Dracula*, taken to Dunkirk by Commander Ewart Brookes. Powered by a steam engine, she started life in 1913 in the service of the Imperial German Navy. Kaiser Wilhelm gave her to Admiral Franz Ritter von Hipper, who took her wherever he went as his admiral's barge. She was with the German fleet when it was scuppered at Scapa Flow in 1918 and was salvaged by the Royal Navy. She was later a private yacht until her owner, Carl Greiner, sent his son Alan to take her to Ramsgate after hearing the Admiralty's plea for small boats, where Commander Brookes took charge of her. Brookes had already spent two days and a night at Dunkirk in command of another craft, which had been sunk beneath him. He was delighted at the speed and power of *Count Dracula*, which lifted 702 British as well as ten Belgian soldiers and took them to larger vessels; he would also come away with a group of Royal Engineers. The following account in his own words is taken from the website of the Association of Dunkirk Little Ships:

> I finally brought her back to Ramsgate with thirty-eight soldiers on board, Royal Engineers, who had spent all the week on the beach by the Casino, building a temporary pier of Thames barges.
>
> I felt rather pleased at the last little jab because at midnight on June 1st, the order was passed: 'all small boats back to England under escort'. German E-boats had come down the coast. The intention was to abandon the Royal Engineers and to allow them to get into the town of Dunkirk as best they could - if they could. A difficult job then, because the Germans were close to the beach and had it under machine gun fire.
>
> A Mr Jeffries from Brighton (a garage owner, I believe) and myself decided to take a chance and see if we could get the Royal Engineers off. We did. All of them. And as they came away, they were exchanging fire with German troops in lorries or armoured cars. A close thing. I received a reprimand for leaving the convoy of small ships but as it was one of many reprimands I had during the war for doing odd things, I didn't worry a great deal.

In May 1940 Robert Walter Timbrell, later a rear admiral in the Royal Canadian Navy, was a sub-lieutenant stationed at the Royal Naval gunnery school at Whale Island, Portsmouth, when he was ordered to take command of MY *Llanthony*, which he soon discovered had been a gentleman's yacht built for Lord Astor of Hever Castle and was at that time owned by the member of Parliament for Birmingham King's Norton, Colonel Lionel Beaumont-Thomas. At Ramsgate Timbrell was assigned a crew consisting of a Royal Navy petty officer, two London Transport bus mechanics and six lumberjacks from Newfoundland. Presumably these had come forward presenting the required attributes for a journey to Dunkirk. His equipment for the trip amounted to an old revolver, a magnetic compass and a chart of the known minefields. More importantly, *Llanthony* had two small tenders, each of which could carry sixteen souls from the beaches at a time.

After fuelling and loading several barrels of freshwater to distribute among the beleaguered troops, they set off across the English Channel. However, long before arriving off the French coast they came across a Thames pleasure steamer in distress, crowded with evacuated troops, which they immediately towed back to Ramsgate. Having done this, they set off again and this time arrived off the beaches and began picking up men. Unfortunately at some point during the operation the *Llanthony* was struck by bombs, which severed the fuel pipes and killed both engines. Consequently she drifted up on to the beach and got stuck. After a potential crisis, a sergeant from a Guards battalion and eight guardsmen came to the rescue. They helped to anchor the boat using a Bren gun carrier while the London Transport mechanics repaired the fuel pipes and managed to restart the engines. A metal plate was fixed over the bomb damage and the yacht returned to Ramsgate with a full cargo of evacuees, including the gallant guardsmen.

Back in Ramsgate Timbrell was put in charge of a small flotilla of boats, mainly fishing trawlers, which he led back to Dunkirk from the helm of the repaired *Llanthony*. The Guards sergeant and one or two of his men volunteered to return with the boats to France to aid the rescue efforts. They gathered together a few weapons, including Bren guns and some sort of anti-tank piece. On the next trip, one of the trawlers hit a mine and was blown up, with all aboard lost. However when the remaining ships came under attack from the *Luftwaffe* the Guards contingent was able to fend them off with their new weapons. They also gave the crew of a German E-boat a nasty surprise when it attempted to attack them only to be driven off.

On the *Llanthony's* final trip, by which time German troops were already fighting within the town, Timbrell was propositioned on the beach by a drunken British soldier who offered to pay for his passage home with a case of looted brandy. He climbed aboard the yacht and spent the entire journey asleep in the wheelhouse.

During all of its trips to Dunkirk, the *Llanthony* itself brought back 280 men. Combining this figure with those saved by the trawlers under his command, Timbrell was responsible for evacuating over 900 servicemen. For his gallantry he was awarded the Distinguished Service Cross (DSC), presented to him personally by King George VI on 3 September 1940.

Boats used by the Royal National Lifeboat Institution (RNLI) were also an obvious fit for the evacuation as many had shallow drafts; most of their craft operating in the south-east of England were called to Dover, where they were fuelled and manned by naval crews. They were then towed across the Channel by drifters to Dunkirk, where most would remain throughout the operation, ferrying men from the beaches out to larger ships.

The boats involved were RNLB *Abdy Beauclerk,* from Aldeburgh; RNLB *Cecil and Lilian Philpot,* from Newhaven; RNLB *Charles Cooper Henderson,* from Dungeness; RNLB *Charles Dibdin,* from Walmer; RNLB *Cyril and Lilian Bishop,* from Hastings; RNLB *Edward Dresden,* from Clacton-on-Sea; RNLB *EMED,* from Walton; RNLB *Greater London,* from Southend-on-Sea; RNLB *Guide of Dunkirk* (new at the time and not stationed yet); RNLB *Herbert Sturmey,* from Cadgwith; RNLB *Jane Holland,* from Eastbourne; RNLB *Louise Stephens,* from Gorleston; RNLB *Lucy Lavers,* from Aldeburgh; RNLB *Lord Southborough,* from Margate; RNLB *Mary Scott,* from Southwold; RNLB *Michael Stephens,* from Lowestoft; RNLB *Prudential,* from Ramsgate; RNLB *Rosa Woodd and Phyliss Lunn,* from Shoreham-by-Sea; RNLB *Thomas Kirk Wright,* from Poole; and RNLB *Viscountess Wakefield,* from Hythe.

Many of these lifeboats would stay in the vicinity of Dunkirk until the end of the operation in case stragglers reached the beaches. Remarkably, only the *Viscountess Wakefield* was sunk during the operation although many others were damaged and towed back to England for repairs.

The Isle of Man Steam Packet Company also had a number of its vessels requisitioned at the outbreak of war, eight of which served at Dunkirk. The SS *Mona's Isle* similar to other steam packet ships was fitted out as an armoured boarding vessel. She was the very first ship to leave Dover for Dunkirk during Operation Dynamo, with the exception of HMS *Wolsey,* which was a destroyer used as a radio link ship but which did not take part in the evacuation as such.

Mona's Isle departed from Dover at 21:00 on 27 May and by midnight had docked at the harbour where she embarked 1,420 troops before leaving again at first light. Returning by Route Z, she came under fire from German shore batteries. Many shells exploded around the craft and her rudder was smashed. The ship still managed to limp back to Dover but not before a Bf 109 had strafed her a few times, killing twenty-three and wounding sixty others. The mission had taken nearly fifteen hours and she was recorded as the first ship to complete a round trip during the evacuation.

Two awards were later made to members of the ship's company for their part in the action. Her commanding officer, Commander John Charles Keith Dowding, received the Distinguished Service Order (DSO), while Petty Officer Leonard Kearley-Pope was awarded the Distinguished Service Medal (DSM) for remaining at a 12-pounder gun for several hours despite suffering multiple wounds. *Mona's Isle* made a second round trip to Dunkirk, bringing out a further 1,200 troops.

Although *Mona's Isle* survived, sadly the company lost three of its other ships during the evacuation: SS *Mona's Queen*, SS *Fenella*, and SS *King Orry*. *Mona's Queen* was also to make a successful round trip under the command of Captain Radcliffe Duggan; she arrived back in Dover during the night of 27 May with 1,200 troops. The next day the ship returned to sea and was shelled off the French coast by shore guns but escaped damage. For her next trip Captain Duggan was replaced by Captain Archibald Holkham. She set out again in the early hours of 29 May, loaded with water canisters for the troops on the beaches who were still short of drinking water. However the ship struck a sea mine outside Dunkirk harbour at 5.30 a.m. and sank in two minutes. Captain Holkham and thirty-one members of the crew were picked up by destroyers, while twenty-four of the crew were lost.

On 29 May the SS *Fenella*, under the command of Captain W. Cubbon, made her first trip to the evacuation area. She started to embark troops from the east pier, and had managed to get 650 on board when she came under heavy fire in the third massed air raid of that day. She was hit by three bombs in quick succession, the first hitting her directly on the promenade deck, the second hitting the pier, blowing lumps of concrete through the ship's side below the waterline, and the third exploding between the pier and the ship's side, wrecking the engine room. The *Fenella* was subsequently abandoned and later sank, but not before the troops were disembarked onto the pier again where they were picked up by the London pleasure steamer the SS *Crested Eagle*, which was also later bombed and beached.

Some weeks later a postcard arrived home from a junior steward on the *Fenella*, Tommy Helsby, who was nineteen years old and hailed from Liverpool. He had been thought lost when the ship sank but had actually been captured by the Germans; in fact, he was the only Steam Packet Company man to be taken prisoner in all of the operations in which its ships took part throughout the war. He had been badly burned and admitted to a hospital in Belgium, where German surgeons had taken care of him. He was repatriated before the end of the war and eventually rejoined the company.

The SS *King Orry* was under the charge of Commander Jeffery Elliot, and on her first trip to Dunkirk succeeded in embarking 1,131 soldiers from the harbour. The ship cast off and made for home in the early hours of 27 May but she soon came under fire from shore batteries. Though they succeeded in inflicting some damage to her, on this occasion she still managed to limp back to Dover where she docked just before noon. She returned to Dunkirk in the late afternoon of 29 May and was attacked by dive-bombers during the crossing but still made it to the harbour. It was then that a second and heavier attack was made on her, which caused her to collide with the east pier although she did manage to secure alongside it. However, it soon became apparent that she was in a dangerous state and could potentially prove a hindrance to other boats, so after midnight she was ordered to leave the harbour. Having done so, she soon began to list heavily to starboard. Her engine room started to flood and she was abandoned and finally sank shortly after 2:00 a.m. on 30 May. Other ships nearby closed in and picked up the survivors.

A fleet of thirty-nine Dutch coasters that escaped the invasion were also used during the evacuation. These were able to approach the beaches very closely due to their flat bottoms and collectively rescued 22,698 men in total. The MV *Rian* saved 2,542 men between 28 and 31 May, under Captain D. Buining – the most men saved by any

Dutch vessel. Other Dutch coasters that saved more than 1,000 men were: MV *Hondsrug*, 1,455; MV *Patria*, 1,400; MV *Hilda*, 1,200; MV *Doggersbank*, 1,200; MV *Horst*, 1,150; MV *Twente*, 1,139; and MV *Friso*, 1,002. Of these, seven were lost.

Sixty-five Belgian craft were also employed, including fifty-four fishing trawlers, six Belgian naval ships and four tugs; the Belgian fishing fleet itself transported 4,300 British and French soldiers to the English coast. After the evacuation was complete many of the Belgian fishing boats were permitted to work out of Brixham Harbour, in Devon, providing a valuable service, fishing for Britain's larder.

The smallest of the little ships was the open-topped fishing dinghy *Tamzine*, which only measured fourteen feet and seven inches in length; she is now preserved at the Imperial War Museum in London. Smaller boats were used such as tenders from larger ships but *Tamzine* was the smallest to get there independently and survive. After ferrying men from the beaches to larger boats offshore, she was finally towed back to England behind a Belgian fishing boat, blood-stained but in one piece.

During the entire evacuation period the Royal Navy lost six destroyers and twenty-four smaller warships, while more than seventy of the little ships failed to return. Most significant, though, was the loss of the destroyers: HMS *Grafton*, HMS *Wakeful*, HMS *Grenade*, HMS *Basilisk*, HMS *Havant*, and HMS *Keith*.

On 27 May HMS *Grafton* had evacuated over 1,600 troops from the beaches of La Panne and Bray-Dunes to the north-east of Dunkirk. She returned on the morning of 29 May and stopped near Nieuwpoort to rescue survivors from the destroyer HMS *Wakeful*, which had been torpedoed by an E-boat and sunk. While in the process of doing this *Grafton* was struck in the stern by a torpedo from the German submarine *U-62*. The resulting explosions killed the captain, Commander Cecil Edmund Robinson, and another officer on the bridge, as well as the canteen manager and thirteen ratings. Thirty-five recently rescued soldiers who were packed on the deck were also killed. The destroyer HMS *Ivanhoe* together with the requisitioned passenger vessel HMS *Malines* managed to take off the survivors, before *Ivanhoe* sank the *Grafton* with gunfire as she was too badly damaged to be saved.

On 27 May HMS *Wakeful* had been responsible for the evacuation of 631 troops. After delivering these to Dover she returned to Dunkirk, where she picked up 640 more. Unfortunately it was during this second mission that she was torpedoed by the German E-boat *S-30*. The destroyer was struck by two torpedoes, one of which hit the forward boiler room. Casualties were very heavy with only one of the 640 Allied troops she had evacuated surviving. Twenty-five of the crew also survived and were picked up by the *Grafton* before she was subsequently sunk herself, as previously described.

During the initial stages of the evacuation HMS *Grenade* had provided cover for other vessels as they evacuated troops, and on 28 May she took part in the rescue of thirty-three survivors from the coaster SS *Abukir,* which had been torpedoed by an E-boat. On the night of 28/29 May she was attacked by Stukas while in Dunkirk's harbour and was hit by two bombs, which set her on fire and claimed the lives of eighteen of those on board. The trawler *John Cattling* then towed her to the west side of the outer harbour so she did not cause any danger to other ships. Here her magazines exploded and she eventually sank.

HMS *Basilisk*, under Commander Maxwell Richmond, made two round trips from Dover on 30 May, evacuating 695 men. On the morning of 1 June she returned to the beaches of La Panne to load more troops, where she was attacked three times by German aircraft. The first attack disabled her and a French fishing trawler *Le Jolie Mascotte* attempted to tow her to safety. No further damage was incurred during the second attack but it caused the French ship to drop the tow. The third attack, around noon, finally sank her in shallow water. The *Le Jolie Mascotte* and the destroyer HMS *Whitehall* rescued eight officers and 123 crewmen from the ship before she went down.

HMS *Havant* arrived off Dunkirk on 29 May and rescued over 2,300 men under the direction of Lieutenant-Commander Anthony Burnell-Nugent. On the morning of 1 June she had embarked 500 troops before going alongside the destroyer HMS *Ivanhoe,* which had been disabled by enemy aircraft. *Havant* took on board all of the troops from *Ivanhoe* and set course for Dover but shortly afterwards was attacked by Stukas. Two bombs exploded in her engine room and another beneath her hull. In the attack eight crewmen were killed and twenty-five were wounded; at least twenty-five of the evacuees on board were also killed. The ship was too badly damaged to be saved and was scuttled by the minesweeper HMS *Saltash,* after an attempt to tow her had failed. HMS *Ivanhoe* managed to get back to Dover on her own steam but took no further part in the evacuation.

HMS *Keith* had been made the flagship of Rear Admiral Frederic Wake-Walker, the overall commander of the evacuation boats. On the morning of 31 May she was off La Panne, under the command of Captain Edward Berthon, when she was attacked by aircraft. A bomb went down the aft funnel and exploded in her number two boiler room, killing everyone inside and starting a fire. She was left without power so the order was given to abandon ship; she sank at roughly 9:45 a.m. Three officers and thirty-three naval ratings were killed during the attack, with eight officers and 123 crewmen being rescued. Rear Admiral Wake-Walker thereafter directed operations from a motor torpedo boat in Dunkirk harbour.

The French Navy also lost three destroyers: *Bourrasque,* which was mined and sunk off Nieuwpoort on 30 May; *Siroco,* which was torpedoed and sunk by the German E-boats *S-23* and *S-26* close to the West Hinder lightship on 31 May; and *Le Foudroyant,* sunk by air attack off the beaches on 1 June.

The following are the daily totals of all Allied troops that were landed back in Britain from all of Dunkirk's evacuation points and ships:

27 May	=	7,669
28 May	=	17,804
29 May	=	47,310
30 May	=	53,823
31 May	=	68,014
1 June	=	64,429
2 June	=	26,256
3 June	=	26,746
4 June	=	26,175
Total	=	338,226

15

HEROES AND VILLAINS

Back in Britain the government was concerned that news about Dunkirk could cause widespread panic among the civilian population. Churchill wanted any information about it drip fed by the media in order to lessen its impact. Clive Bossom was serving in the Royal East Kent Regiment, known as 'The Buffs', and relates a story with an interesting twist to this account. He had only received his regular commission on 1 September and when his battalion set out for France two weeks later, on 16 September, he was sent to the depot at Canterbury to receive a crash course in the art of war. He recalled:

A few months later I was posted to our base camp at Le Mans. I was slightly disillusioned with my first command. One elderly corporal who obviously had discovered the delights of French wine, a handful (in every sense of the word) of unwanted scallywags and one mad, temperamental cook. Even with my newly experienced crash course on military knowledge, I was hard-pressed to keep my fifteen men fully occupied with training and trying to turn them out to look anything like guardsmen.

After a few weeks of this I thought I deserved forty-eight hours compassionate leave. I wrote myself a pass allowing me to visit my recently acquired American step-grandmother, Madeleine Dittenhofer, who was living gracefully at the Hotel Crillon in Paris. Unfortunately once there I ran into a senior staff officer in the hotel lobby who enquired whether I was on his staff. When he was informed I was on 'compassionate leave' he immediately despatched me back to the depot in Canterbury. As a result I missed Dunkirk by several weeks.

Back in the UK I was posted to a company of the 11th Battalion The Buffs stationed near Mereworth Castle in Kent (home of Esmond Harmsworth, 2nd Viscount Rothermere, chairman of Associated Newspapers). Lorna and Esme Harmsworth, great friends of mine, lived in the castle. They invited me over for tennis and a swim and insisted I stay for an early supper. At supper all the young sat at one end of the long dining room table, at the other end sat Esmond Rothermere, deep in conversation with two of his editorial staff from the *Daily Mail*. Being extremely inquisitive I edged up as near as possible to try and eavesdrop on their very serious conversation. Only partly could I hear but the gist seemed to be that Churchill had informed all editors that they should break the story of Dunkirk as slowly and gently as possible. On no account make any dramatic announcement which could cause an immediate panic.

I returned to my mess and announced to those still present that the French and Belgian armies had surrendered, the BEF was in full retreat and that the German army was almost at our gates. Having made this dramatic announcement I retired to bed, only to be awoken brusquely at 3:00am by two very grim intelligence officers from Army HQ who demanded to know how and where I had got this information. I was in a real dilemma. I did not want to implicate Viscount Rothermere, who certainly had not breathed a word to me about Dunkirk, so I simply told the truth explaining how foolish I had been to eavesdrop and even more foolish to pass on this garbled version of what I had overheard.

In reality, because of the fast pace of developments most people in Britain knew absolutely nothing of what was occurring on the Continent: in fact they believed the British army to be invincible. So when word got around Bristol that they were bringing the soldiers home, Doreen Govan, a resident of the city, explains that people were confused. They could only assume that whatever soldiers they were, they would be coming home victorious. With this attitude widespread, when it was announced that the army would be arriving at Stapleton Road station, women and children in their droves went down to cheer them on. Those who still had Union Jacks or favours left over from the coronation of King George and Queen Elizabeth took them to wave. There was great excitement, but the sight that met their eyes was not at all what they had expected, as Doreen explains:

> I shall never forget what we saw that day. Train after train was pulling in and unloading soldiers from the carriages. The men were dirty, unshaven and desperately tired: most of the uniforms were tattered. Some soldiers were being helped along between two comrades, some were on crutches, others wearing dirty blood-stained bandages. Word got round that there were French and Belgian soldiers among them. How we cheered those soldiers as they were transferred into buses to be taken to their next destination, which turned out to be Eastville Park. Despite the battle fatigue the soldiers smiled and waved back and some of them threw foreign coins out to the children below. We heard later that the soldiers were bewildered at the enthusiastic welcome home. 'After all, we were defeated' they were alleged to have said. The buses took them off to Eastville Park, which had been hastily commandeered but not barbed-wired. What seemed like hundreds of khaki army tents had been put up in neat rows and the soldiers were posted there for the wounded to be treated and to be given rest before being sent back to their regiments to go where they were needed next.

As an army reservist, the father of Mrs V. J. Lewis, who lived in Coventry and worked at the Courtaulds factory that had then begun to make silk for parachutes, had been called up at the start of the war. He had proceeded to France with the BEF, after which the family heard very little from him except a brief card to say he was well. Then, one morning at about 2:00 a.m., pebbles were thrown at her mother's window. Her husband was standing outside the house. He explained that he had escaped from the beaches of Dunkirk on a boat and after arriving in England had come directly home to let his wife know that he was safe. He stayed a while and then attempted to get back to his regiment. Around the country and under different circumstances, people in this way were beginning to learn the truth about the disaster unfolding in France and coming to terms with its consequences.

As well as the heroic actions of those aboard the ships, there were boundless acts of bravery during the battle that raged around Dunkirk while the troops were being evacuated. Harold Ervine-Andrews, for instance, was a twenty-eight-year-old captain serving in the 1st Battalion, East Lancashire Regiment, who was awarded the Victoria Cross for his gallantry on the night of 31 May/1 June. The company he commanded was holding a position on the Canal de Bergues when it came under intense German fire. The following announcement that accompanied his citation for the decoration was published in *The London Gazette* on 30 July 1940:

His Majesty The King has been pleased to approve of the award of the Victoria Cross to the undermentioned: - Lieutenant (acting Captain) (now Captain) Harald Marcus Ervine-Andrews, The East Lancashire Regiment.

For most conspicuous gallantry on active service on the night of 31 May-1 June, 1940. Captain Ervine-Andrews took over about a thousand yards of the defences in front of Dunkirk, his line extending along the Canal de Bergues, and the enemy attacked at dawn. For over ten hours, notwithstanding intense artillery, mortar, and machine-gun fire, and in the face of vastly superior enemy forces, Captain Ervine-Andrews and his company held their position.

The enemy, however, succeeded in crossing the canal on both flanks; and, owing to superior enemy forces, a company of Captain Ervine-Andrews' own battalion, which was dispatched to protect his flanks, was unable to gain contact with him. There being danger of one of his platoons being driven in, he called for volunteers to fill the gap, and then, going forward, climbed onto the top of a straw-roofed barn, from which he engaged the enemy with rifle and light automatic fire, though, at the time, the enemy were sending mortar-bombs and armour-piercing bullets through the roof.

Captain Ervine-Andrews personally accounted for seventeen of the enemy with his rifle, and for many more with a Bren gun. Later, when the house which he held had been shattered by enemy fire and set alight, and all his ammunition had been expended, he sent back his wounded in the remaining carrier. Captain Ervine-Andrews then collected the remaining eight men of his company from this forward position, and, when almost completely surrounded, led them back to the cover afforded by the company in the rear, swimming or wading up to the chin in water for over a mile; having brought all that remained of his company safely back, he once again took up position.

Throughout this action, Captain Ervine-Andrews displayed courage, tenacity, and devotion to duty, worthy of the highest traditions of the British Army, and his magnificent example imbued his own troops with the dauntless fighting spirit which he himself displayed.

A far less glorious act was perpetrated by the Germans on 27 May, in what is called the Le Paradis massacre. The incident occurred after soldiers belonging to the 2nd Battalion, the Royal Norfolk Regiment, had become isolated. They occupied and defended a farmhouse in the hamlet of Le Paradis, near the village of Lestrem south of Dunkirk, against an attack by the 14th Company, SS *Totenkopf* Division, under the command of *Hauptsturmführer* Fritz Knöchlein. After running out of ammunition the British surrendered and the Germans led them across the road to a wall, where they were promptly lined up and machine gunned. Ninety-seven men died, but miraculously two survived their injuries: Private Albert Pooley and Private William O'Callaghan. After the Germans left, the two men managed to escape.

The following day the Germans returned to the scene and forced local French civilians to bury the bodies. Pooley and O'Callaghan hid for several days until they were captured by a group of non-Waffen SS German troops and taken away as prisoners of war. After the war, Fritz Knöchlein was convicted by a war crimes court, with the two survivors acting as witnesses against him. For his part in the massacre he was executed in 1949. Another mass grave found near Le Paradis in 2007 suggests that around twenty men of the Royal Scots who surrendered to an SS unit may also have been killed in a separate massacre.

A similar fate befell troops of the 144th Infantry Brigade of the 48th (South Midland) Infantry Division, who were holding a road through the village of Wormhoudt on 28 May, also south of Dunkirk. Having exhausted their ammunition, the troops were soon overrun and surrendered hoping to be treated as prisoners-of-war according to the Geneva Convention. Following their surrender, a group of men, which included soldiers from the 2nd Battalion, Royal Warwickshire Regiment, 4th Battalion, Cheshire Regiment, the Royal Artillery and the French garrison of a nearby military depot, were taken to a barn in La Plaine au Bois just outside of Wormhoudt. During the march to the barn the SS soldiers already began to illustrate their brutality by shooting those wounded and in difficulty.

Nearly 100 men were packed inside the small barn when SS troops threw stick-grenades inside, killing many outright, although several were saved by the courage of two British soldiers, Sergeant Stanley Moore and Company Sergeant Major Augustus Jennings, who threw themselves on top of the grenades to suppress the force of the explosion and shield their comrades from the blast. On realising this, the Nazis began shooting their remaining prisoners instead.

In the ensuing panic several British soldiers, including Private Bert Evans, managed to escape to tell the story; others, such as Gunner Brian Fahey, were left for dead. A total of eighty men were killed, including the senior British officer in the group, Captain James Lynn-Allen, who was shot in the head while helping others to escape; fifteen men in the group died shortly afterwards of their wounds. Those that did survive were luckily taken under the care of regular German army medics, who treated their wounds and sent them to hospital before they were forwarded to prisoner-of-war camps. Bert Evans, the last survivor of the massacre, died in 2013.

It was alleged that the troops that carried out the atrocity were soldiers of the 2nd Battalion of the 1st SS Panzer Division *Leibstandarte* SS Adolf Hitler, under the command of *Hauptsturmführer* Wilhelm Mohnke. However Mohnke, who went on to become an SS *brigadeführer* and survived until 2001, was never prosecuted over the massacre – or anybody else for that matter.

Lord Gort and his headquarters staff were evacuated from Dunkirk on 31 May, arriving back in England on 1 June, leaving Major-General Harold Alexander in command of a 4,000-strong British rearguard. Most of these men were themselves evacuated on the night of 2/3 June, with Alexander leaving on the very last ship. General Alexander had remained until the last possible moment, calling out repeatedly across the quayside through a megaphone: 'Is anyone there?' Similarly, Captain William Tennant patrolled the beaches looking for stragglers. Once he was satisfied that there were no more British troops remaining, he sent the message to Admiral Ramsay: 'BEF EVACUATED'. For the next few hours ships continued to pick up French soldiers that had been able to get away. Then, after the last ships had finally sailed, what remained of the rearguard and 40,000 French troops surrendered on 4 June.

Despite sustained efforts, the Germans had been unable to capture Dunkirk during the evacuation and prevent the BEF from escaping. As a last resort, on 31 May General Georg von Küchler, who had led the 18th Army, had been given command of all German forces on the Dunkirk perimeter. He launched an all-out offensive along the entire front, but the French still managed to hold them back until the final ships had sailed. At 10:20 a.m. on 4 June, a swastika flag was hoisted over the docks: the Battle of Dunkirk was finally over.

Between 28 May and 4 June, while the evacuation was taking place, General Weygand had attempted one last operation to exploit the only apparent weakness of the German forces, which lay in the fact that they could be potentially trapped themselves between the Allied armies. He therefore instigated an attack northwards over the Somme to rescue the encircled Allied forces in the Dunkirk pocket and from there mount a decisive counter-attack. The following encounter became known as the Battle of Abbeville, which took place near the French town of that name. The assault was carried out by the 2nd and 4th DCRs of the French army and the British 1st Armoured Division, and comprised 500 tanks and four Infantry divisions. However, in spite of initial Allied success the attack ultimately failed through poor communications and lack of backup.

Between 10 May and the end of the evacuation, the BEF lost 68,000 soldiers: 3,500 were killed and 13,053 wounded, with the vast majority becoming prisoners-of-war. They had to abandon almost all of their equipment in France, from tanks and field guns to ammunition and other small stores. Much of this was left forlorn on the beaches surrounding Dunkirk. Some military chiefs and politicians began to call the evacuation a miracle, but in his speech to the House of Commons on 4 June, Winston Churchill stressed to the nation: 'We must be very careful not to assign to this deliverance the attributes of a victory. Wars are not won by evacuations.' This speech also included one of his most famous quotes:

We shall go on to the end, we shall fight in France, we shall fight on the seas and oceans, we shall fight with growing confidence and growing strength in the air, we shall defend our Island, whatever the cost may be, we shall fight on the beaches, we shall fight on the landing grounds, we shall fight in the fields and in the streets, we shall fight in the hills; we shall never surrender ...

16

OPERATION CYCLE

Although the British Expeditionary Force had been evacuated, the story of Britain's war on the western front in 1940 was certainly not over. For a start, there were still British forces on the Continent, including the 51st (Highland) Infantry Division, which had gone to help out on the Maginot Line as Saar Force. Their fate still hung in the balance. Although the French had been heavily beaten in the north, they had not surrendered, and Britain still had an obligation to fight alongside its main ally.

On 5 June the Germans launched a second operation, known as *Fall Rot* (Case Red), designed to finish off what remained of France's fighting ability. During the events of *Fall Gelb* the Allies had collectively sent their best forces north in a bid to hold the Germans back in the Low Countries. They had lost sixty-one divisions, virtually all of the BEF and the valuable military assistance of Belgium and Holland. In a war that would depend on mobility, they had also lost most of their tanks and much of their other heavy equipment.

The German front line stretched from Sedan to the English Channel: everything to the north of this was now under enemy occupation. In order to stop the *Wehrmacht* from advancing any further south General Weygand was left with only sixty-four French divisions supplemented by the 51st (Highland) Infantry Division. The Germans, by contrast, still had 142 divisions and, just as importantly, they now had total air supremacy over the whole theatre of operations, with the exception of the English Channel where Fighter Command still ruled the roost on a knife's edge.

Hitler's directive number thirteen, issued on 24 May, gives a clear indication how he envisaged the next stage of the war against the Allies. Of course, its first objective, to prevent the BEF escaping back across the English Channel, had failed, although the British had been beaten and eliminated from the equation which, as far as the Germans were concerned, was a satisfactory outcome. The rest of the directive included the following:

The Army will then prepare to destroy in the shortest possible time the remaining enemy forces in France. This operation will be undertaken in three phases:

Phase 1: A thrust between the sea and the Oise as far as the lower Seine below Paris, with the intention of supporting and securing with weak forces the later main operations on the right flank.

Should the position and reserves available permit, every effort will be made, even before the conclusion of hostilities in Artois and Flanders, to occupy the area between the Somme and the Oise by a concentric attack in the direction of Montdidier, and thereby to prepare and facilitate the later thrust against the lower Seine.

Phase 2: An attack by the main body of the Army, including strong armoured forces, southeastwards on either side of Reims, with the intention of defeating the main body of the French Army in the Paris-Metz-Belfort triangle and of bringing about the collapse of the Maginot Line.

Phase 3: In support of this main operation, a well-timed subsidiary attack on the Maginot Line with the aim of breaking through the Line with weaker forces at its most vulnerable point between St-Avold and Sarreguemines in the direction of Nancy-Lunéville.

Should the situation allow, an attack on the upper Rhine may be envisaged, with the limitation that not more than eight to ten divisions are to be committed.

Following Dunkirk, France was in upheaval with millions of refugees trying to escape the Nazis. Families loaded their belongings on to any available motor vehicles or horse-drawn carts, while others simply pushed or pulled hand carts. It is estimated that anything up to ten million French citizens fled, with the vast majority heading south to places such as Bordeaux or Marseille. The population of Chartres, for instance, reduced from 23,000 to only 800. This massed movement of people became known as *L'Éxode*, 'The Exodus'.

After their success in the north, when the *Wehrmacht* launched the opening phase of Operation *Fall Rot* on 5 June, which was to flood the area between the Rivers Somme and Oise, they expected a relatively easy passage. However the French put up much stronger resistance than they had anticipated. One reason why the French 1st Army Group collapsed after it moved up to the K-W Line was because this allowed the Germans to drive a wedge between them and their supplies. In the south the situation was very different, as below the German front line the French armies were closer to their supply and communications lines and maintained an unbroken link with them: here they had access to things like repair shops, ammunition dumps and all other types of stores. All of this helped the troops to function more effectively and kept valuable equipment in the field.

Another factor in this stauncher resistance was the fact that the French armies in the south were being steadily strengthened. By now they had been able to replace the tanks that the 1st, 2nd and 4th DCRs had lost in combat, so they were pretty much back to full strength. Further, around 112,000 French soldiers that had been evacuated from Dunkirk had been rested and reequipped at camps in southern England and repatriated by the Royal Navy through ports in Normandy and Brittany such as Cherbourg and Brest. They had now returned to fight again and morale was high among all participating forces.

With the forces available to him General Weygand considered his best option was to implement what was known in military terms as a 'hedgehog defence'. This was a tactic used against a mobile armoured enemy, in which the defenders would deploy in-depth in heavily fortified positions that had all-round defence capabilities; the attackers would be able to move between the individual hedgehog positions but the defenders would be able to counter-attack from within their strongpoints. If successful this would keep large numbers of attacking troops tied up while at the same time draining their resources.

General Weygand used towns and villages as the central points for his 'hedgehogs' and fortified them along a 360-degrees perimeter. Behind the perimeter, infantry and armoured units would be formed up ready to counter-attack or relieve the units defending the perimeter if necessary; there would also be concentrations of artillery within the central positions. Gradually, the tactic began to pay off.

Forty-eight hours after the start of *Fall Rot* General Fedor von Bock's Army Group B, which had committed forty-seven divisions, had hardly moved. Along the River Aisne, General Erich Hoepner, in command of XVI Corps, had deployed more than a thousand armoured fighting vehicles, which included two Panzer divisions and a motorised division. However the French held them back, and before long Hoepner had lost eighty tanks with nothing to show for it. At Amiens, the Germans were repeatedly driven back by powerful French artillery concentrations from within the strongpoints. Although Hoepner struggled to get his troops across the Aisne, General Günther von Kluge's 4th Army was more successful on the River Somme, where it did succeed in capturing vital bridgeheads.

Frustrated by Weygand's new tactics, the Germans called in the *Luftwaffe* to deliver a decisive blow against the French gun positions, and by the end of the third day of the attack the Germans were beginning to make headway as their enemy began to weaken. To the south of Abbeville, the French 10th Army, under General Robert Altmayer, had its front broken and was forced to retreat towards Rouen and south along the River Seine.

General Erwin Rommel, at the head of the 7th Panzer Division, headed west over the River Seine and through Normandy to capture the port of Cherbourg. On the way he came face-to-face with the British 51st (Highland) Infantry Division. At the time of Dunkirk the division had been pulled back to a new line along the River Somme near Abbeville, where it was attached to IX Corps, commanded by General Marcel Ihler, now part of the French 10th Army. It was given the task of holding a line that went from Érondelle to the coast, a distance of some twenty-three miles, roughly four times longer than a division would normally be expected to hold. As a result it was very thinly stretched.

Peter Hairs, who was serving as a fighter pilot in No. 501 Squadron, has a memory of the 51st from the period between Dunkirk and the commencement of operation *Fall Rot*. At the time his squadron was based at Anglure, to the south of Reims, with the Advanced Air Striking Force and was one of the few RAF units still serving in France:

The date I was shot down in France was, I believe 3 June 1940. At the time the squadron was climbing in line astern when there was a sudden explosion somewhere underneath my seat. As I was not tail-end-Charlie I assumed I must have been hit by some keen French AA gunner and it was not until later that I was told by the chaps flying behind me that a Me 109 had swooped down and fired at me from below with cannon shells. I still have bits of shrapnel in my lower back which were disclosed on an X-ray taken by a chiropractor a few years ago. I landed (wheels up) in a field and a French soldier approached brandishing a rifle. Despite my limited knowledge of the language he obviously realised I was on his side and did not shoot. A number of local people also appeared from the woods nearby (what they were doing there in the middle of nowhere I have never been able to understand) and then two British army officers came crashing through the hedge in a jeep. They took me to their unit, gave me lunch and then drove me to the local railway station where I took a train to Paris. I spent the night there and the next day travelled to Châteaudun only to find that the squadron had moved to Le Mans where I eventually caught up with them.

I believe I was shot down somewhere near Soissons at a place named Saint-Léger-aux-Bois as I still have one of my own visiting cards with a note written on the back by myself at the time as follows: '9th Lancers - Saint-Léger-aux-Bois – 51st Div'. This obviously refers to the unit that looked after me.

Whilst on the subject of events in France there was an occasion when I was flying from Rouen (Boos) to Le Mans and did not have a map for the first part of the trip. I was not unduly worried as I was quite sure I would find Paris and would then be OK as I did have a map of that area. However there was no sign of the city when I would have expected to see it. I did nevertheless find an aerodrome at which I landed. It was quite deserted and scattered with bomb craters so I taxied over to the perimeter fence, got out of my Hurricane, and asked a Frenchman who happened to be walking by 'Ou est Paris?' in my best schoolboy French. He looked a little surprised but pointed in a southerly direction. I took off, flew in the direction indicated and sure enough was soon in sight of the Eiffel Tower. The aerodrome was, I believe, Beauvais.

There was another occasion when the whole squadron was lost and as we were running short of fuel it was necessary for each of us to find an appropriate landing place. I spotted a large grass free area which had signs of vehicles having driven over it, so it looked pretty firm and safe for a forced landing. It proved to be in fact an aerodrome under construction. I found a small group of RAF personnel there and they were able to arrange for some cans of fuel to be brought. I met the officer who was in charge of the stores and strangely enough he was a chap who was at school with me.

The note made by Peter Hairs is interesting because the 9th Queen's Royal Lancers were not technically part of the 51st (Highland) Infantry Division. One of the other major formations still deployed in this part of France following the evacuation from Dunkirk, they belonged to the 2nd Armoured Brigade of the 1st Armoured Division, commanded by Major General Roger Evans. They had been fighting at Abbeville with the French 10th Army but for a very short time had provided support for the 51st.

Between 5 and 6 June the 51st (Highland) Infantry Division came under sustained attack from Rommel's tanks, with the 7th Battalion, Argyll and Sutherland Highlanders taking the initial hit and suffering very heavy losses. The whole division was forced to slowly fall back to positions along the River Bresle.

On 9 June, the French commander at the port of Le Havre sent word to both General Ihler and Major General Victor Fortune, the commander of the 51st, explaining that the Germans had captured Rouen and in so doing had cut their supply lines. The enemy was now moving swiftly towards the coast. Ihler and Fortune decided that their only course of action was to try and evacuate their troops through the port of Le Havre, and a request was sent to the Admiralty for sufficient ships.

The 51st Division consisted of three brigades and its ancillary troops. Fortune decided to detach one of his brigades, the 154th, from his main body to form the basis of Arkforce, under the command of Brigadier Arthur Stanley-Clarke; Arkforce also included two artillery regiments, engineers and a brigade from the Beauman Division. This was an improvised division made up largely of territorial units that had been employed up until then for pioneer and labour duties, and which had now been designated a fighting force under the command of Major General Archibald Beauman. Arkforce was to establish a defensive line about nineteen miles to the east of Le Havre that would allow the rest of the division and IX Corps to retreat towards the port for evacuation. They moved out on the night of 9/10 June towards Fécamp, but during the move lost all communications with the division. Stanley-Clarke made the fortuitous decision to move his own troops to Le Havre.

On 9 June the Admiralty sent orders to Admiral Sir William James, the commander-in-chief of Portsmouth Command, instructing him to arrange an evacuation from Le Havre, codenamed Operation Cycle. He immediately sent a flotilla of ships to France, led by HMS *Codrington*, commanded by Captain G. L. Warren. The flotilla included the British destroyers HMS *Ambuscade*, HMS *Bulldog*, HMS *Boadicea*, HMS *Harvester*, HMS *Broke*, HMS *Saladin*, and HMS *Fernie*; there were also two Canadian destroyers, HMCS *Restigouche* and HMCS *St Laurent*, the New Zealand sloop HMNZS *Wellington*, the corvette HMS *Gardenia*, the minelayer HMS *Hampton*, as well as troop ships and other supporting vessels, including a number of Dutch schuyts, flat-bottomed sailing boats used in the Netherlands originally for fishing or carrying light cargoes. On arrival they discovered that the *Luftwaffe* had severely bombed the port, making the evacuation difficult but still achievable.

Beach parties landed at Le Havre to take control of the evacuation on 10 June, and after a twenty-four-hour postponement, the evacuation began in earnest on 11 June. The embarkation was hindered somewhat by the damage the *Luftwaffe* had inflicted on the port. The troopship SS *Bruges* was crippled by air attack and had to be beached, but nevertheless the operation went smoothly, with the largest number of troops being removed on the night of 12/13 June. By dawn the evacuation was complete and 11,059 British troops had been rescued, with Arkforce among them, although the rest of the 51st (Highland) Infantry Division had not made it to the port in time.

On 10 June Admiral James visited Le Havre himself and ordered his destroyers to check out the smaller harbours to the east of the port to decide whether further troops could be rescued from them. An armada of sixty-seven merchant ships and 140 smaller craft had been assembled for the purpose. One possible location was Saint-Valery-en-Caux, where Allied troops were descending on the harbour and local beaches while others established a defensive perimeter to hold the Germans at bay. However, extremely heavy fog restricted the movement of the ships and none arrived.

At the very eastern end of the perimeter, a successful evacuation was eventually made from Veules-les-Roses, where 2,137 British and 1,184 French soldiers were rescued under heavy fire from German artillery that had set up positions on the nearby cliffs, which also caused damage to the destroyers HMS *Bulldog,* HMS *Boadicea* and HMS *Ambuscade.*

Just before dawn the troops at the harbour and on the beaches of Saint-Valery-en-Caux, which included most of what remained of the 51st (Highland) Infantry Division, were ordered to withdraw back towards the town while a new evacuation plan was decided upon. However, Major-General Fortune discovered that the French commander had already negotiated their surrender with General Rommel. Roughly 6,000 men of the division were subsequently taken prisoner on 12 June. Fortune was among those captured – one of the most senior British officers to be taken prisoner during the entire Second World War. After their surrender the men of the division were marched to Germany via Belgium; their destination was Stalag XX-A at Toruń, in Poland. Their capture also left the door open for General Rommel and the 7th Panzer Division to proceed on to and capture the port of Cherbourg on 19 June.

Serving in a unit of the Royal Army Ordnance Corps attached to the 51st (Highland) Infantry Division was Richard Seddon, who in 1997 wrote an account for me of his service in France and his own lucky escape, which included the following:

On 10 June, our unit was at the tail end of a large convoy trying to reach Saint-Valery-en-Caux on the French coast. I was in the very last truck, because I could speak French and stay with any breakdown whilst it was put right and then get it back in its right place in the convoy - if, that is, we could find where on earth the convoy had got to. As 'other ranks' we were forbidden maps or even to know the route and destination.

We did not know then that the whole Dunkirk withdrawal was over, and as Vivian Rowe describes in *The Great Wall of France*, the French 10th Army and the 51st (Highland) Infantry Division were cut off and Fécamp was already in German hands; due, as Winston Churchill related in *The Second World War Vol II* (1949), to a case of gross mismanagement by the French command.

At noon my truck and the mechanics were at the bottom of a hill with a breakdown, when big bangs somewhere over the crest ahead told us that the front of the convoy was being attacked - from the sound of it by General Rommel's tanks near Saint-Valery-en-Caux where later that day almost the entire 51st (Highland) Infantry Division was to be captured, including our own small RAOC unit - all except us, thanks to the breakdown possibly arranged by my guardian angel. We had guessed that something dodgy was going on, because, approaching Saint-Valery, a written order had been handed up from a military policeman at a crossroads, ordering 'change of route make for Fécamp'.

As I crawled up the hill in the shadows of the roadside hedge to take a look, I was joined by a French 10th Army infantry platoon in pale blue uniforms. Our main convoy was about a mile ahead on the wide plateau of the hilltop, and the tanks sparsely dotted about on the right-hand distance. The convoy was halted and being attacked noisily with some trucks on fire.

The Frenchmen suddenly obeyed a shouted command and went down the hill and away, leaving me alone.

I dodged back down the hill to rejoin the others. As a lance corporal with four privates and a truck I was now in charge; and we held a quick council of war. So far, the Germans did not know we were there. The five of us only had ten rounds of rifle ammunition each and I decided not to waste it on tanks; and obeying the last order, we piled into my truck and set off to get help from Fécamp. Were we lured to that trap by an agent posing as a British military policeman - or was the mismanagement not entirely on the French side? At no time did anyone suggest surrender; though the mechanic and my driver had driven off, and I later learned they had surrendered. We had a vague idea of bringing a unit from Fécamp, with anti-tank guns to knock out the German tanks.

After driving towards the coast for about two miles, we ran into loud machine-gun fire coming from somewhere, and, abandoning the truck which was rather conspicuous, we went down to the shingle beach below the cliffs. We knew that to Fécamp was some ten miles south-west along the shore. The tide was rising, and the tideline on the chalk cliff-face was depressingly above our heads. We gambled on having about two hours to make it.

Everything was open to aerial attack; and under the cliffs, as we trudged, we watched a fishing lugger half a mile off shore going to Fécamp, until two German planes flew over and shot it to a standstill with well-aimed cannon fire. The German pilots could have seen us if we moved about and if they had not been so busy; but they flew away. Then, like a London taxi, a British destroyer came gliding along and hove to by the lugger. They saw us and flashed a signal when we waved. We were a bit puzzled when they then sailed away, and we set off once more for Fécamp, but after we had clambered over the fallen chalk from the cliffs for about twenty minutes, another destroyer hove in sight, which we learned later was HMS *Boadicea*. Their whaler with oarsmen and a petty officer coxswain came into the heavy surf regardless of any Germans on the cliff top, and took us on board - plus one or two army and civilian stragglers who had joined us. As I checked the beach for any others, the whaler had to move out beyond the breakers, and I had to swim to it, holding my rifle above the waves.

Naval historian Peter C. Smith later described in *Hold the Narrow Sea* how the German planes attacked and damaged the first destroyer which was HMS *Bulldog*, and also HMS *Boadicea* who stopped and took us on board, and how they rescued my small group of British soldiers and French civilians. He recounted how the remaining troops on shore had been captured.

The German planes soon returned in force. Three heavy bombs hit HMS *Boadicea* killing eight of the crew. One blew up the boiler room and main steam pipe; another hit the stern and jammed the rudder to starboard and the third failed to explode and remained in the bilges. All this left us with a list and a bulging bulkhead. We had no engines, and no electrics, so no radio and drifted helpless on the calm sea in darkness and silence. Yet, in the small hours, in darkness, the damaged HMS *Ambuscade*, limping home unexpectedly from a similar encounter, discovered the stricken, blacked out *Boadicea* adrift, and, all night and all the next day, towed her gently to Portsmouth. During the day, the Captain read the funeral service with the crew and my squad at attention, when the flag-draped bodies of the gallant dead were consigned to the sea.

While all of this was taking place Peter Hairs and No. 501 Squadron were themselves preparing to evacuate. They had moved from Le Mans to Dinard on 11 June. One of their aircraft, Hurricane L1868, had to be temporarily left behind. Although it was in good shape, the engine failed to start so a small detachment of ground crew was left behind to try and remedy the trouble. Peter was detailed to fly back to Le Mans to pick up the Hurricane and another squadron pilot, John Gibson, flew him there in a French Potez 585. He wrote:

On arrival I found that the Hurricane's engine was still not behaving itself. The mechanics continued working on it and in the meantime my flight commander, PAN Cox (Philip Anthony

Neville) flew over in his Hurricane. He landed and suggested that if the recalcitrant engine failed to start we would destroy the aircraft and both fly back in his machine. He would sit on my lap, as he was not so tall as me and operate the throttle and control column while I coped with the rudder! We hoped this would work but never found out because at long last the crew managed to get the engine started; they hastily replaced the panels and PAN and I took off. The crew set off by road in their truck and all was well. There was not a lot of time for this rescue operation as the German army were advancing rapidly and were likely to arrive at Le Mans at any moment.

PAN Cox mentioned above was a particularly likeable and popular member of the squadron. I first met him at St Athan where he was my flight commander and then he joined 501 Squadron in France, where he again became my flight commander. Unfortunately he was shot down and killed over Dover towards the end of July. He was one of far too many excellent pilots who lost their lives. They were all fine young men.

The squadron eventually flew to RAF St Helier in the Channel Islands on 17 June, from where they carried out patrols over Cherbourg to cover the exodus of service personnel heading out of the port before Rommel and his troops arrived on 18 June. Peter Hairs admitted that his records of France are a little 'scrappy' due to the fact that his logbook from the period together with most of his equipment was dumped in the harbour at St-Malo, from where the ground crew and pilots not allocated aircraft were embarked.

On 19 June, No. 501 Squadron returned to England with their eight surviving Hurricanes. They were reformed and based at Croydon for about two weeks before being posted to Middle Wallop in time for the start of the Battle of Britain.

17

A SECOND BEF

Lieutenant General Alan Brooke, who had commanded II Corps of the British Expeditionary Force in France and Belgium, returned from Dunkirk on 30 May and on 2 June he was summoned to a meeting at the War Office in London. He met with the new chief of the imperial general staff, General Sir John Dill, who had replaced General Edmund Ironside on 27 May. Winston Churchill had appointed Ironside commander-in-chief of Home Forces: in other words the man who was given the responsibility of coordinating Britain's ground defence in the event that the Nazis attempted an invasion of the country. At their meeting, Brooke was informed that he was to return to France to command a second BEF.

Having already escaped from France and being well aware of the military mismanagement of the first BEF by the French, Brooke made it quite clear to both Dill and the secretary of state for war, Anthony Eden, that the enterprise was almost pointless unless it was meant to be nothing more than a gesture of good will towards the French. However, it was an order and Brooke accepted it; but he must have been devastated on being further informed that once in France his troops would again come under the authority of General Weygand.

The troops for this new force would comprise those already serving on the Continent that had not been evacuated at Dunkirk and new units that would be dispatched from Britain. The main troops already in France were the 51st (Highland) Infantry Division and the

1st Armoured Division. Of course, nobody could have predicted at that time that within the next ten days the 51st would be defeated around Saint-Valery-en-Caux and its main body of men taken prisoner.

The 1st Armoured Division, commanded by Major General Roger Evans, began to arrive in France on 14 May. Lord Gort had been pressing for more armoured support for weeks, but when the division did eventually arrive it was seconded to the French 10th Army. The division consisted of the 2nd Armoured Brigade, under Brigadier Richard McCreery; the 3rd Armoured Brigade, under Brigadier John Crocker; and the 1st Support Group, led by Brigadier Frederick R. Morgan. Unfortunately they had no infantry support available because their dedicated units had been transferred to aid the 30th Infantry Brigade. At the time of Brooke's meeting with Dill, the division was still fighting alongside the French at Abbeville and had already suffered heavy losses.

Brooke's forces would also include lines of communication troops and the mysterious Beauman Division, touched upon earlier, which appears to have been a ragtag army of misfits that had been left in France following Dunkirk: after the BEF had moved up to the K-W Line, a lot of support troops or units still under training were left in the area below the River Somme. These troops largely came under the jurisdiction of Brigadier Archibald Beauman from his headquarters at Rouen. There were units of Royal Engineers, Royal Army Ordnance Corps and Royal Corps of Signals as well as lines of communication troops acting as pioneers helping to build and maintain the various bases that supported the BEF, or posted there to protect bases and other facilities such as railways and ports.

After the Germans began their offensive, rail movements between the bases and the front line quickly became difficult due to congestion; the roads also began to clog up with refugees and retreating French and Belgian troops. On 18 May Beauman was ordered by Major General Philip de Fonblanque, the general officer commanding lines of communication troops, to strengthen his defences. He formed a small mobile force that he named Beauforce, which was made up of Territorial infantry battalions that had previously been used to protect his lines and undertake pioneer work. A second formation, called

Vicforce, was also formed out of five provisional battalions that had been employed at various depots, together with reinforcement drafts recently arrived from Britain. This second brigade-sized unit was named after its first commanding officer, Colonel C. E. Vickery.

Beauman positioned his forces along the rivers Andelle and Béthune, in order to protect Rouen and the port of Dieppe. A further force, known as Digforce, was then established by combining units of the Auxiliary Military Pioneer Corps to make up several battalions under Lieutenant Colonel J. B. H. Diggle. These troops were mainly reservists who were not ready to join their units in the front line and had been detailed for construction and labour duties in the rear area.

On 29 May, these three formations were combined to form the Beauman Division, and Beauman himself was promoted to acting major-general in order to lead them. This was the only example of a British army division being named after its commander since the Peninsular War. The use of the word 'division' was to cause a little confusion, as General Weygand and the French assumed it to be a proper fighting formation complete with its own artillery, engineers and signals, rather than an odd collection of largely untrained troops armed only with light weapons and shovels.

In early June, the men of the Beauman Division continued to construct defences along the Andelle–Béthune line, which stretched for fifty-five miles. On 6 June reinforcements of three battalions of infantry as well as some artillery and engineer units arrived. However a complete brigade was subsequently detached to join the part of the 51st (Highland) Infantry Division in Arkforce, which as we have seen was intended to cover the retreat of the main part of the division to Le Havre. Beauman was evidently finding it difficult to maintain contact with all his widely dispersed men and issued the following orders stating that units should hold on 'as long as any hope of successful resistance remained' and that 'brigade commanders will use their discretion as regards withdrawal'.

The Beauman Division would first see action on 8 June when elements of the 5th and 7th Panzer divisions began to advance towards Rouen, with their initial attacks arriving at Sigy-en-Bray and Forges-les-Eaux; at the latter the Germans tricked the British by using captured French tanks to drive through their roadblocks.

Once successfully through the lines, they turned and attacked the novice soldiers from the rear. Despite the support of parts of the 1st Armoured Division, the Allied line had soon been penetrated in several places and the Beauman Division was pushed back. A brave stand was made in the late afternoon by a unit called Syme's Battalion (presumably after its colonel), which had apparently been formed from depot troops the week before and had absolutely no battle experience whatsoever. They managed to stall the Germans for several hours outside Rouen before they were eventually forced to retreat to the south of the River Seine along with the rest of the division.

During the second week of June new forces sailed from Portsmouth to the port of Brest to bolster Brooke's second BEF. These were the 52nd (Lowland) Infantry Division, commanded by Major General James Drew, made up of units of Royal Artillery and Royal Engineers; as well as the 155th Infantry Brigade (Brigadier Thomas Grainger-Stewart); the 156th Infantry Brigade (Brigadier J. S. N. Fitzgerald); and the 157th Infantry Brigade (Brigadier Sir John Laurie). This force was also supplemented by the 1st Canadian Infantry Division, under the command of Major General Andrew George Latta McNaughton. Among the Canadian infantry units that landed at Brest with the division were The Royal Canadian Regiment (RCR), The 48th Highlanders of Canada, and the Hastings and Prince Edward Regiment.

It was hoped that these troops would be enough to help stabilise the French defensive effort, and if that failed to create a redoubt in the Brittany Peninsula. Brooke requested that the 3rd Infantry Division, under Major General Bernard Law Montgomery and which had also just returned from Dunkirk, be made ready to join his new command as soon as possible.

While Brooke's troops gathered in France and he took stock of what forces were actually available to him – as opposed to what he had been led to believe would be available – the RAF found themselves in constant action supporting the French.

By 13 June the Germans had begun to make advances across the River Seine to the west, and the French forces around Paris had begun to retreat. This left General Altmayer's 10th Army isolated with their backs to the coast. The remaining units of the Advanced Air

Striking Force were ordered to retreat towards Nantes and Bordeaux and from there make a maximum effort to support the French. Fairey Battles were used to fly armed reconnaissance sorties over the River Seine and attack German columns, while Bristol Blenheims of Bomber Command were also deployed to attack enemy road and rail movements.

While the military struggles continued, on the political front a penultimate session of the Supreme War Council met at the Château du Muguet, near Briare in France, on 11–12 June. The French government had been forced to leave Paris and the meeting took place at General Weygand's army headquarters. The British were represented by Winston Churchill, Anthony Eden, General Sir John Dill, General Hastings Ismay (Churchill's chief military advisor), General Sir Edward Spears (British representative to the French prime minister) and other staff officers. They met with the French prime minister Paul Reynaud and other dignitaries, including Charles de Gaulle, who had been promoted to brigadier general on 24 May. On 5 June, de Gaulle had been appointed Under Secretary of State for National Defence and War, and had been put in charge of coordination with the British forces.

What would prove to be the final meeting of the council took place at the Préfecture in Tours on 13 June. The British delegation was composed of Churchill, Lord Halifax (Secretary of State for Foreign Affairs), Lord Beaverbrook (Minister of Aircraft Production), Sir Alexander Cadogan (Permanent Under Secretary of State for Foreign Affairs), General Ismay and General Spears. Among those accompanying the French prime minister was Paul Baudoin, the Under Secretary of State to the Prime Minister and a member of the French war committee, as well as Generals Weygand and de Gaulle.

The atmosphere at this final session was very different from the preceding one at Briare, where Churchill had been sympathetic and understanding of France's predicament. Now it was down to business, with the British focusing on the situation from their own perspective.

Reynaud declared that unless immediate help was forthcoming from the USA, the French government would have little choice but to surrender. General Weygand also stated that, in his opinion, an armistice should be sought immediately. This was an awkward proposition because Britain and France had agreed never to conclude a separate peace deal with the Germans. However, by this point France was evidently incapable of sustaining its war effort. Having said that, the French Cabinet was not totally in support of Reynaud and Weygand; General de Gaulle, for instance, was certain that France could continue by using guerilla tactics. Churchill hoped that Weygand would relinquish his command of the French armies in favour of de Gaulle, but the general stood fast.

Churchill was shocked by this development. He insisted, 'We must fight, we will fight, and that is why we must ask our friends to fight on.' Reynaud understood Britain's stance, acknowledging that as an island he could see how it could continue the war. He also affirmed that France could still pursue the struggle from its North African possessions, but only if there was a realistic chance of success. That success could only be guaranteed if America was prepared to join in the fight. The French leader called for British understanding, asking again for France to be released from her obligation not to broker a separate peace with the Nazis, explaining that his country could do no more militarily.

The day ended in confusion as Churchill returned to London without speaking to the French Cabinet, as had been promised by Reynaud. The ministers were dismayed and angry and felt abandoned. Spears believed that this event played its part in swaying the majority of the Cabinet towards surrender. He later suggested that by the night of 13 June any possibility of France remaining in the war had almost disappeared.

In the meantime, the 157th Infantry Brigade of the 52nd (Lowland) Division had occupied defensive positions south of the Siene and been put under the command of the French 10th Army. Lieutenant General Brooke placed all the British units that were now fighting with the 10th Army under the command of Lieutenant General James Marshall-Cornwall and collectively named them Norman Force.

By now it was clear to Brooke that his second BEF was doomed. The 51st (Highland) Infantry Division no longer existed; the 1st Armoured Division was depleted; and the Beauman Division was in total disarray. He sent an urgent request to the War Office asking for his troops to be evacuated, and during the night of 14 June he received orders to prepare British forces to leave through the port of Cherbourg; he was also told that he was no longer under the command of the French. He ordered Marshall-Cornwall to withdraw his forces towards Cherbourg immediately. Although they were no longer obliged to follow French instructions, Brooke decided to continue to cooperate with their ally for the time being.

As by then only the 157th Infantry Brigade had actually arrived at the front line, Brooke ordered the rest of the 52nd (Lowland) Division to adopt a defensive stance near Cherbourg to cover the evacuation of the rest of his force. The AASF was also directed to send the last bomber squadrons back to Britain and use its fighter aircraft to cover the evacuation.

The French government had declared Paris an open city on 10 June, which effectively meant that all defensive measures had been abandoned. This was done so that the Germans could enter the city without being opposed: in doing this there would be no need for them to bomb or otherwise attack the city. The military concept of declaring somewhere an open city was aimed at protecting its landmarks and resident civilians from unnecessary violence. The Germans entered the city peacefully on 14 June and a gigantic swastika flag was raised above the Arc de Triomphe. By the time the tanks rolled through the streets, some two million Parisians had already fled. To a large extent the Germans did respect the heritage and people of Paris, although the Gestapo would arrest, interrogate and spy on those denizens they suspected of subversive activity.

While all of this was taking place the German advance over the Seine had come to a standstill while bridges were built over the river for the Panzers to cross. On the morning of 15 June the 157th Infantry Brigade and elements of the French 10th Army made contact with the enemy to the east of Conches-en-Ouche. They were ordered to retreat to the area near Verneuil, where the British contingent took over an eight-mile front. German forces followed up quickly and on 16 June, General Altmayer ordered the army to fall even further back to the Brittany Peninsula.

France is and was a big country, and while the last remaining British effort was taking place in and around Normandy and Brittany, the rest of the country was also under attack. On the western front, the German implementation of Operation *Fall Rot* was going well, but Hitler's directive had also called for an attack on the Maginot Line. On 15 June Army Group C, led by General Wilhelm Ritter von Leeb, launched Operation *Tiger,* a frontal assault across the Rhine, one element of the much larger Operation *Fall Braun*, the overall name for the invasion in the east across the German border. Prior to this all of their attempts to break through the Maginot Line had failed. One assault lasted for eight hours on the extreme north of the line, costing the Germans forty-six dead and 251 wounded, while the French had only two soldiers killed.

Operation *Tiger* marked a change in strategy with regards to the Maginot Line. The Germans would now carry out a full and direct offensive, employing the full might of their army. When, on 14 June, Paris fell, the German 1st Army went over to the offensive and attacked the Maginot Line between Saint-Avold and Saarbrücken, achieving penetrations in several places. The *Wehrmacht* employed a three prong strategy: first, to weaken the forts' defensive capability through concentrated heavy artillery and bombing; second, to move in close and blind the defenders by destroying apertures with line-of-sight fire from high-velocity 88 mm cannon; and finally, direct combined-arms assault.

Despite having superior weapons, all German assaults at each of the main forts on the Maginot Line had failed. The bunkers were so strong that they had hardly been scratched. Intense barrages by siege cannon and Stuka dive-bombers placed 2,000-lb armour-piercing bombs right on top of the emplacements, but still they caused little or no damage. German assault teams attempting to blow up the forts were unable to get close enough to deliver their explosives. The French pounded their every move with accurate and deadly fire. At the Ouvrage Simserhof, for instance, soldiers from the German 257th Division tried and failed to get close to the fort as almost 15,000 French artillery shells rained down on them. Most of the forts had been designed so that they could be covered by supporting fire from the next emplacement along the line. One fortress, at Schoenenbourg, fired 15,802 75-mm rounds at attacking German infantry. Consequently and by return it was the most heavily shelled of all the French positions.

The same day that Operation *Tiger* was launched, Operation *Kleiner Bär* began as Army Group C's XXXVII Corps crossed the Rhine and advanced through the Alsace region of north-east France, near Colmar, towards the Vosges Mountains. It possessed 400 artillery pieces bolstered by heavy artillery and mortars. The area around Colmar was being guarded by the French 104th and 105th divisions, both of which retreated to the safety of the mountains on 17 June.

On the same date, General Heinz Guderian's XIX Corps, which had been an essential part of Army Group A's spearhead towards the Channel ports, had backtracked to help out in the east. They had reached the Swiss border and in so doing had cut off the Maginot defences from the rest of France. Most units surrendered on 25 June; the Germans claimed to have taken 500,000 prisoners.

One or two of the main fortresses did continue to resist despite repeated appeals for them to surrender from both the Germans and General Georges. The last forts finally capitulated on or around 4 July under protest. Of the fifty-eight major fortifications on the Maginot Line, just ten were captured by the *Wehrmacht* in battle.

Another development to all of these events was the declaration of war on Britain and France by Italy on 10 June, which opened up another front in the Alps. Italy was not really prepared for war but Mussolini hoped to profit from Hitler's success. He had reportedly said to Marshal Pietro Badoglio, his army chief of staff, 'I only need a few thousand dead so that I can sit at the peace conference as a man who has fought.'

The French Army of the Alps, commanded by General René Olry, consisted of 190,000 troops along the Alpine Line. The Italians sent 450,000 men against them, but Olry had no problems stopping their advance. He proved a hard enemy for the Germans to deal with when they decided to enter the theatre. Despite these efforts, Olry's surrender would be a forced inevitability due to the wider political situation, but the performance of the French army in this sector was far more successful than on other fronts and is claimed to be one of the reasons why some areas of the country were later preserved from occupation.

18

OPERATION AERIAL (NORTHERN SECTOR)

Operation Aerial (also Ariel) was the code name given to the final evacuation of British and Allied troops from north-west of France between 15 and 25 June 1940. The participating ports were grouped to form two sectors. Admiral Sir William James, the commander-in-chief of Portsmouth Command, who had already successfully managed Operation Cycle, was given the job of lifting troops from Cherbourg and St-Malo, the most northerly of the ports. Admiral Sir Martin Dunbar-Nasmith VC, commander-in-chief of both Plymouth Command and Western Approaches Command, based at Plymouth, would control the evacuation from Brest, Saint-Nazaire and La Pallice. The evacuation would later also include ports on the Gironde Estuary, Bayonne and Saint Jean-de-Luz.

Despite the fact that the 7th Panzer Division was closing in on Cherbourg, its evacuation proceeded smoothly. Admiral James arranged for a flow of independently routed troop ships and other craft to use Southampton, Poole and Weymouth. Most of the 52nd (Lowland) Infantry Division and the remnants of the 1st Armoured Division embarked between 15 and 17 June, while the following day Lieutenant General James Marshall-Cornwall's Norman Force was rescued. When the final vessels sailed out of the port on the afternoon of 18 June, a total of 30,630 men had been extracted; this included 9,000 troops that had been moved to Cherbourg from Le Havre during Operation Cycle. The next day Rommel's Panzer troops finally took charge of the port.

After the debacle at Dunkirk, Hitler was determined that the *Luftwaffe* would prevent further Allied evacuations. *I. Fliegerkorps*, commanded by Generaloberst (Colonel General) Ulrich Grauert, was assigned to the Normandy and Brittany sectors, and between 9 and 10 June its aircraft subjected Cherbourg to around fifteen tonnes of bombs. Yet during the actual evacuation period itself, bombing on the harbour was relatively light.

Further south at St-Malo, it was the turn of the 1st Canadian Division to be rescued between 16 and 17 June, during which a total of 21,474 men were evacuated. Interestingly, as well as using ships from Portsmouth Command, here the Admiralty called on the authorities in Jersey to provide all available craft to help in the evacuation.

Apparently the potato season was in full swing in the Channel Islands and a number of large cargo vessels were in the harbour at St Helier. These were dispatched to St-Malo along with a flotilla of smaller vessels organised by William Le Masurier, the commodore of St Helier Yacht Club. Luckily, the German troops that had been pressing down on St-Malo were suddenly diverted to attack the airport at Rennes instead. This gave the rescuers enough time to safely lift all the Allied troops present and take them to England without needing to go via Jersey. As well as going to Plymouth, some of the craft went to Dartmouth and other anchorages.

Among those evacuated from St-Malo was Bill Ward, who we met earlier in the book. He was a militiaman serving with the 2/4th Battalion, King's Own Yorkshire Light Infantry. On arriving in France his battalion had been used for labour duties, and in the first instance went to Caen to help build sidings for an ammunition dump; later his unit was swallowed up by the Beauman Division. His epic story of reaching St-Malo, similar to that of Richard Seddon, shows the desperate nature of what these men went through. Many would make their way to the evacuation ports in small groups using their own initiative and dodging the enemy as they went.

Bill Ward takes up the story around the time that the 1st Canadian Infantry Division was being re-embarked from St-Malo and returning to England, which would have been between 16 and 17 June. He remembers his unit becoming part of an emergency division and being sent north by train to help hold the Germans back around Rouen. They de-trained somewhere near Pont de l'Arche on the south bank of the River Seine, to the south east of Rouen, as he recalled:

We had been ordered to hold the line of the Seine to the east of Pont de l'Arche and were split into companies. Our company was asked to hold the most eastern section. Whether the Germans were near or not we had no idea and so we set off marching in sections down the road. A steep hill rose on our right and to the left were fields of ripe corn. We reached a road and hamlet at the foot of the hill; at the junction a team of French artillery men had an anti-tank gun pointing uphill. A steady stream of black French colonial troops were making their way down the hill. It seemed a dangerous place to be but our new platoon commander, Peter Lambeth, who had been posted to us, told me a reverse slope was a classic position to hold and that was what we were going to do. So, in an amateur way, we dug our positions.

Late that afternoon there was a series of enormous explosions from the direction of the river. It was the French engineers destroying the bridges over the Seine. We settled down to wait. Later, we heard the rattle of tracked vehicles on the far side of the hill, so at dawn our platoon commander decided to send a patrol to look. I was chosen with a fellow lance corporal and was sent up the hill and along the line of a hedge, to get a view over the top of the hill. We could see numerous armoured vehicles and lorries. All of them looked black with white crosses and swastikas.

Standing up in the turret of an armoured vehicle which was coming along the road, was a young man wearing a French steel helmet. It must have been a souvenir but at the time, I thought the man was French, so I stood up beside the road. On seeing me, he ordered his gunner to open fire. At the same time the French gunners at the bottom of the road opened up with ferocious explosions. My colleague put the Bren gun he was carrying on my shoulder and began to fire. We then went through the hedge and down the hill as fast as we could. I was deafened by the noise. A German motorcycle and side car was slewing off the road by the armoured vehicles, already firing at us before he stopped. The platoon commander ordered us to withdraw down the hill.

The journey downhill was incredible; young Vallans was hit with a bullet which tore a strip out of his trousers and under pants. This we patched up as best we could with our first aid equipment.

Crossing the road we came under fierce and intense fire from the motorcyclist. Our platoon commander, Peter Lambeth, was hit by a bullet in his leg. Wally Arnold, his batman and I dragged him to safety, behind a cottage, where we tried to patch him up. We could see the bullet but Peter wouldn't let me try and get it out with my knife - and I don't blame him. The machine gunner could see us, but we lay flat on our stomachs and he could not depress the gun sufficiently enough to hit us. The cottage wall was disintegrating behind us.

We found ourselves in some rose bushes and I picked a flower for each member of the section, who put them in the button holes of their battle dress blouses. It brought a bit of hope to our somewhat depressed feelings. The bullets seemed very close now, so with Wally on one side of Peter and me on the other, we made a hasty but clumsy dive for the bottom of the garden, through the wooden fence and into the field full with corn.

We set off through the corn after the others. Peter was wonderfully courageous, hopping on one leg, while hanging on to Wally and myself. It must have been painful but he never complained. Further motorcyclists and armoured vehicles went down a track on our right leading to the river Seine. The armoured vehicles gave no quarter to those who surrendered to them. The Germans made them put their rifles on the road, which they ran over, and then opened fire on them. It was horrendous!

We lay flat in the corn, quiet and out of sight, when we encountered a motorcycle and side car, coming down the lane on our left. Once again the gunner couldn't depress his machine gun far enough, and although he took the tops off the corn above our heads, we remained safe. So, there we decided to stay. Peter's leg was painful, so I had another go at bandaging it. The blood drying on my hands prickled sharply. We finished the water in our water-cans and listened to the German machine gunners, talking nearby.

All day long, from somewhere to the north, heavy artillery bombarded the south bank of the Seine. As we lay in the corn, we could watch the blur of each shell, as it went over the fields, followed by a dull thud and a cloud of smoke. I made drawings of these impacts in my sketch book. We dozed and afterwards, I made a foray to the road. It was narrow, metalled and raised, with a ditch on either side. Coloured French colonial troops were dodging along. One stopped and asked if I was 'blesse' (injured), I replied 'no', and wished him well.

Eventually night fell and a great dark yellow moon appeared in a mauve sky. We could still hear the advanced German soldiers talking nearby but we got on our feet, put our arms round Peter and shuffled to the road. I knew the 23rd Psalm by heart and quickly recited it to my friends. I went ahead: a milk van had rolled over into the field on the right, so I went to collect water from its engine in my steel helmet. The vehicle was smashed and there were bullet holes all over it. The driver was lying dead across his seat and there was no water or milk.

The banks on either side of the road were lined with wounded or dead people. One of them groaned and I could see he was a priest who had been shot. I gave him what was left of my water and he blessed me.

We carried on but Peter kept getting cramp. He bravely continued, until eventually, we reached the river bank. It was thick with vegetation into which we scrambled and lay puffing. I went down to the water, filled my steel helmet and brought it back to Peter and Wally. The water stank like sewerage, and tasted like it as well. Nonetheless, we all took a good, long drink.

We decided that I should go and look for a boat. First, I scoured the side of the river on which we were, but then decided I should swim across the river and look on the other side. It was starting to get light to the east. I stripped down to my vest and under pants. Peter gave me his .38 pistol which I hung by its lanyard around my neck. We shook hands and I waded in. There was a mist over the river as I set off. The Seine was wide at Pont de l'Arche and the pistol became heavy, so I wriggled out of the lanyard and let it go. As I swam, a German sentry watching the river heard me through the mist and opened fire. This didn't deter my stroke and the bullets plopped into the water beside me. It's funny how bullets seem to stop at once in the water.

I crawled over the slippery slimey bank and started my search for a boat, attracting gun fire from the side of the river I had just left. I found a decayed boat, in a derelict state, which I couldn't move. Daylight was gaining and as I moved along the bank a machine gun opened up. The wire fence was cut and sprung apart and I made a dash up the bank. I scrambled through nettles and shoulder high reeds, straight into the fire of a French sniper. I shouted 'Ne tiree pas, je suis anglais', as a great lump of bark flew off a tree by my head. To my amazement a sniper appeared from behind a bush in front of me. There was an anxious few moments as I looked down the barrel of his gun, and at his finger on the trigger. I must have been a comic sight in my under pants and vest. He lowered his rifle and reached deep into the pocket of his overcoat, drawing out a bottle of wine, which he handed to me. I might have been a tee-totaller, but I was extremely thirsty, and I more or less emptied the bottle at one gulp. He hurriedly snatched it back but gave me his overcoat and beckoned me to follow him to his motor bike. I did so, and he took me into Pont de l'Arche. There I met a well-spoken French officer and was told that a small group of English tank men, called Queen's Bays (2nd Dragoon Guards) were a few miles downstream. I was also shown our Sergeant Major suffering from shell shock, who was locked - raving - in a little out house. We then went hunting for clothes. I found a pair of trousers, which had come from a tailor's dummy, blown out of a shop by the bridge. They were fawn coloured and would pass for British army uniform: and they were comfortable. Soon a couple of French boys came back with a battle dress blouse. There were no papers on it but it did for me.

This was a sad day, I had lost all the drawings I had done so far, but it wouldn't be too long before I was getting more done. I took the French lieutenant downstream and showed him where Peter and Wally were still hidden in the undergrowth, on the other side of the river. He promised to get me a boat that night. However, the enemy was very active and Wally decided to swim across the river, just as I had done earlier. Peter Lambeth was taken prisoner and remained so for the rest of the war.

The 30 cwt lorry from the Queen's Bays turned up and I crawled in the back and someone handed me a bottle of beer, which I thankfully cleared. At the Queen's Bays, Major (Lord) Scott, gave me a woollen light weight blanket which some years later my mother made into a dressing gown. At their camp I managed to sleep. Then someone asked for volunteers to go and raid the nearby NAAFI. As a gratefully rescued soldier I went in the lorry with the driver Topper Brown and a couple of lads from the KOYLI. We drove a few miles to the village square where there was a marquee full of NAAFI supplies: bacon, sausages, chocolate, beer, dry bread and blanco, which we gave to the French. They would find it inedible!!

Then it was back to join the Queen's Bays and to our horror they had been attacked by a German armoured patrol. Their one remaining armoured car had been destroyed by close range shell fire; one or two soldiers lay scattered on the ground. We quickly swung out on to the road, Topper putting his foot down to the floor, and headed south. We decided to go to Marseille, but we didn't have a map. I then remembered seeing a wine advert on the walls of most cafés in the area for 'Byrhh'. The advert included a large scale map of France. We stopped at the next café we came to. It was deserted but there was a map on the wall, which I carefully took down and folded, so we could read it from our current position. We continued at top speed, with two of our boys pointing their Bren gun over the tail board of the lorry and about three others armed with rifles in the back. We then noticed a line of dust going ahead of us in the road. Dawning on us what it might be, Topper turned the lorry at right angles into the trees on the roadside. It was a Stuka and we felt safe hidden by the foliage, and there we stayed until the aeroplane had disappeared.

As night was coming on, we looked for somewhere to camp. Then we saw a pair of splendid wrought iron gates at the entrance to a château park. We tugged them half open just enough to get through, went in and closed them behind us. There was a good gravel drive slightly uphill to a fine château. We would be less obvious in the grounds than in the house. We pulled off under the trees, lit a fire and kept a good look out. I had captured a chicken at a farm, wrung the poor creature's neck and hung it in the back of the van. On the way along it had started clucking, so someone had beheaded it and now it was broiled for our supper. A bit crude but we were hungry. A series of guards were chosen, two at a time, while the rest lay on the lorry tarpaulin. I was about the only one with a blanket.

In the very early hours of the morning while it was still pitch black, a sentry shook me with a whispered warning. There was a light under one of the trees a few yards down the path, and when I looked, right enough there was a dim light at the foot of the tree. I borrowed his rifle, fixed his bayonet and quietly (apart from my heart thumping) attacked the light. I gave a good thrust with the rifle, and buried the bayonet into solid tree. It was moss growing round the foot of the tree that was luminous.

The next morning we were up and about early and fetched water from a stream that ran through the trees nearby. We then tucked into our last slice of bread. We also had a little sip of tea left. Then, someone heard the gates we had come through being opened. We were staggered; it was a German motorcycle and side car out of which the gunner had climbed to open the gates. The likelihood of an armoured vehicle being close behind it dawned on us at once. We threw everything into the back of the lorry. I jumped into the cab with Topper, who was still crunching his slice of bread and as soon as I was assured that everyone else was in the back, we were off at top speed. Fortunately the drive carried on around the side and to the back of the château. We had no idea where we were going but happily there was another set of - less elaborate - gates. They were open and we went straight through them onto a narrow road lined with trees. Our Bren gun chattered away at the motorcycle which was now following us, and which was soon joined by an armoured car. We really got up speed. Topper had removed the governor on the engine and the lorry went like a sports car. We sped up a hill and the armoured car and motorcycle were left far behind.

Of all people, we met a guardsman, upright and marching. He was carrying a Bren gun and decided to join us on our way. Then into the road dashed two or three soldiers. They were ack-ack gunners with a Bofors gun and a truck to tow it, which had pulled in. We had a quick conference and decided they should leave the gun and join us. Before doing so, they unscrewed the barrel of the Bofors gun and tumbled it down a slope. They next unhitched the carriage and we helped to push it out the way, then we were off again.

It was rumoured that the Germans were occupying several villages on the road but we roared through each of them at top speed. The gun truck doing its best to keep up. We were now on the road to St-Malo and I think we were told in Avranches that it was still in French hands. At last we saw the town and ran into an enormous queue of British Army vehicles. There was a fuel dump beside the road. Then, immediately behind us, drew up an American ambulance with five very confident young lady nurses. They had been captured by the Germans and then released.

We could see the harbour now and I noticed a beautiful salmon pink yacht, in which we could no doubt get across the Channel, or at least to the Channel Islands. But as we marched in file, myself leading and carrying - I think it was the guard's Bren gun - we were stopped by a staff officer, red tabs and all and directed to the racecourse. Little or nothing was going on there. I personally burgled the NAAFI and stuffed my jacket with Wills Gold Flake packets. I didn't smoke myself but I thought the money would be useful if I could sell them. Our little army then marched to the harbour. A hospital ship was alongside the quay but we were stopped at the gangway as we were armed. Unpatriotically we threw all our weapons in the water. An officer standing nearby, said we could be court-martialed for this and

I said 'provided it was in England we didn't care', and on board we marched, where we were ordered to remove our boots and go up on deck into the bows. The ship was the *St Andrew* and to our delight we sailed within minutes. There were Stukas circling overhead and dropping bombs into the sea, more to discourage us than hit us but it was noisy and frightening. We got something to eat, a blanket each and got down to sleep under the anchor winches. It wasn't the end of our campaign but we sailed top speed to England and arrived in Dartmouth in the early morning. I tried to get some sleep on the quayside, when a well-dressed man, seeing I was still awake asked if my parents knew I was safe. I told him 'no' so he took my phone number and rang up father. It must have caused great rejoicing, as the beaches at Dunkirk had already been cleared. We went to Dartmouth, marching through the streets with a lone piper from a Scottish regiment in front. The town turned out and clapped us as if we were victors not a defeated army. I felt proud though. At the marine barracks I sold my Gold Flake, had a bath with a crowd covered in oil from a torpedoed ship, got new uniform and was sorted out a train with others from my unit, who were dispatched north. I couldn't believe it, when we were bussed from Sheffield station to the army barracks to which I had first been called up. My family all came to see me in turn and how happy a reunion it was. There were many years of war ahead.

From entries in the Admiralty's War Diaries covering the evacuation from St-Malo we can date Bill Ward's story exactly. The HS *St Andrew,* which was a hospital ship, sailed from Plymouth on 16 June and departed from St-Malo with its evacuees on 18 June, arriving in Dartmouth the following day.

19

OPERATION AERIAL (SOUTHERN SECTOR)

During Operation Aerial, Admiral Dunbar-Nasmith had two tasks at the ports in the southern sector. As well as rescuing a large number of British, Polish and Czechoslovakian troops, he also had the job of trying to stop the French Atlantic fleet from being surrendered to the Germans.

About 85,000 Polish troops had been deployed to France, under the command of General Władysław Sikorski, and were still in the process of being established as fighting formations when the Battle of France erupted. This army was partially destroyed during the hostilities, but over 24,000 men would be evacuated to the United Kingdom where they would form a Polish Free Army.

Similarly, the Czech army in exile in France formed a division consisting of about 5,000 men, commanded by General Rudolf Viest. During the battle this unit was involved in heavy fighting, but most of its personnel were evacuated to reform in Britain as the 1st Czechoslovak Mixed Brigade Group.

In the first instance, it seems that Dunbar-Nasmith was not completely aware of the urgency of the situation and his first action was to send senior naval officers to Brest and Saint-Nazaire on 16 June to begin the process of evacuating stores and equipment. This he thought would take about a week to complete. In Britain the War Office had a clearer picture of what was happening, and he was ordered to begin the evacuation of troops immediately.

The evacuation from Brest occurred between 16 and 17 June, during which a total of 28,145 British and 4,439 Allied personnel were rescued. This included a large number from the RAF, mainly ground crews of the Advanced Air Striking Force. There was very little interference from the *Luftwaffe*, who carried out no heavy air raids against the port during the extraction process.

Churchill was worried that the French Atlantic Fleet, which was anchored at Brest, would ultimately fall into enemy hands and had ordered Dunbar-Nasmith to do all he could to persuade the French naval commanders to sail to Britain. However, at 16:00 on 17 June most of this armada set sail for French North African ports such as Casablanca and Dakar, with only a small number steering a course for Britain.

The evacuation from Saint-Nazaire did not go as smoothly as at some of the other ports and certainly drew more attention from the *Luftwaffe*. Saint-Nazaire is situated at the mouth of the River Loire, which is subject to very strong currents so the larger ships had to wait along the shore at Quiberon Bay before moving to the port to pick up evacuees or otherwise have them ferried and boarded offshore. Fifty miles up the river is the port city of Nantes, from where Dunbar-Nasmith was led to believe that somewhere between 40,000 and 60,000 Allied troops were evacuating to Saint-Nazaire, hoping to be evacuated, but he had no idea of when they were expected to arrive.

Lifting this number of men would be a huge undertaking. Dunbar-Nasmith accordingly assembled an impressive rescue force consisting mainly of the destroyers HMS *Havelock*, HMS *Wolverine* and HMS *Beagle*; the passenger liners MV *Georgic*, SS *Duchess of York*, RMS *Franconia* and RMS *Lancastria*; the Polish ships MS *Batory* and MS *Sobieski*; and several commercial cargo ships. Waiting at anchor in Quiberon Bay these ships were very vulnerable to air attack, but British fighter aircraft managed to restrict the *Luftwaffe* to minelaying. However, this in itself caused delays because special ships fitted out as minesweepers would have to sweep and clear the channels of mines before the evacuation ships could move.

The evacuation started on 16 June when MV *Georgic*, HMS *Duchess of York* and the two Polish ships sailed to the port and lifted 16,000 troops before taking them to Plymouth. During the hours of darkness, ships continued to load equipment from the harbour, and two further destroyers, HMS *Highlander* and HMS *Vanoc*, arrived to lend a hand.

Hawker Hurricane fighter aircraft of No. 73 Squadron flew their last sorties from their base at Nantes before flying off to southern England. Unserviceable Hurricanes were burned by their ground crews, who then made their way towards Saint-Nazaire to be evacuated aboard the ill-fated liner RMS *Lancastria*.

The *Lancastria* was built on the River Clyde by William Beardmore and Company for Anchor Line, a subsidiary of Cunard. She was launched in 1920 and was originally called the RMS *Tyrrhenia*. Designed to carry 2,200 people, including three passenger classes and a crew of 375, she made her maiden voyage from Glasgow to Quebec City in June 1922. In 1924 she was refitted for two classes, renamed *Lancastria* and sailed scheduled routes between Liverpool and New York until 1932, after which she was employed as a cruise ship. She was requisitioned by the Ministry of War Transport as a troopship in October 1939 and became His Majesty's Transport (HMT) *Lancastria*.

On 13 June 1940 she was in Liverpool in readiness for dry-docking and essential repairs, including the removal of 1,400 tons of surplus oil fuel. Her crew had been given shore leave although her chief officer, Harry Grattidge, remained with the ship for the initial stages of dry-docking. Around midday he went to the Cunard office, where he was instructed to recall the crew immediately because the ship had to set sail at midnight. Remarkably, all but three of the crew returned to the ship in time, although naturally the repairs had not been implemented.

The *Lancastria* first sailed to Plymouth under the command of Captain Rudolph Sharp and from there, accompanied by another of Cunard's requisitioned ships, the RMS *Franconia*, set off for Brest with orders to proceed to Quiberon Bay. Approaching their final destination the *Franconia* was attacked by a single Junkers Ju88 bomber, which caused sufficient damage for her to be returned to Liverpool.

Later that day the *Lancastria* was ordered to a spot roughly five nautical miles south of Chémoulin Point and nine nautical miles west of Saint-Nazaire, where she arrived early in the morning of 17 June. Here she was loaded with men while at anchorage, with the evacuees being ferried out to her in tugs, tenders and other small craft.

Nobody knows how many people were onboard the ship, but by mid-afternoon on 17 June, estimates vary from around 4,000 to an incredible 9,000; the general consensus is 6,000 plus. Captain Sharp had been instructed by the Admiralty to disregard the limits set down under international law and to load as many men as possible. For a ship that could only comfortably support 2,200, we can only imagine how cramped it must have been, particularly on the upper decks, where men would have occupied every available space.

What is known is that there was a varied group of people on board. As well as RAF personnel there were many of Major-General de Fonblanque's lines of communication troops and men of the Beauman Division. There were certainly Royal Army Service Corps and Auxiliary Military Pioneer Corps troops on board. There were also many civilians, such as embassy staff and employees of Fairey Aviation of Belgium (*Avions Fairey*), the Belgian-based subsidiary of the British Fairey Aviation company that built aircraft for the Belgian government. Its workers had been evacuated to France in order to relocate to British aircraft factories and had ended up at Saint-Nazaire, from where they were taken out to the *Lancastria*.

The *Lancastria* was only one of a number of ships in the area, which soon drew the attention of the *Luftwaffe*. At around 13:50 aircraft attacked and hit the nearby 20,000-ton Orient liner SS *Oronsay*. Although a bomb hit her bridge, destroying her compass and all her navigating equipment, she survived the attack and fortunately there were no fatalities.

The *Lancastria* was by now fully loaded and was given the all-clear to depart, but unfortunately the Royal Navy had no spare destroyers to provide her with an escort. Captain Sharp, concerned about the possibility of being a target for German submarines if she set sail alone, decided to wait for the *Oronsay* to accompany her along with the first available escort destroyer.

While the ship waited a further air raid began, and consequently, at around 15:48, she received four direct hits from Junkers Ju88s belonging to *Kampfgeschwader* 30. This caused the ship to list, first to starboard and then to port, before she finally rolled over and sank, all within the space of twenty minutes.

The sea where the ship went down was covered with leaking oil including the 1,400 tons that had not been removed in Liverpool, much of which was now burning on the surface. Many of the survivors drowned or were choked by the smoke. The ship only carried 2,000 lifejackets and it is probable that some of these would not have been accessed in time. German aircraft also flew over the scene repeatedly, strafing the men in the water with machine guns and using tracer bullets to light up more of the oil slick.

The actual air raid finished at approximately 16:30 and a number of both French and British vessels came to pick up survivors. For instance, the trawler HMS *Cambridgeshire*, which was the first vessel to arrive, took on board around 900, most of which were then transferred to the steam merchant ship *John Holt*. There were 2,447 survivors in total but the number of those who died is unknown. Over the years The *Lancastria* Association, established to preserve the memory of those who perished, has researched a list of 1,738 people who were known to have been killed. However the real figure is unquestionably much higher than that: modern estimates range from between 3,000 and 5,800 fatalities, which would represent the biggest loss of life in British maritime history.

The seriously wounded were taken to Saint-Nazaire for medical treatment but most of those whom were rescued were ferried back to Plymouth. The destroyers HMS *Beagle* and HMS *Havelock* took 600 and 460 respectively; the *John Holt* carried 829; the tanker *Cymbula* another 252; and the liner RMS *Oronsay* 1,557. Lesser numbers were also evacuated in other ships.

Coming amidst the news of so many unfolding disasters, Winston Churchill initially forbade newspaper editors to publish the story, and consequently the sinking did not become common knowledge in Britain for a number of years. The families of those who were known to have perished were simply told that their loved ones died fighting with the BEF in France. Churchill intended to lift the ban after a few days but the disaster was quickly followed by the French surrender, the fear of invasion and the start of the Battle of Britain. Under the intense pressure of these momentous occasions Churchill forgot to lift the ban until he was reminded of it again later in the war.

Later, on the night of 17 June, HMS *Cambridgeshire* was ordered to evacuate the commander-in-chief of the BEF, Alan Brooke and his staff. Because the ship had been involved in the rescue of men from the *Lancastria*, there were no rafts or lifejackets onboard and the decks were strewn with discarded clothing. The ship sailed from Saint-Nazaire at 15:00 on 18 June and arrived in Plymouth late on the afternoon of the following day, having acted as an escort to a convoy of evacuation ships en route.

After the sinking of the *Lancastria* the evacuation from Saint-Nazaire continued, with a convoy of ten ships lifting 23,000 men just after dawn on 18 June; this left only 4,000 still to be evacuated. However, the next part of the operation became slightly frantic as Dunbar-Nasmith was informed that the Germans were about to storm the port. At 11:00 a.m. that same day, further ships picked up the last 4,000 men but failed to retrieve a large amount of military equipment and supplies in their haste to escape.

The next day the Germans had still not arrived, but Dunbar-Nasmith was led to believe that some 8,000 Polish soldiers had reached the port. Seven transport ships and six destroyers were accordingly sent to pick these men up but they could only find 2,000. These men represented the final evacuation from Saint-Nazaire. In total, 57,235 troops had been rescued, 54,411 of which were British, with most of the others being Polish.

Further south, the final place due for evacuation in accordance with Operation Aerial was La Pallice, the commercial deepwater port of the city of La Rochelle. Unfortunately, when the senior naval officer reached here on 16 June, he discovered quantities of soldiers waiting to be lifted but no transports, as all of the ships he had been promised had been sent to Brest and Saint-Nazaire instead. He decided to requisition some cargo ships that he found in the harbour and embarked the troops on these, although again all their vehicles and equipment were left behind. This convoy eventually got away safely on 18 June.

On two occasions after La Pallice had been cleared, Dunbar-Nasmith was informed that further troops had reached the port.

Twice he ordered ships to fetch them away. On 19 June around 4,000 Polish troops were embarked, but the following day very few men were found. As well as the Poles, 2,303 British soldiers were also rescued from La Pallice. This marked the end of Operation Aerial as it had originally been planned; but by now things had moved on again and there were stories of more troops gathering even further south.

The ships that were left empty at La Pallice and therefore not required were sent further south again to Bordeaux, which nestled along the River Gironde. There were now practically no British troops left in France but there were embassy and consular staffs to be brought away, as well as considerable numbers of Polish and Czech troops and British and foreign civilians desperate to leave France before the German conquest was complete.

The first British ships arrived in the Gironde estuary on 16 June. These were the cruiser HMS *Arethusa* and the destroyer HMS *Berkeley*. They carried the senior naval officers given the task of directing these final rounds of evacuations. After delivering her passengers, the *Arethusa* was stationed off Bordeaux to act as a radio and communications centre. The next day all British and some Allied shipping in the port was ordered to make their way to England, while the embarkation of Czech and Polish troops and civilians began. Similar traffic continued through the next two days, with several thousand souls evacuated.

On 19 June the destroyer HMS *Berkeley* took aboard the various embassy and consular staffs that had made their way to Bordeaux and transferred them to the *Arethusa*. The *Berkeley* was then relieved by the cruiser HMS *Galatea* and sailed back to Plymouth with the president of Poland, Władysław Raczkiewicz, and many of his ministers and a number of other important dignitaries on board. Embarkation of Allied troops and civilians continued meanwhile from Le Verdon-sur-Mer, at the mouth of the River Gironde, where a large contingent of 6,000 Polish troops had arrived.

The operation continued to stretch further south where the Polish ships MS *Batory* and MS *Sobieski* and the liners MV *Ettrick* and SS *Arandora Star* went to Bayonne, where between 19 and 20 June they rescued roughly 9,000 men. These ships then continued on to Saint Jean-de-Luz, very close to the border with Spain, where poor weather delayed the start of the evacuation until 24 June. The British ambassador to France, Sir Ronald Campbell, stayed with the French government, which had moved from Paris to Bordeaux, until 23 June, then made his way to Arcachon before finally being evacuated from Saint Jean-de-Luz.

On the political front, Paul Reynaud had resigned as prime minister of France on 16 June, in the belief that he had lost the support of his Cabinet. He was succeeded by Marshal of France Philippe Pétain, who delivered a radio address to the French people announcing his intention to seek an armistice with Nazi Germany. At 18:36 on 22 June the French effectively surrendered, when they signed the armistice near Compiègne, which would take effect after midnight on 25 June. Signatories for Germany included Wilhelm Keitel, the commander-in-chief of the *Wehrmacht*, while those on the French side were more junior, such as General Charles Huntziger. This agreement established a German occupation zone in northern and western France that encompassed all English Channel and Atlantic ports. Italy also received a small zone in the south-east, and an unoccupied zone would be governed by the newly formed Vichy government led by Philippe Pétain which, though officially neutral, was generally aligned with the Nazis.

When Hitler received word from the French government that they wished to negotiate an armistice, he symbolically selected the Compiègne Forest as the site for the negotiations, as this was the site of the 1918 armistice ending the First World War. Hitler considered this location to be the ultimate revenge for Germany over France. With that said, in the final sentence of the preamble the drafters inserted the following: 'Germany does not have the intention to use the armistice conditions and armistice negotiations as a form of humiliation against such a valiant opponent.' Furthermore, in Article 3, Clause 2, the drafters stated that their intention was not to heavily occupy France after the cessation of hostilities.

So, on 21 June 1940, in the very same railway carriage in which the 1918 armistice had been signed, which had been retrieved from a museum and placed on the precise spot where it was located in 1918, Hitler sat in the same chair in which Marshal Ferdinand Foch had sat when he faced the representatives of the defeated German Empire.

After listening to the reading of the preamble, Hitler left the carriage, just as Foch had done in 1918, leaving the negotiations to the high command of the armed forces, namely Keitel. The negotiations lasted one day, until the evening of 22 June 1940. General Huntziger had to discuss the terms by telephone with the French government representatives in Bordeaux, mainly with the newly nominated defence minister, General Maxime Weygand.

Soon news of the armistice had reached the French authorities in the various ports, who informed the British that all evacuations must end at noon on 25 June. Despite this, the last troopship did not leave until 14:30 on that day after a total of 19,000 military personnel, mostly Polish troops, were rescued from Bayonne and Saint Jean-de-Luz.

In defiance of French instructions, a final set of evacuations took place from ports along the Mediterranean coast of France, including Sète, from 24 and 26 June. From here, another 10,000 troops, mostly Polish and Czechoslovakian, as well as a few civilian refugees embarked for Gibraltar before moving on to England. One of the Czech soldiers was Franta Belsky, who prior to the war had been an art student in London, as he recalled:

> I had just started at the Central School of Art in London and hearing that a Czechoslovak army was being formed in France, I trotted off to the embassy and joined up - I was eighteen. We were impatient for the first transport to go and I waited and sculpted and had time to take my entrance to the Royal College of Art before we left.
>
> We crossed the Channel with British troops but as civilians - oh, those eggs and bacon served to them. We entrained at Le Havre for a journey across chaotic France, taking five days and four nights. We kept stopping all the way and I kept asking the railwaymen for coloured chalks and started decorating the front of the engine, gradually down the sides of the train: with a panorama of the Prague castle, slogans, songs, fighting soldiers.
>
> On arrival at the depot camp in Agde (a concentration camp built for the Spanish Civil War Republican refugees) I was called to the education officer: would I like to stay as the resident artist? 'Sir, I came to fight; kindly send me to a unit', was my reply.

I still designed a few field post stamps and badges before getting to a battery of First World War horse drawn 75's.

We were idealistic students, all lumped together under ex-Foreign Legion NCOs. We decided to ask for a transfer to a new crack anti-tank battery. We lived to see the Fall of France - the sister battery had eleven survivors. Cut off from everywhere except the Southern ports my lot made for Sète. Rumours abounded that we were going to Africa, to the Foreign Legion - we would have gone anywhere.

Back in London, unknown to us, the exiled president Edvard Beneš asked Churchill for help. Instantly he diverted cargo ships to pick us up, take us to Gibraltar and from there to England, where we landed five weeks after the Dunkirk evacuation. We entered the British Army, swore allegiance to The King and regrouped in Cholmondeley Park.

After the war Franta Belsky became a notable sculptor, Among his most important works is the Royal Air Force Memorial in Prague, which celebrates Czechs who served with the RAF during the war.

Collectively, operations Cycle and Aerial accounted for the rescue of 191,870 military personnel. This figure comprised 144,171 British, 18,246 French, 24,352 Polish, 4,938 Czechs and 163 Belgians; also rescued were 310 artillery guns, 2,292 vehicles, and 1,800 tons of stores. However, most equipment, especially tanks and other heavy vehicles, had to be left behind. When combined with Operation Dynamo, a total of 558,032 men were rescued from the French ports.

Although the BEF had now been completely evacuated and all British forces had been returned home, there was still one pressing issue which Churchill felt he had to deal with. Although the French army had surrendered, its navy, one of the greatest in the world, remained intact. Churchill was still fearful that its ships would be delivered up to the Nazis, even though their commander, Admiral François Darlan, insisted that they would not. However, Churchill was not prepared to take the gamble and tried to convince his War Cabinet that attacking the French fleet was their best course of action. The Cabinet was not convinced as they still considered France to be a friendly power. Churchill demanded that the French fleet either surrendered to Britain, or sailed to British ports. Darlan refused, and Churchill finally got the backing of his War Cabinet and ordered an attack on the French ships.

On 3 July the British surrounded the French fleet at the port of Mers-el-Kebir outside Oran in Algeria. Churchill sent Darlan a message to sail his ships to Britain or the USA, or to scuttle them within six hours. The French showed the British an order they had received from Darlan instructing them to sail the ships to the USA if the Germans broke the armistice and demanded them.

Meanwhile, the British intercepted a message from the Vichy government ordering French reinforcements to move urgently to Oran. Churchill was through playing games and ordered the attack to his commanders. An hour and a half later the British attacked. In less than ten minutes, 1,297 French personnel were dead and three battleships were sunk. One battleship and five destroyers managed to escape.

While the French were furious over these events, the reaction in England was the exact opposite. The day after the attack Churchill went to the House of Commons to explain why he had ordered it. For the first time since taking office as prime minister, Churchill received a unanimous standing ovation.

Britain now stood completely alone, with only her Commonwealth partners to lend support. The Germans were positioned all along the French Atlantic and Channel coasts, and Hitler ordered his military chiefs to draw up plans for the invasion of the country belonging to his one undefeated enemy. For the people of Great Britain the darkest days were still ahead, as Churchill announced to the nation:

What General Weygand has called the Battle of France is over ... the Battle of Britain is about to begin. Upon this battle depends the survival of Christian civilisation. Upon it depends our own British life, and the long continuity of our institutions and our Empire. The whole fury and might of the enemy must very soon be turned on us. Hitler knows that he will have to break us in this island or lose the war. If we can stand up to him, all Europe may be freed and the life of the world may move forward into broad, sunlit uplands.

But if we fail, then the whole world, including the United States, including all that we have known and cared for, will sink into the abyss of a new dark age made more sinister, and perhaps more protracted, by the lights of perverted science. Let us therefore brace ourselves to our duties, and so bear ourselves, that if the British Empire and its Commonwealth last for a thousand years, men will still say, this was their finest hour.

APPENDIX I

Corps and divisional units serving with the First British Expeditionary Force, excluding Royal Artillery, Royal Engineers, Royal Corps of Signals and Headquarters Troops.

1st Army Tank Brigade: Brigadier D. H. Pratt DSO MC
    4th (Battalion) Royal Tank Regiment
    7th (Battalion) Royal Tank Regiment
1st Light Armoured Reconnaissance Brigade: Brigadier Charles Wake Norman CBE
    1st East Riding Yeomanry
    1st Fife and Forfar Yeomanry
    12th Royal Lancers (Prince of Wales's)
5th Infantry Division: Major General Harold Franklyn KCB DSO MC
13th Infantry Brigade: Brigadier Miles Christopher Dempsey GBE KCB DSO MC
    2nd Battalion, Cameronians (Scottish Rifles)
    2nd Battalion, Royal Inniskilling Fusiliers
    2nd Battalion, Wiltshire Regiment
17th Infantry Brigade: Brigadier Montagu George North Stopford GCB KBE DSO MC
    2nd Battalion, Royal Scots Fusiliers
    2nd Battalion, Northamptonshire Regiment
    6th Battalion, Seaforth Highlanders

I Corps: Lieutenant General Michael George Henry Barker CB DSO
    Corps Troops:

4th Battalion, Cheshire Regiment (Divisional Machine Gun Battalion)
6th Battalion, Argyll and Sutherland Highlanders (Machine Gun Battalion)
6th Battalion, King's Own Royal Regiment (Lancaster) (Pioneer)
7th Battalion, King's Own Royal Regiment (Lancaster) (Pioneer)
1st Infantry Division: Major General Harold Rupert Leofric George Alexander KG GCB OM GCMG CSI DSO MC
13th/18th Royal Hussars (Divisional Cavalry)
2nd Battalion, Cheshire Regiment (Machine Gun Battalion)
1st Guards Brigade: Brigadier Merton Beckwith-Smith DSO MC MA
    3rd Battalion, Grenadier Guards
    2nd Battalion, Coldstream Guards
    2nd Battalion, Hampshire Regiment
2nd Infantry Brigade: Brigadier Charles Edward Hudson VC CB DSO & Bar MC
    1st Battalion, Loyal Regiment (North Lancashire)
    2nd Battalion, North Staffordshire Regiment
    6th Battalion, Gordon Highlanders
3rd Infantry Brigade: Brigadier T. N. F. Wilson
    1st Battalion, Duke of Wellington's Regiment
    2nd Battalion, Sherwood Foresters
    1st Battalion, King's Shropshire Light Infantry
2nd Infantry Division: Major General H. C. Lloyd
4th/7th Royal Dragoon Guards (Divisional Cavalry)
2nd Battalion, Manchester Regiment (Machine Gun Battalion)
4th Infantry Brigade: Brigadier E. G. Warren
    1st Battalion, Royal Scots
    2nd Battalion, Royal Norfolk Regiment
    1/8th Battalion, Lancashire Fusiliers
5th Infantry Brigade: Brigadier G. I. Gartlan CBE DSO MC
    1st Battalion, Queen's Own Cameron Highlanders
    2nd Battalion, Dorsetshire Regiment
    7th Battalion, Worcestershire Regiment
6th Infantry Brigade: Brigadier Noel Mackintosh Stuart Irwin CB DSO & Two Bars MC
    1st Battalion, Royal Welch Fusiliers
    1st Battalion, Royal Berkshire Regiment
    2nd Battalion, Durham Light Infantry
48th (South Midland) Infantry Division: Major General Augustus Francis Andrew Nicol Thorne KCB CMG DSO & Two Bars DL
4th Battalion, Cheshire Regiment (Machine Gun Battalion)
143rd Infantry Brigade: Brigadier James Muirhead MC
    1st Battalion, Oxfordshire and Buckinghamshire Light Infantry
    1/7th Battalion, Royal Warwickshire Regiment

8th Battalion, Royal Warwickshire Regiment
144th Infantry Brigade: Brigadier James Melvill Hamilton
    2nd Battalion, Royal Warwickshire Regiment
    5th Battalion, Gloucestershire Regiment
    8th Battalion, Worcestershire Regiment
145th Infantry Brigade: Brigadier Archibald Cecil Hughes
    2nd Battalion, Gloucestershire Regiment
    4th Battalion, Oxfordshire and Buckinghamshire Light Infantry
    1st (Buckinghamshire) Battalion, Oxfordshire and Buckinghamshire Light Infantry
II Corps: Lieutenant General Alan Francis Brooke KG GCB OM GCVO DSO & Bar
Corps Troops:
    8th Battalion, Middlesex Regiment (Machine Gun Battalion)
    4th Battalion, Gordon Highlanders (Machine Gun Battalion)
    8th Battalion, King's Own Royal Regiment (Lancaster) (Pioneer)
    9th Battalion, King's Own Royal Regiment (Lancaster) (Pioneer)
3rd Infantry Division: Major General Bernard Law Montgomery KG GCB DSO PC
    15th/19th The King's Royal Hussars (Divisional Cavalry)
    1/7th Battalion, Middlesex Regiment (Machine Gun Battalion)
    2nd Battalion, Middlesex Regiment (Machine Gun Battalion)
7th Guards Brigade: Brigadier John A. C. Whitaker
    1st Battalion, Grenadier Guards
    2nd Battalion, Grenadier Guards
    1st Battalion, Coldstream Guards
8th Infantry Brigade: Brigadier Frank Hole Witts DSO MC
    1st Battalion, Suffolk Regiment
    2nd Battalion, East Yorkshire Regiment
    4th Battalion, Royal Berkshire Regiment
9th Infantry Brigade: Brigadier W. Robb
    2nd Battalion, Lincolnshire Regiment
    1st Battalion, King's Own Scottish Borderers
    2nd Battalion, Royal Ulster Rifles
4th Infantry Division: Major General Dudley Graham Johnson VC CB DSO & Bar MC
5th Royal Inniskilling Dragoon Guards (Divisional Cavalry)
2nd Battalion, Royal Northumberland Fusiliers (Machine Gun Battalion)
10th Infantry Brigade: Brigadier Evelyn Hugh Barker KCB KBE DSO MC
    2nd Battalion, Bedfordshire and Hertfordshire Regiment
    2nd Battalion, Duke of Cornwall's Light Infantry
    1/6th Battalion, East Surrey Regiment
11th Infantry Brigade: Brigadier Kenneth Arthur Noel Anderson KCB MC

2nd Battalion, Lancashire Fusiliers
1st Battalion, East Surrey Regiment
5th (Huntingdonshire) Battalion, Northamptonshire Regiment
12th Infantry Brigade: Brigadier John Ledlie Inglis Hawkesworth KBE
    CB DSO and Bar
    2nd Battalion, Royal Fusiliers
    1st Battalion, South Lancashire Regiment
    6th Battalion, Black Watch (Royal Highland Regiment)
50th (Northumbrian) Motor Infantry Division: Major General Giffard Le
    Quesne Martel KCB KBE DSO MC
4th Battalion, Royal Northumberland Fusiliers (Motorcycle Battalion)
150th Infantry Brigade: Brigadier Cecil William Haydon DSO MC
    4th Battalion, East Yorkshire Regiment
    4th Battalion, Green Howards
    5th Battalion, Green Howards
151st Infantry Brigade: Brigadier J. A. Churchill
    6th Battalion, Durham Light Infantry
    8th Battalion, Durham Light Infantry
    9th Battalion, Durham Light Infantry
25th Infantry Brigade: Brigadier William Havelock Ramsden CB CBE
    DSO MC
    1/7th Battalion, Queen's Royal Regiment (West Surrey)
    2nd Battalion, Essex Regiment
    1st Battalion, Royal Irish Fusiliers
III Corps: Lieutenant General Sir Ronald Forbes Adam GCB DSO OBE
Corps Troops:
    1/9th Battalion, Manchester Regiment (Machine Gun Battalion)
    1/6th Battalion, South Staffordshire Regiment (Pioneer)
42nd (East Lancashire) Infantry Division: Major General William George
    Holmes KBE CB DSO and Bar
125th Infantry Brigade: Brigadier G. W. Sutton
    1st Battalion, Border Regiment
    1/5th Battalion, Lancashire Fusiliers
    1/6th Battalion, Lancashire Fusiliers
126th Infantry Brigade: Brigadier Eric Grant Miles CB DSO MC
    1st Battalion, East Lancashire Regiment
    5th Battalion, King's Own Royal Regiment (Lancaster)
    5th Battalion, Border Regiment
127th Infantry Brigade: Brigadier John George Smyth VC MC PC
    4th Battalion, East Lancashire Regiment
    5th Battalion, Manchester Regiment
    1st Battalion, Highland Light Infantry

44th (Home Counties) Infantry Division: Major General Edmund Archibald Osborne CB DSO

131st Infantry Brigade: Brigadier John Edward Utterson-Kelso CB DSO OBE MC

    2nd Battalion, Buffs (Royal East Kent Regiment)

    1/5th Battalion, Queen's Royal Regiment (West Surrey)

    1/6th Battalion, Queen's Royal Regiment (West Surrey)

132nd Infantry Brigade: Brigadier James Stuart Steele GCB KBE DSO MC

    1st Battalion, Queen's Own Royal West Kent Regiment

    4th Battalion, Queen's Own Royal West Kent Regiment

    5th Battalion, Queen's Own Royal West Kent Regiment

133rd Infantry Brigade: Brigadier N. I. Whitty DSO

    2nd Battalion, Royal Sussex Regiment

    4th Battalion, Royal Sussex Regiment

    5th Battalion, Royal Sussex Regiment

Saar Force: Major General Victor Morven Fortune KBE CB DSO

51st (Highland) Infantry Division: Major General Victor Morven Fortune KBE CB DSO

152nd Infantry Brigade: Brigadier H. W. V. Stewart DSO

    2nd Battalion, Seaforth Highlanders

    4th Battalion, Seaforth Highlanders

    4th Battalion, Queen's Own Cameron Highlanders

153rd Infantry Brigade: Brigadier G. T. Burnet MC

    4th Battalion, Black Watch (Royal Highland Regiment)

    1st Battalion, Gordon Highlanders

    5th Battalion, Gordon Highlanders

154th Infantry Brigade: Brigadier A. C. L. Stanley-Clarke DSO

    1st Battalion, Black Watch (Royal Highland Regiment)

    7th Battalion, Argyll and Sutherland Highlanders

    8th Battalion, Argyll and Sutherland Highlanders

Divisions undergoing training or performing labour duties.

12th (Eastern) Infantry Division: Major General Roderic Loraine Petre CB DSO MC

35th Infantry Brigade: Brigadier Euston Edward Francis Baker CB CBE DSO MC

    2/5th Battalion, Queen's Royal Regiment (West Surrey)

    2/6th Battalion, Queen's Royal Regiment (West Surrey)

    2/7th Battalion, Queen's Royal Regiment (West Surrey)

36th Infantry Brigade: Brigadier George Rowland Patrick Roupell VC CB

    5th Battalion, Buffs (Royal East Kent Regiment)

    6th Battalion, Queen's Own Royal West Kent Regiment

    7th Battalion, Queen's Own Royal West Kent Regiment

37th Infantry Brigade: Brigadier R. J. P. Wyatt MC

2/6th Battalion, East Surrey Regiment
6th Battalion, Royal Sussex Regiment
7th Battalion, Royal Sussex Regiment
23rd (Northumbrian) Infantry Division: Major General A. E. Herbert
8th Battalion, Royal Northumberland Fusiliers (Motorcycle Battalion)
9th Battalion, Royal Northumberland Fusiliers (Machine Gun Battalion)
69th Infantry Brigade:
    5th Battalion, East Yorkshire Regiment
    6th Battalion, Green Howards
    7th Battalion, Green Howards
70th Infantry Brigade: Brigadier Philip Kirkup DSO OBE MC TD
    10th Battalion, Durham Light Infantry
    11th Battalion, Durham Light Infantry
    1st Battalion, Tyneside Scottish
46th (West Riding) Infantry Division: Major-General H. O. Curtis
2/7th Battalion, Middlesex Regiment (Machine Gun Battalion)
137th Infantry Brigade:
    2/5th Battalion, West Yorkshire Regiment
    2/6th Battalion, Duke of Wellington's Regiment
    2/7th Battalion, Duke of Wellington's Regiment
138th Infantry Brigade: Brigadier Edward John Grinling DSO MC TD
    6th Battalion, Lincolnshire Regiment
    2/4th Battalion, King's Own Yorkshire Light Infantry
    6th Battalion, York and Lancaster Regiment
139th Infantry Brigade:
    2/5th Battalion, Leicestershire Regiment
    2/5th Battalion, Sherwood Foresters
    9th Battalion, Sherwood Foresters

APPENDIX II

German Divisions in Army Groups A, B and C
Army Group A:
Officer in Command: General Gerd von Rundstedt
Chief of Staff: Lieutenant General Georg von Sodenstern

4th Army:
Officer in Command: General Günther von Kluge
Chief of Staff: Major General Kurt Brennecke
II Corps: General of Infantry Adolf Strauß
 12th Infantry Division: Major General Walther von Seydlitz-Kurzbach
 32nd Infantry Division: Lieutenant General Franz Böhme
V Corps: General of Infantry Richard Ruoff
 211th Infantry Division: Major General Kurt Renner
 251st Infantry Division: Major General Hans Kratzert
 263rd Infantry Division: Major General Franz Karl
VIII Corps: General of Infantry Walter Heitz
 8th Infantry Division: Major General Rudolf Koch-Erpach
 28th Infantry Division: Lieutenant General Hans von Obstfelder
 87th Infantry Division: Major General Bogislav von Studnitz
 267th Infantry Division: Major General Ernst Feßmann
XV Corps: General of Infantry Hermann Hoth
 5th Panzer Division: Major General Max von Hartlieb-Walsporn
 7th Panzer Division: Major General Erwin Rommel
 62nd Infantry Division: Major General Walter Keiner

12th Army:
Officer in Command: General Wilhelm List
Chief of Staff: Major General Eberhard von Mackensen
III Corps: General of Artillery Curt Haase
    3rd Infantry Division: Major General Walter Lichel
    23rd Infantry Division: Major General Walter von Brockdorff-Ahlefeldt
    52nd Infantry Division: Major General Hans-Jürgen von Arnim
VI Corps: General of Engineers Otto-Wilhelm Förster
    16th Infantry Division: Brigadier General Heinrich Krampf
    24th Infantry Division: Brigadier General Justin von Obernitz
XVIII Corps: General of Infantry Eugen Beyer
    5th Infantry Division: Major General Wilhelm Fahrmbacher
    21st Infantry Division: Brigadier General Otto Sponheimer
    25th Infantry Division: Major General Erich Clößner
    1st Mountain Division: Major General Ludwig Kübler

16th Army:
Officer in Command: General of Infantry: Ernst Busch
Chief of Staff: Brigadier General Walter Model
VII Corps: General of Infantry Eugen Ritter von Schobert
    36th Infantry Division: Major General Georg Lindemann
    68th Infantry Division: Brigadier General Georg Braun
XIII Corps: Major General Heinrich von Vietinghoff
    15th Infantry Division: Brigadier General Friedrich-Wilhelm von
        Chappuis
    17th Infantry Division: Brigadier General Herbert Loch
    10th Infantry Division: Brigadier General Konrad von Cochenhausen
XXIII Corps: Major General Albrecht Schubert
    34th Infantry Division: Brigadier General Hans Behlendorff
    58th Infantry Division: Brigadier General Iwan Heunert
    76th Infantry Division: Brigadier General Maximilian de Angelis
    26th Infantry Division: Brigadier General Sigismund von Förster

Panzer Group Kleist:
Officer in Command: General of Cavalry Paul Ludwig Ewald von Kleist
Chief of Staff: Brigadier General Kurt Zeitzler
XIV Corps: General of Infantry Gustav Anton von Wietersheim
    2nd Infantry Division (motorised): Major General Paul Bader

13th Infantry Division (motorised): Brigadier General Friedrich-Wilhelm von Rothkirch und Panthen

29th Infantry Division (motorised): Brigadier General Willibald von Langermann und Erlencamp

XXXXI Corps: Major General Georg-Hans Reinhardt

    6th Panzer Division: Brigadier General Werner Kempf

    8th Panzer Division: Colonel Erich Brandenberger

XIX Corps: General of Cavalry Heinz Guderian

    2nd Panzer Division: Major General Rudolf Veiel

    1st Panzer Division: Major General Friedrich Kirchner

    10th Panzer Division: Major General Ferdinand Schaal

Reserves:

XXXX Corps: Major General Georg Stumme

    6th Infantry Division: Major General Arnold Freiherr von Biegeleben

    9th Infantry Division: Major General Georg von Apell

    4th Infantry Division: Major General Erick-Oskar Hansen

    27th Infantry Division: Major General Friedrich Bergmann

    71st Infantry Division: Major General Karl Weisenberger

    73rd Infantry Division: Major General Bruno Bieler

Army Group B:

Officer in Command: General Fedor von Bock

Chief of Staff: Lieutenant General Hans von Salmuth

6th Army:

Officer in Command: General Walther von Reichenau

Chief of Staff: Major General Friedrich Paulus

XVI Corps: General of Cavalry Erich Hoepner

    33rd Infantry Division: Major General Rudolf Sintzenich

    3rd Panzer Division: Brigadier General Horst Stumpff

    4th Panzer Division: Brigadier General Ludwig Ritter von Radlmeier

IV Corps: General of Infantry Viktor von Schwedler

    205th Infantry Division: Major General Ernst Richter

XI Corps: Major General Joachim von Kortzfleisch

    7th Infantry Division: Brigadier General Eccard Freiherr von Gablenz

    211th Infantry Division: Brigadier General Kurt Renner

    253rd Infantry Division: Major General Fritz Kuhne

31st Infantry Division: Major General Rudolf Kämpfe
IX Corps: General of Infantry Hermann Geyer
XXVII Corps: General of Infantry Alfred Wäger
    269th Infantry Division: Major General Ernst-Eberhard Hell

18th Army:
Officer in Command: General Georg von Küchler
Chief of Staff: General of Artillery Erich Marcks
X Corps:
    1st SS Panzer Division Leibstandarte SS Adolf Hitler
    227th Infantry Division
    1st Cavalry Division
XXVI Corps:
    256th Infantry Division
    254th Infantry Division
    SS 'Der Führer' Division

Reserves:
    208th Infantry Division
    225th Infantry Division
    526th Infantry Division
    SS 'Verfügungstruppe' Division
    7th Airborne Division
    22nd Air Landing Infantry Division
    9th Panzer Division
    207th Infantry Division

Army Group C:
Officer in Command: General Wilhelm Ritter von Leeb

1st Army:
Officer in Command: General Erwin von Witzleben
XII Corps:
    75th Infantry Division
    198th Infantry Division
    268th Infantry Division

XXIV Corps:
    60th Infantry Division
    168th Infantry Division
    252nd Infantry Division
XXX Corps:
    79th Infantry Division
    93rd Infantry Division
    258th Infantry Division
XXXVII Corps:
    257th Infantry Division
XLV Corps:
    95th Infantry Division
    167th Infantry Division

7th Army:
Officer in Command: General Friedrich Dollmann
XXV Corps:
    557th Infantry Division
    6th Mountain Division
XXVII Corps
    218th Infantry Division
    221st Infantry Division
XXXIII Corps
    239th Infantry Division
    556th Infantry Division
Reserves:
    197th Infantry Division
    213th Infantry Division
    215th Infantry Division
    246th Infantry Division
    262nd Infantry Division
    554th Infantry Division
    555th Infantry Division

ACKNOWLEDGEMENTS

My main sources of information has been *Hutchinson's Pictorial History of the War*, published by Virtue and Company Ltd periodically during the Second World War.

The memories of Billy Drake, Tony Ancrum, Peter Hairs, Paul Farnes and James O'Meara have been adapted from my book *Voices from the Battle of Britain*, published by David and Charles 2010. Particular thanks to Mark O'Meara who provided the written memories of his late father, Squadron Leader James O'Meara.

The memories of John Peyton and Clive Bossom were first written for the book *Politicians at War* by Henry Buckton, published by Leo Cooper Pen and Sword Books, 2003. Copyright: Henry Buckton.

The memories of Doreen Govan and Mrs V. J. Lewis are taken from the book *The Children's Front* by Henry Buckton, published by Phillimore & Co Ltd, 2009. Copyright: Henry Buckton.

Memories of Erwin Rommel taken from *Blitzkrieg, 1940*, Eye Witness to History, www.eyewitnesstohistory.com (2002).

Many thanks to Jason Carley, *The Association of Dunkirk Little Ships* www.adls.org.uk for information on the little ships ML *Advance*, MY *Bluebird of Chelsea*, MY *Chico*, MY *Cordelia*, Barge *Count Dracula* and MY *Llanthony*.

INDEX